J2EE™ Connector Architecture and Enterprise Application Integration

The Java™ Series

Lisa Friendly, Series Editor
Tim Lindholm, Technical Editor
Ken Arnold, Technical Editor of The Jini™ Technology Series
Jim Inscore, Technical Editor of The Java™ Series, Enterprise Edition

Ken Arnold, James Gosling, David Holmes
The Java™ Programming Language, Third Edition

Joshua Bloch
Effective Java™ Programming Language Guide

Greg Bollella, James Gosling, Ben Brosgol, Peter Dibble,
Steve Furr, David Hardin, Mark Turnbull
The Real-Time Specification for Java™

Mary Campione, Kathy Walrath, Alison Huml
The Java™ Tutorial, Third Edition:
A Short Course on the Basics

Mary Campione, Kathy Walrath, Alison Huml, Tutorial Team
The Java™ Tutorial Continued:
The Rest of the JDK™

Patrick Chan
The Java™ Developers Almanac 2000

Patrick Chan, Rosanna Lee
The Java™ Class Libraries, Second Edition, Volume 2:
java.applet, java.awt, java.beans

Patrick Chan, Rosanna Lee
The Java™ Class Libraries Poster, Sixth Edition, Part 1

Patrick Chan, Rosanna Lee
The Java™ Class Libraries Poster, Sixth Edition, Part 2

Patrick Chan, Rosanna Lee, Doug Kramer
The Java™ Class Libraries, Second Edition, Volume 1:
java.io, java.lang, java.math, java.net, java.text, java.util

Patrick Chan, Rosanna Lee, Doug Kramer
The Java™ Class Libraries, Second Edition, Volume 1:
Supplement for the Java™ 2 Platform,
Standard Edition, v1.2

Kirk Chen, Li Gong
Programming Open Service Gateways with Java™
Embedded Server

Zhiqun Chen
Java Card™ Technology for Smart Cards:
Architecture and Programmer's Guide

Li Gong
Inside Java™ 2 Platform Security:
Architecture, API Design, and Implementation

James Gosling, Bill Joy, Guy Steele, Gilad Bracha
The Java™ Language Specification, Second Edition

Mark Hapner, Rich Burridge, Rahul Sharma, Joseph Fialli,
Kim Haase
Java™ Message Service API Tutorial and Reference:
Messaging for the J2EE™ Platform

Jonni Kanerva
The Java™ FAQ

Doug Lea
Concurrent Programming in Java™, Second Edition:
Design Principles and Patterns

Rosanna Lee, Scott Seligman
JNDI API Tutorial and Reference:
Building Directory-Enabled Java™ Applications

Sheng Liang
The Java™ Native Interface:
Programmer's Guide and Specification

Tim Lindholm and Frank Yellin
The Java™ Virtual Machine Specification, Second Edition

Vlada Matena and Beth Stearns
Applying Enterprise JavaBeans™:
Component-Based Development for the J2EE™ Platform

Roger Riggs, Antero Taivalsaari, Mark VandenBrink
Programming Wireless Devices with the Java™ 2
Platform, Micro Edition

Rahul Sharma, Beth Stearns, Tony Ng
J2EE™ Connector Architecture and Enterprise Application
Integration

Henry Sowizral, Kevin Rushforth, and Michael Deering
The Java 3D™ API Specification, Second Edition

Sun Microsystems, Inc.
Java™ Look and Feel Design Guidelines: Advanced Topics

Kathy Walrath, Mary Campione
The JFC Swing Tutorial:
A Guide to Constructing GUIs

Seth White, Maydene Fisher, Rick Cattell, Graham Hamilton,
Mark Hapner
JDBC™ API Tutorial and Reference, Second Edition:
Universal Data Access for the Java™ 2 Platform

Steve Wilson, Jeff Kesselman
Java™ Platform Performance:
Strategies and Tactics

The Jini™ Technology Series

Eric Freeman, Susanne Hupfer, Ken Arnold
JavaSpaces™ Principles, Patterns, and Practice

Jim Waldo/Jini™ Technology Team
The Jini™ Specifications, Second Edition,
edited by Ken Arnold

The Java™ Series, Enterprise Edition

Rick Cattell, Jim Inscore, Enterprise Partners
J2EE™ Technology in Practice:
Building Business Applications with the Java™ 2 Platform,
Enterprise Edition

Patrick Chan, Rosanna Lee
The Java™ Class Libraries Poster, Enterprise Edition,
version 1.2

Nicholas Kassem, Enterprise Team
Designing Enterprise Applications with the Java™ 2
Platform, Enterprise Edition

Bill Shannon, Mark Hapner, Vlada Matena, James
Davidson, Eduardo Pelegri-Llopart, Larry Cable,
Enterprise Team
Java™ 2 Platform, Enterprise Edition:
Platform and Component Specifications

http://www.javaseries.com

J2EE™ Connector Architecture and Enterprise Application Integration

Rahul Sharma
Beth Stearns
Tony Ng

✦Addison-Wesley

Boston • San Francisco • New York • Toronto • Montreal
London • Munich • Paris • Madrid
Capetown • Sydney • Tokyo • Singapore • Mexico City

Library of Congress Cataloging-in-Publication Data
Sharma, Rahul.
    J2EE Connector architecture and enterprise application integration / Rahul Sharma,
  Beth Stearns, Tony Ng.
        p.   cm.
    Includes bibliographical references and index.
    ISBN: 0-201-77580-8 (pbk.)
    1. Java (Computer program language)   2. Application software.   3. Computer
  architecture.   I. Stearns, Beth.   II. Ng, Tony.   III. Title.

  QA76.73.J38 S454 2001
  005.2'762—dc21

                                                                2001045992

The publisher offers discounts on this book when ordered in quantity for special sales. For more information, please contact:

Pearson Education, Inc.
Pearson Education Corporate Sales Division
201 W. 103rd Street
Indianapolis, IN 46290
(800) 428-5331
corpsales@pearsoned.com

ISBN: 0-201-77580-8
Text printed on recycled paper
1 2 3 4 5 6 7 8 9 10—MA—0504030201
First Printing, December 2001

To the dearest dad. We all miss you.
—Rahul

To "Papie" Tonton. Gros Bisous.
—Beth

To Sophia.
—Tony

Contents

Foreword

STANDARDS can redefine a marketplace—consider the impact that SQL had in launching the relational database market. Standards can also create new markets—without HTML, HTTP, and SSL, we would still be waiting for the World Wide Web. That is why the Java community is so excited about Web Services and the Java™ 2 Enterprise Edition (J2EE™) Connector Architecture: we expect a similarly dramatic impact on application integration.

By application integration (or simply "integration"), I do not just mean Enterprise Application Integration (EAI), which I would characterize as Intranet integration, which happens behind the firewall. I am also including business-to-business application integration (B2BI) wherein the applications from one company directly interoperate with the applications of a business partner across the Internet or a Virtual Private Network. In fact, EAI and B2BI are already converging: individual business units increasingly have their own IT infrastructure and applications. So just as Web technologies are widely used on our Intranets, we can expect XML, Web Services, and J2EE adapters to become common on our corporate networks. But I would take this one step further. The majority of new applications today are built to plug into the Web. Going forward, we should demand that both commercial off-the-shelf applications as well as "home grown" applications be "integration ready" out of the box—ready to plug into this emerging integration "backplane" of Web Services.

Technology alone is never sufficient to drive this level of change. There also must be a compelling business case. Today, large companies depend on tens of thousands of applications. Most of these applications operate in silos, interconnecting only with their close peers. And the trend is toward proliferation. At the same time, the rigors of competition are forcing our businesses to specialize—to focus on only what they do well. But as we divest and outsource, we are forced to more closely integrate with our business partners.

Integration "after the fact" is such a pain point that some application vendors are now suggesting that the only antidote is to purchase every business application from a single supplier so that they are "pre-integrated"—call this "worst of breed."

For larger businesses such a prospect is absurd. What about the legacy applications and data? What about the increasing demand for vertically specialized applications? What about the in-house software essential for competitive differentiation?

So, while integration may well be the biggest source of information technology (IT) pain today, the integration solutions market nevertheless remains fragmented. Growth is stilted by a lack of standards. Instead of a unifying architecture, we have numerous small vendors offering highly proprietary technologies:

1. **Proprietary protocols**—The litmus test for a proprietary protocol is whether the same software stack has to run on both sides of the network. The Web analogy is compelling—without HTML and HTTP, a World Wide Web of heterogeneous clients talking to heterogeneous servers would not have happened. Proprietary protocols simply do not work for the scale of integration we need on the Web. Beware: While XML is a standard, XML document-passing conventions can still be highly proprietary. That's why the emerging family of Web Services standards is so essential—SOAP, WSDL, UDDI, ebXML, BTP, and so on. Without such standards, users will be unable to mix and match integration solutions as they have Web technologies.

2. **Proprietary adapters**—Adapters map between new standards (such as Java technology and the J2EE platform) and legacy technologies (including COBOL/CICS). Even with the emergence of XML and Web Services, adapters remain essential because very little of today's legacy is going to directly support Web Services. Adapters solve what could be called the "last mile" problem of integration—how do I get from my XML/Web Services "backbone" into the legacy? Without a standard model for adapters, it's nearly impossible to get critical mass. Instead of an enterprise software vendor delivering standard adapters with its product, adapters are "one-off" by a small integration vendor or the system integrator.

3. **Proprietary containers**—Protocols and adapters are hosted in containers. Virtually all integration solutions on the market today depend on proprietary containers. These containers are themselves proprietary not just because the adapters and protocols are. Consider that little investment protection is offered for the additional programming required to move data from one integration platform to another:

   - Synchronous and asynchronous messaging (for hub-and-spoke as well as peer-to-peer integration server networks)

   - Security (authentication, authorization, privacy, nonrepudiation)

   - Transactions, compensating actions, and guaranteed delivery

   - Message (data dependent) routing, load balancing, and failover

   - Rules management, workflow, and multi-vendor collaboration

- Naming/directory (LDAP, UDDI)

- Transformation

- Repository and content management

- Session management and protection

- Caching for efficient re-use of content and data

In the first case—proprietary protocols—the answer is XML and Web Services. In the second case, for proprietary adapters, the answer is the J2EE Connector Architecture (JCA). What about the third case—proprietary containers? The key insight is to recognize that "integration logic" is not fundamentally different from "business logic." Look at the considerations enumerated in the case of proprietary containers. All are equally applicable to the hosting of general-purpose applications, in addition to the integration glue.

Today, the industry is rapidly coalescing around the Java/J2EE platform and the .NET alternative from Microsoft. Both platforms have a compelling shared vision of Web Services, a vision that is already being proven out with direct interoperability testing between the two. The additional value proposition for Java, however, in the first place, is that Web Services bindings can be generated transparently for existing J2EE applications (programmers use what they already know), and, in the second place, that the J2EE Connector Architecture is commercially viable today. Indeed, software vendors like PeopleSoft, Siebel, SAP, and many others are working to deliver standard JCA adapters for their enterprise suites. We also have leading systems integrators like Accenture, CSC, EDS, KPMG, and so on developing standards-based integration practices around this new framework. Of course, the major J2EE product systems vendors—BEA, Sun, IBM, HP, Oracle, Compaq, NEC, and so on—are also very much behind using Java technology as a basis for integration. All this gives the J2EE-based integration critical mass.

Of course, this new standard integration platform needs more time to cook. Web Services standards continue to progress. Guaranteed delivery, nonrepudiation, and compensating actions are three key areas of ongoing investment. Also, the JCA-compliant adapters are still being built, and vendors like BEA have extended JCA to allow bi-directional communications and support for asynchronous processing (via the Java Message Service).

How, then, should organizations deal with this coming tsunami of standards-based integration? By treating integration challenges both tactically and strategically: Tactically, get the job done, with a mix of best-fit standard and proprietary technologies. But strategically bet on the emerging standards. In particular, do not make long-term or large commitments to proprietary integration frameworks.

For those who may still have doubts, we have just witnessed a very similar transformation. Four years ago there were literally dozens of application servers promoting all sorts of proprietary programming models. We said then that J2EE would drive rapid consolidation in this market, and that those who ignored J2EE would sacrifice their investment. The large majority of those proprietary technologies are now gone. Those that remain have redesigned their product around J2EE.

The smart money is on history repeating itself for Web-based application integration. The compelling demand for standardization will drive this market—standards like Web Services and the J2EE Connector Architecture. As with all technology transformations, right now there are compelling opportunities to gain competitive advantage—competitive advantage for software vendors, for systems integrators, for end-users, and especially for integration vendors. Hopefully, understanding and adopting that competitive advantage is why you bought this book.

Scott Dietzen, Ph.D.
Chief Technology Officer, Server Division
BEA Systems

Preface

THIS book provides an in-depth coverage of the Java™ 2, Enterprise Edition (J2EE™) platform Connector architecture. The Connector architecture is an integral part of the J2EE platform, and, as a key component in the platform's support for application integration, it ensures that J2EE applications can connect to and use a multitude of EISs and legacy systems. The Connector architecture, because it defines a standard set of contracts for handling connections, transactions, and security, makes it easier for vendors to develop products that can hook into the J2EE platform. Vendors follow the guidelines of these Connector contracts to develop special software modules, called resource adapters, that enable this linkage between their underlying products and the J2EE platform.

This book is written for application component developers who are building applications that run on the J2EE platform. It is also of interest to independent software vendors (ISVs) and others who develop resource adapters for specific EISs, such as legacy and database systems.

Conventions Used in This Book

This book uses certain graphical and typographical conventions.

The graphical conventions used here are based on the Unified Modeling Language (UML) standard. UML is a modeling language for object-oriented development. In general, object-oriented modeling decomposes systems into collaborating objects. The resulting model captures the underlying semantics of a problem. UML defines different models for representing systems, and graphical diagrams to depict these models, including a class model, a state model, a use case model, an interaction model, an implementation model, and a deployment model.

We only use a subset of the UML diagrams in this book. The diagrams of most interest to readers are the class diagrams, which depict static structure, and sequence, object, and collaboration diagrams, which depict dynamic object interactions.

Note that we use the terms application server, server, and J2EE application server interchangeably. Unless otherwise noted, these three terms all refer to a J2EE application server.

For those interested in more information about UML, we refer you to the following sources:

- *UML Distilled*, Second Edition, Fowler, Scott, 2000, Addison-Wesley
- *Instant UML*, Muller, 1997, Wrox Press Ltd.

Graphics

Many of the graphics in this book depict UML diagrams. The conventions used in these diagrams follow the UML standard. Because different notations can be used to represent the same model, we have included a figure that illustrates how we use these UML conventions in this book.

Briefly, Figure 1 illustrates the arrows and connectors used in standard UML diagrams, along with different types of associations.

Typographic Conventions

Table 1 describes the typographic conventions used in this book.

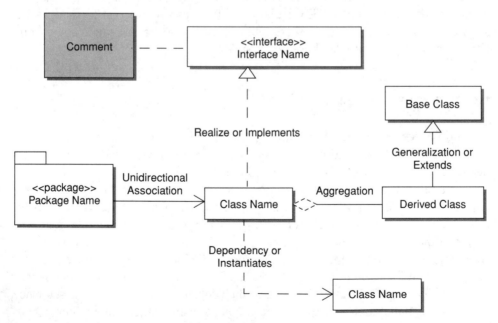

Figure 1   UML symbols and associations

Table 1 Typographic Conventions

Typeface or Symbol	Meaning	Example
AaBbCc123	The names of commands, files, and directories; interface, class, method, variable, and deployment descriptor element names; programming language keywords	Edit the file `InventoryManagerEJB.java`. Uses a `ConnectorFactory` object. Invokes the `getConnection` method.
AaBbCc123	Book titles, new words or terms, or words to be emphasized.	Read Chapter 2 in *EJB 1.1 Specification.* This is a *local transaction.* You *must* be careful when using this option.

Other Sources of Information

You should refer to other publications related to J2EE and to the J2EE Web site, `http://java.sun.com/j2ee/`. The following books, both online and in print, are of particular interest to those developing J2EE Connectors and other application components.

- *Java 2 Platform, Enterprise Edition Connector Specification*, 2000, Sun Microsystems, Inc. Available at `http://java.sun.com/j2ee/docs.html`.

- *Java Message Service API,* 2000, Sun Microsystems, Inc. Available at `http://java.sun.com/j2ee/docs.html`.

- *Java™ 2 Standard Edition Platform (J2SE™),* 2000, Sun Microsystems, Inc. Available at `http://java.sun.com/products`.

- *Java™ Authentication and Authorization Service (JAAS) 1.0 Specification,* 2000, Sun Microsystems, Inc. Available at `http://java.sun.com/security/jaas/doc`.

- *Java™ 2 Platform, Enterprise Edition, Platform and Component Specifications*, Shannon, Hapner, Matena, Davidson, Pelegri-Llopart, Cable, Enterprise Team, 2000, Addison-Wesley.

- *Enterprise JavaBeans™ 2.0 Specification,* Copyright 2001, Sun Microsystems, Inc. Available at `http://java.sun.com/j2ee/docs.html`.

- *Designing Enterprise Applications with the Java™ 2 Platform, Enterprise Edition, Version 1.0.*, Kassem, Enterprise Team, 2000, Addison-Wesley.

- *Applying Enterprise JavaBeans™, Component-Based Development for the J2EE™ Platform*, Matena, Stearns, 2001, Addison-Wesley.

- *JDBC™ API Tutorial and Reference, Second Edition, Universal Data Access for the Java™ 2 Platform*, White, Fisher, Cattell, Hamilton, Hapner, 1999, Addison-Wesley.

- *JDBC™ 2.0 API Specification*, 1999, Sun Microsystems, Inc. Available at `http://java.sun.com/products/jdbc`.

- *JDBC 2.0 Standard Extension API Specification*, 1999, Sun Microsystems, Inc. Available at `http://java.sun.com/products/jdbc`.

- *RMI over IIOP 1.0.1 Specification*, 2000, Sun Microsystems, Inc. Available at `http://java.sun.com/products/rmi-iiop`.

Contents of the Book

As noted previously, we've written this book for two distinct audiences: application developers and software product vendors (including ISVs) who are building resource adapters and enterprise information systems. Application developers work within the Information Technology (IT) department of an enterprise. Their charter is to link the underlying infrastructure products, whether they were developed in-house or purchased from a third-party vendor, with the J2EE application server and platform technologies. Application developers need to know how to use the resource adapters provided by the product vendors and ISVs, and vendors need to know how to construct resource adapters that conform to the Connector architecture specifications.

We have organized this book into sections so that it is easier for readers to access the information they need. Before we get into the specifics of using or building resource adapters, we have included an introductory section that provides background information of interest to all readers. This first section, consisting of Chapters 1 and 2, provides a general introduction to application integration and the J2EE Connector architecture.

The next section is primarily for application developers who need to know how to use a resource adapter. This section describes the Connector application programming model. Chapters 3 through 9 describe how to use a resource adapter from an application developer perspective.

Chapters 10 through 12 focus on the details of the Connector system contracts. These chapters are written for product vendors and ISVs interested in building a resource adapter. Product vendors and ISVs will probably want to focus on Chapter 10 and Chapter 11, which provide the details for building and deploying a resource adapter.

The book begins with an introduction to enterprise application integration, a term that is often abbreviated to EAI. Chapter 1, Enterprise Application Integration, describes the state of enterprise application integration today and shows how it has evolved to this point. Much of the J2EE Connector architecture addresses the problem of application integration, particularly Web-driven application integration. Because more and more services are provided through the Web, it is essential that enterprises have an efficient solution for EAI.

Enterprises must also integrate their enterprise information systems (EISs) with their Web services. EISs encompass the information infrastructure—the business processes and data—of an enterprise. Often, these are the legacy applications, database management systems, and so forth, that the enterprise relies on for its business functioning. This chapter describes the different approaches to integrating the often disparate pieces of an enterprise's information infrastructure, and it shows how the J2EE Connector architecture helps with this process.

Chapter 2, J2EE Connector Architecture Overview, provides an introduction to the Connector architecture. It presents the architecture's concepts and introduces the three system contracts defined by the architecture: the connection, transaction, and security contracts. The Connector architecture is designed for applications running on the J2EE platform. For those not quite as familiar with the J2EE platform, this chapter also includes a description of the platform's components and technologies.

Chapter 3, Managing Connections, starts the application programming model section. This chapter focuses on how application developers can best use the connection pooling mechanisms defined by the Connector architecture's connection management contract. The chapter describes the interfaces that support connection pooling and shows application developers how to use these interfaces so that their applications can connect to an EIS.

Application developers also need to know how to effectively use the transactional support provided by the J2EE platform, and specifically by the Connector architecture. The architecture supports both local and global transactions, and developers use different application programming interfaces to implement these approaches. Chapter 4, Working with Transactions, describes basic transactional concepts and illustrates how to develop transactional applications on the J2EE platform.

Security is also important for EAI. Chapter 5, Managing Security, describes the support for secure connections to EISs that the Connector architecture provides. The Connector architecture builds on the J2EE platform security model. The J2EE model defines the security applied to a client's access to the Web tier, and from there to the EJB tier. The Connector architecture defines a security management contract that extends the J2EE security model to include the connection between the EJB and EIS tiers. This security contract enables a J2EE server to manage security while it creates connections to an EIS and accesses EIS resources.

This chapter introduces the reader to the Connector's security contract and describes the basic J2EE security concepts and terminology. It presents the security model as it relates to the process of signing on to an EIS and illustrates that process with an example scenario.

The Connector architecture supports synchronous and asynchronous messaging systems. These types of messaging systems underlie communication between an application server and an EIS. Often, asynchronous messaging is the preferred communication mode because it allows a message sender to continue processing without waiting for the message to be received and acknowledged. It offers improved performance over synchronous messaging and eliminates some of the dependencies between sender and receiver, or EIS and application. Chapter 6, Asynchronous Messaging, describes the Java Message Service (JMS), the standard Java API (application programming interface) defined for enterprise messaging systems, and shows how the Connector architecture accomplishes asynchronous messaging within this framework.

Chapter 7, Common Client Interface, describes the interfaces and methods of the Common Client Interface (CCI), which is a set of APIs between application components and EIS resource adapters. The CCI provides a common API across heterogeneous EISs, so that vendors specializing in application integration do not have to adapt their products to each individual EIS whose client API they want to support. By building their products to the CCI API, application integration product vendors have a standard way to plug in their resource adapters to different EISs. In addition to describing the interfaces and methods, the chapter provides an example that illustrates how to use the CCI.

Chapter 8, Tools and Frameworks, describes how to integrate application development tools with EIS resource adapters using the Connector architecture, particularly the Common Client Interface API. Integrating tools with resource adapters is particularly challenging because of the heterogeneous nature of EISs—they differ in their client APIs, their support for transactions and security, and in their application programming models. The Connector architecture promotes the use of tools so that development and system integration are simplified.

Chapter 9, XML and the Connector Architecture, provides overview information about XML (eXtensible Markup Language) and shows how to work with XML data within the J2EE and Connector framework. This chapter has a two-fold approach. It describes the current means for incorporating XML data, but, more important, it gives some insight into XML-related tools that are expected to be available in the near future.

ISVs, once they have a good grasp of the underlying contracts, need to know how to build a resource adapter module. A resource adapter is a system-level software driver that provides the connection to the vendor's EIS. A resource adapter implements the EIS side of the Connector system contracts, and it provides a client level API that applications can use to connect to the adapter's underlying EIS.

Chapter 10, Building a Resource Adapter, describes the steps involved in building a resource adapter. It illustrates these steps with code examples for a sample resource adapter.

Chapter 11, Resource Adapter Packaging and Deployment, describes how to package and deploy a resource adapter that you have developed. Packaging and deployment are essential steps for bringing a resource adapter to market. The Connector architecture specifies a standard packaging format for a resource adapter. The deployment process installs components such as adapters into the enterprise's operational environment. By following the Connector architecture's packaging and deployment formats, you are assured that a resource adapter will work on any J2EE application server.

This completes the application programming model section of the book. From this point on, we focus on the system-level aspects of the Connector contracts. These next three chapters—one on each system contract—are meant to provide an "under the covers" view of the contracts. Although the intended audience for these chapters is application server vendors and resource adapter providers, application developers may find this information useful.

Chapter 12, Connection Management Contract, looks at the Connector architecture's connection management contract from a system-level viewpoint. It examines in detail the contract's interfaces and classes. It also explains how connections are handled in both two-tier and multi-tier environments and how a connection pool is implemented. Its focus is on managing connections in different environments so that scalability is enhanced.

Chapter 13, Transaction Management Contract, explains the system-level details of the Connector architecture's transaction management contract. It examines the methods of the local and global transaction interfaces and explains the different levels of transactional support that a J2EE application server provides. It also illustrates how the contract mandates the handling of this transactional support.

Chapter 14, Security Management Contract, similar to the previous two chapters, explains the system-level details of the Connector architecture's security management contract. Not only does it present and explain the interfaces and classes that the contract supports, it also shows how to use the contract to identify and authenticate users and determine their authorization and access control privileges.

The Connector architecture is constantly evolving and including new Java technologies. Chapter 15, Future Directions, describes the new technologies that will be included in the architecture. It particularly focuses on the features that the 2.0 version of the architecture is expected to support. These features will enhance EIS pluggability into the J2EE platform.

We have also included three chapters from three different resource adapter vendors. Chapter 16, written by engineers working with SAP, describes the architecture of the SAP connector, and shows how the connector manages connections, transactions, and security. It also describes the CCI provided for the SAP connector and uses an example to illustrate how to use this resource adapter in an application. Chapter 17, written by IBM Corporation, describes how developers can use the IBM J2EE Connector architecture-based tools to develop enterprise applications. This chapter focuses on using VisualAge for Java to develop an application that uses a CICS ECI connector to execute a CICS transaction within a WebSphere Application Server environment. Chapter 18, provided by BEA Systems, Inc., describes how they have implemented the J2EE Connector architecture specification in their WebLogic Server product.

Last, the book includes an appendix that contains the API reference and a glossary of terms. The reference section contains all the classes and interfaces defined by the Connector architecture as well as the methods within each interface or class.

Acknowledgments

WE would like to thank the following individuals who participated in the Connector architecture expert group and made valuable contributions to the architecture's design and specification: Pete Homan and Deb June (BEA), Charlton Barreto (Borland), Yoshi Otagiri and Ivar Alexander (Fujitsu), Tom Freund and Michael Beisiegel (IBM), Tony Plan and Pavan Bhatnagar (IPlanet), Guy Bieber (Motorola), Dan Coyle (Oracle), Jack Greenfield (Rational), Marek Barwicki (SAP), Fred H. Carter (Sun Microsystems), Rajini Balay and K. Swaminathan (Sybase), Jon Dart (Tibco), and Lester Lee (Unisys).

We especially want to thank Vlada Matena, who worked closely with Rahul Sharma, and was instrumental in starting the Connector architecture. We also want to thank our associates at Sun who provided technical input and guidance for the development of the architecture, particularly Shel Finkelstein, Mark Hapner, Vlada Matena, Bill Shannon, Sekhar Vajjhala, Jean Zeng, and Pong Ching.

In addition, we want to thank the following individuals whose work on the J2EE Reference Implementation and Compatibility Test Suite gave us a platform and standard against which we could test the architecture's concepts: Liz Blair, Anand Dhingra, Helen He, Gursharan Singh, and Sheetal Vartak.

Likewise, we want to thank the following individuals for reviewing the drafts of this book: Lance Anderson, Herb Jellnek, Ram Jeyaraman, Robert McCarter, Vijay Sarathy, Herb Jellneck, Mark Hershey, and Robert McCarter.

Last, we want to acknowledge the following people who helped us accomplish the many tasks necessary to publish this book: Jeff Jackson, for his unflagging and enthusiastic encouragement; Lisa Friendly and Jim Inscore, for helping coordinate all those publication details; and Mike Hendrickson, Ross Venables, and Elizabeth Ryan, among others at Addison-Wesley, who have continued to be the best publishing team with whom we've had the pleasure to work.

CHAPTER 1

Enterprise Application Integration

ENTERPRISE computing has progressed enormously in just the last few years. Especially with the advent of the Web, not only is it possible for diverse organizations to automate and integrate their businesses and computer operations, it is imperative that they do so. Suddenly, as corporations become Web-enabled and find themselves relying on myriad applications, the ability to evolve and integrate existing applications becomes significant.

Virtually all enterprise organizations at some time face the problem of integrating different applications and database systems. In addition, enterprise organizations must constantly evolve. This need to evolve occurs as enterprises strive for competitive advantages. In today's economy, it is rare for an organization to continue to be successful by merely maintaining the status quo. In a sense, enterprises are forced to evolve to stay at the forefront of their industries. Enterprises frequently find themselves having to merge with other enterprises, reorganizing their internal structure, and adopting new technologies and platforms as they strive for competitive advantages. More and more, they are adopting an e-business strategy. The failure of the "dot-com" business-to-consumer (B2C) economy has not affected the need for traditional enterprises to adopt an e-business strategy.

Enterprises still consider the e-business model to be an effective medium. The e-business model is particularly useful for managing purchasing and supply-chain issues, managing customer relationships and providing customer service, and providing Web-based applications and services. (An example of such a Web-based service is an online customer service application for bill payment and presentment.) Because it is imperative that enterprises adapt to business- and technology-driven changes, they need an e-business model more than ever to adapt their existing business processes, applications, and enterprise systems to these changes.

Furthermore, it is not a simple matter for an enterprise to discard its existing applications, or even overhaul its established business processes, to effect a change in its business model. These kinds of changes are financially expensive to undertake and daunting in terms of human resources. Many enterprises cannot afford to make such changes or discard existing systems. Thus it is critical for enterprises to be able to leverage their investments in their existing enterprise infrastructure and applications.

In these situations, enterprise application integration assumes a great importance. Enterprise application integration (EAI) enables an enterprise to integrate its existing applications and systems and to add new technologies and applications to the mix. EAI also helps an enterprise to model and automate its business processes.

Enterprise application integration has always focused on a company's IT department integrating new software modules or applications with its existing systems. How did a company handle these integration scenarios before the advent of EAI, J2EE, and the Connector technology? Companies handled such integration with a great deal of difficulty and significant expense, often bringing in teams of expensive consultants with little guarantee that they would deliver satisfactorily. Several years after undertaking these projects, it was not uncommon for companies to throw up their collective "corporate hands," write off the hundreds of thousands—if not millions—they had spent, and walk away from the project.

Enterprise organizations also must weigh the cost of replacing existing systems with new systems against the cost of merging existing systems with new systems. Discarding existing systems is never an easy choice: companies have invested huge sums of money to install, use, and customize these systems. Not only are their personnel comfortable with using these systems, even if the software is rife with drawbacks, but often the company's way of doing business has evolved to fit with these systems. It's difficult to just walk away from such an investment. Likewise, bringing in a replacement system has its costs: there's the purchase price of the new system, plus the training and customization costs. The investment in the new system can be as large, if not larger, than the investment in the existing system.

Companies also have the option of keeping their existing systems and finding the means to combine their functionality. In addition to retaining the existing systems, companies can integrate them with new applications to enhance functionality. The key with this option is the cost of integrating the separate applications and systems. EAI has grown out of this need to simplify the process of integrating applications and data.

1.1   What Is Enterprise Application Integration?

Enterprise application integration (EAI) entails integrating applications and enterprise data sources so that they can easily share business processes and data. Integrating the applications and data sources must be accomplished without requiring significant changes to these existing applications and the data.

Before EAI, integrating applications and data within a corporate environment was an expensive and risky proposition. Companies were trying to combine applications that often ran on different hardware platforms and had no protocols for communicating with other software packages outside of their own narrowly defined realm. In a sense, companies had "islands" of business functions and data, and each island existed in its own, separate problem domain. (See Figure 1.1.)

How did an enterprise try to fix this situation? The company would bring in a team of consultants and embark on a long and expensive process of determining the feasibility of integrating their systems, designing the integration approach, and finally developing and implementing the procedures (both manual and computerized) to achieve the integration. Sometimes the analysis phase determined that it was not economical or possible to integrate the particular systems. Even when the integration did go forward, it might take years to accomplish. There was often no guarantee of success. Projects were often abandoned because of cost overruns or the belated recognition of significant difficulties. Even when projects were completed, the resulting patchwork solution might be fraught with its own set of problems.

EAI represents a different approach to this problem. EAI defines semantics for application and data integration. That is, EAI defines a standard methodology, or approach, for applications and data sources to communicate. By supporting this standard, applications can easily communicate with other applications and data sources. The pieces in the integration puzzle—such as an underlying database

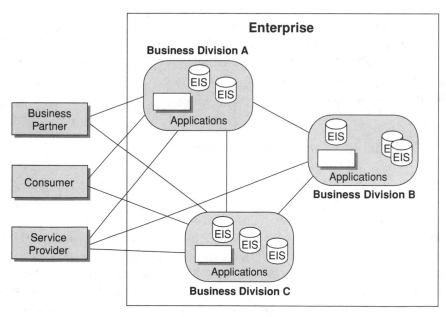

Figure 1.1   A Typical Enterprise Domain

management system (DBMS)—can change, but because of this common methodology, the replacement piece can be plugged in and the communication can continue uninterrupted.

There are many real-world examples of EAI, particularly in the banking and financial services and the telecommunications industry. Take AT&T, for example. AT&T started as a phone service provider, then added cable television services and wireless service. Later it became a broadband provider. The company has grown and evolved by merging with other companies and acquiring other businesses. As a result of this growth, and before its current plans to break into four different companies, AT&T needed to integrate its online customer services. It had to integrate its bill presentment for all services, payment for services, and its overall customer service. This entailed integrating access to the existing applications that provided these services.

By focusing on integrating business processes and data, EAI encompasses both the distribution of such processes and data and the concept of reusing modules. Most important, EAI approaches this integration as a process separate from the different applications. That is, someone can integrate various applications with each other, and with underlying data sources, without having to understand or know the details of the applications themselves.

EAI is best suited for environments that are heterogeneous rather than homogeneous. Heterogeneous environments are those whose applications and data do not all reside within the same environment, such as in the AT&T example just discussed. A company may have reached this point because of acquisitions or mergers with other companies in which they have been compelled to absorb some other company's systems into their own environment. They may have been trying to increase their capacity—or to avoid replacing existing systems—by patching their own internally developed systems or other purchased systems onto their core systems. Or, they may be supporting large numbers of users on distributed systems with a multitude of platforms.

1.2   Web-driven Application Integration

With the advent of the Web, enterprise application integration has taken on a larger significance beyond that of merging application systems solely within an enterprise. Enterprise servers now handle and maintain huge amounts of data and business logic. Furthermore, because the Web enables easy information and service access, it has become a principal means of communication. An enterprise must be able to make its business data accessible to others, from internal employees to external partners, suppliers, and buyers. Employees require access to the enterprise data to keep abreast of company policies and developments and to carry on the internal business of the company. For example, employees file their expense reports through a Web interface. Business partners may be communicating important technological information. Buyers and suppliers need access to enterprise data to facilitate the parts ordering and delivery process.

Providing services through the Web is rapidly becoming the emerging trend. Enterprises are recognizing that it is important for them to provide more of their services, such as customer support and product catalogs, through the Web. Enterprises have come to see that having such services available both in a traditional manner and over the Web enhances their business. The technology scenario is evolving at a breathtaking pace, and EAI is now increasingly being driven by Web-driven requirements and technologies.

Web-driven application integration, by making data and services more easily and widely accessible, places additional security requirements on an enterprise. All access to enterprise servers must happen in a secure manner. No company can risk losing data, or worse, having the integrity of their data compromised in any way. Likewise, such server access must also be transactional to maintain data integrity.

And, last, it's necessary for all this to happen in an environment that is scalable. Whether an enterprise starts large or small, the need for access to its systems is bound to multiply. An enterprise cannot risk using a system that is not able to scale to many users over time. For example, an online stock trading application offered by the financial services industry must be able to handle transactions whose numbers can increase rapidly. It is best, too, if the enterprise can retain the flexibility to develop and add in new applications and extend its existing applications.

As more businesses establish a Web presence, Web-driven EAI becomes more essential. Enterprises need to integrate their existing applications and enterprise systems to drive their business-to-consumer and business-to-business interactions, plus their other Web services. In fact, success in e-business is driven by an enterprise's ability to integrate existing applications and extend the reach of these applications to Web-based access.

Up till now, applications were classified as either front-office or back-office applications. Front-office applications are considered to face the customer or end user. Front-office applications include applications for customer relationship management and marketing automation. Back-office applications provide the information infrastructure for running the back-end business processes of an enterprise. Applications provided by an enterprise resource planning (ERP) system are good examples of back-office applications. Traditional EAI focused on integrating the front- and back-office applications. However, traditional EAI is becoming Web-driven EAI. Rather than being targeted to the front end or the back end, most EAI applications are now integrated for the front and back ends and Web enabled.

Just as it is imperative for an enterprise information system (EIS) to move to a Web-based architecture, enterprise applications need to be deployed on widely adopted, standard application platforms. Enterprises now regard application servers as mature platforms for developing Web-based applications. As Figure 1.2 shows,

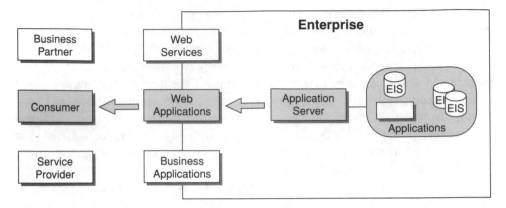

Figure 1.2   Web-driven Application Integration

application servers are particularly appropriate for the B2C and business-to-business (B2B) areas that place so much stress on application integration. The application server provides a natural point of integration between an enterprise's existing enterprise information systems and the Web-based applications. The application server also helps handle transactions and can be scaled as needed. The J2EE application platform is the technology of choice for enterprises and application vendors.

Figure 1.2 illustrates this Web direction to which enterprises are currently moving. The success of the Java programming language and the J2EE platform are also responsible for this Web-driven application integration, in large part because they make it easier to develop and implement Web-based applications.

To maximize this Web-driven application integration, enterprises are turning to the Java programming language and the J2EE platform. Java is a platform-independent computer language that is designed for the Web, and it is a successful, widely adopted platform for enterprise application development.

In addition to the Java platform, enterprises are using eXtensible Markup Language (XML) to exchange corporate data across application domains. XML is a platform-independent way of representing data formats, and it is invaluable for exchanging data among different entities. There is a synergy between XML and Java. XML is to data what the Java programming language is to application services. Because of XML's platform-independent features, it serves as a foundation for the current generation of Web technologies.

1.3   Enterprise Information Systems

Before delving into the details of EAI, it is useful to understand the definition of an enterprise information system. An enterprise requires certain business processes and underlying data to run its business. An enterprise information system encompasses these business processes and information technology (IT) infrastructure. The enterprise business processes include applications for handling payroll processing, inventory management, manufacturing production control, and financial accounting (accounts payable and accounts receivable).

We define an enterprise information system as an application or enterprise system that provides the information infrastructure for an enterprise. An EIS consists of one or more applications deployed on an enterprise system. An EIS provides a set of services to its users. Services exposed to clients may be at different levels of abstraction—including the system level, data level, function level, and business object or process level.

Graphically this might look as shown in Figure 1.3. In this EIS environment, the applications reside on the application server. The application server has a vendor-specific infrastructure, particularly regarding such services as transaction processing, security, and load balancing. The applications that sit on the server may be supplied by different vendors, or they may be developed in house by the IT department. Applications have been written in various languages, such as COBOL, C, and C++. Clients can access the different applications by means of application programming interfaces (APIs). An API is some routine that allows a client to do such operations as create a purchase order or update a customer record. The data access interface represents the means of access to the legacy datastores or relational databases. The

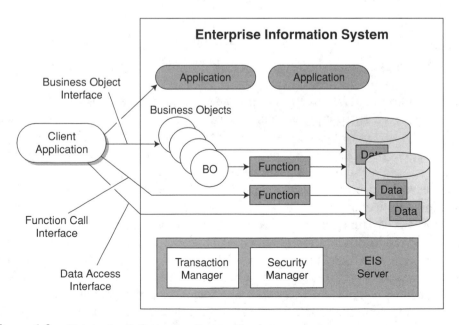

Figure 1.3   Enterprise Information System Environment

business object interfaces are abstractions representing the business-specific logic for accessing functions and data.

Many different applications and systems qualify as EISs. EISs include the following:

- Enterprise applications that have been developed by an enterprise specifically to meet its business needs. These are considered to be custom applications. Legacy applications typically run on different computing environments. In addition, they are developed using different programming languages, such as C and COBOL.

- Applications that are part of an ERP suite of applications. ERP applications cover a wide range of functions, including inventory management, production control, human resources. Logistics applications are another set of ERP applications.

- Transaction programs running on a mainframe transaction processing system.

- Legacy databases that manage data critical to the business processes of an enterprise.

For a variety of reasons, EISs vary greatly even within the same enterprise. EISs usually vary because

- Enterprises purchase or implement different EISs over a period of years as their business needs grow.

- Enterprises deploy enterprise applications on different platforms or architectures.

- Enterprises customize an EIS to fit their own unique business needs.

An enterprise develops EISs over time, as a need for a particular EIS arises. For example, an enterprise may start out by purchasing a manufacturing system. Over the years, as its business grows, it incrementally adds different accounting packages, customer support, human resources, and so forth. It may be able to add some systems to the platform that hosts its manufacturing operations. However, other packages require different platform capabilities, or have only been developed for a particular platform or architecture. Not only does the enterprise add the new software systems, it also buys additional hardware that may be completely different from its original configuration. (The AT&T example mentioned earlier is another good illustration of this process.) It is easy to see that when an enterprise has been in business for a long time, it may very well be using EISs that have been developed and installed on different computing platforms and architectures.

It is not uncommon for a large, established enterprise to have a few applications that run on a mainframe transaction processing system. These mainframe-based systems may have been purchased years ago. The same enterprise runs other applications that may be part of an integrated ERP suite of applications.

In addition, it is typical for an enterprise to customize its applications to its own enterprise-specific business processes. This level of customization can vary greatly. For example, an enterprise may purchase an off-the-shelf ERP application, and then customize the application so that it addresses its specific business processes. At the same time, it may develop other applications internally, using its own employees or consultants. These internally developed applications are completely custom applications, designed to specifically meet the enterprise's business needs.

1.4   Challenges in EIS Integration

EISs differ significantly, in terms of their level of technological support, administrative and technological restrictions; their ability to integrate with other systems and their exposure to low-level system details, as follows:

- **Level of technological support**—EISs vary greatly in their level of technological advancement. For example, support for transactions and security differs vastly. Some EISs are rather primitive, and they may offer no support for transactional access. Or, if they do offer some support, it is limited in scope. Other EISs are more advanced in supporting a transaction and security infrastructure. They may allow transactional access to their resources. Or, they may support a two-phase commit protocol and distributed transactions and thus may be able to participate in transactions with other EISs.

- **Administrative and technological restrictions**—Many EISs impose specific technology and administrative restrictions on their users. These EISs are legacy systems or applications that have been in existence for a long time and their usage requirements may be more rigidly structured. For example, in some legacy systems, it may be difficult to create new user accounts. Other legacy systems are difficult to extend to support development of new applications. An enterprise with such a legacy system must adapt to its shortcomings, but it still must find a way to integrate the legacy system with other systems and new Web-based applications.

- **Ability to integrate with other systems**—EISs also differ in terms of their application programming models and client APIs, which makes it difficult to integrate these different EISs. These differences exist because most EISs were developed using architectures and technologies that best suited a certain class of enterprise applications and were prevalent at the time the application was initially developed. In addition, these EISs were developed when integration and interoperability with other types of systems and EISs may not have been the primary design goals.

- **Exposure to low-level system details**—Client APIs for these EISs may differ in the low-level transaction and security management details they expose to application developers, and this makes it more complex to integrate EISs. The application developer must understand the programming details of the EIS's low-level client API to properly integrate with the EIS. For example, suppose an EIS defines its client API using a C library. The C library defines methods that client applications use to manage transactions and perform transactional access to the EIS. Such a library may even expose the distributed communication mechanisms between client applications and the EIS. The application developer now has the added task of understanding this C library—and the low-level mechanisms exposed through this API—to use the client API. This additional complexity increases the development effort in enterprise application integration.

Given the complex nature of application development and EIS integration, it is important that developers use standardized application development tools and integration frameworks.

Transactional access to EISs is also important in terms of EIS integration. Enterprises run their businesses using the information stored in their EISs—the success of an enterprise critically depends on this information. An enterprise cannot afford to have an application cause inconsistent data or compromise the integrity of data stored in an EIS. Various applications require ensured transactional access to the EISs.

Secure access to its EISs is also of critical importance to an enterprise. An enterprise must be able to depend on the information in its EIS for its business activities. Any loss or inaccuracy of information, or any unauthorized access to the EIS, is extremely costly to an enterprise.

Scalability is another important requirement. Over time, enterprises can expect to increase their relationships to suppliers, buyers, and partners. Their applications, particularly those that access EISs, must be scalable and able to support a large number of clients. To accomplish this, use of connection pooling becomes an important requirement for EIS integration.

Additionally, enterprises must consider their existing application investment and a cost-effective integration plan. Most enterprises and EISs have invested sizable amounts in their existing application code and infrastructure. Although they recognize the need to migrate to a J2EE platform, they must accomplish this migration incrementally rather than in one step. An incremental migration lets them get maximum use from their existing systems, but still gradually add new functionality as J2EE components and make more of their existing applications J2EE accessible. During this migration process, they can rely on application server and system software vendors to manage the system-level complexity of transactions and security, and thus let their application developers focus on solving business domain problems.

1.5 Enterprise Application Integration Approaches

There are several approaches to achieving enterprise application integration. We have identified five approaches that we feel are used to integrate existing enterprise information systems with enterprise applications. These approaches are

- Using a two-tier client server
- Using synchronous adapters
- Using asynchronous adapters
- Using a message broker approach
- Using an application server-based approach

1.5.1 Two-Tier Client-Server Approach

This approach is based on the two-tier client-server model used by applications that are not based on the Web. It was a widely used approach prior to the advent of Web-based applications, but is less used now.

With this approach, an EIS provides an adapter that defines an API for accessing the data and functions of the EIS. A client application accesses data and functions exposed by an EIS through this adapter interface. The client uses the programmatic API exposed by the adapter to connect to and access the EIS. The adapter implements the support for communication with the EIS and provides access to EIS data and functions.

Communication between an adapter and the EIS use a protocol specific to the EIS. This protocol may provide support for security and transactions. It also supports content propagation from an application to the EIS. Most adapters expose an API to the client that abstracts out the details of the underlying protocol and the distribution mechanism between the EIS and the adapter. (See Figure 1.4.)

Although a resource adapter is specific to a particular EIS, an EIS may provide more than one adapter that a client can use to access the EIS. Because the key to EIS adapters is their reusability, EISs, or independent software vendors (ISVs), try to develop adapters that employ a widely used programming language and expose a client programming model that has the greatest degree of reusability.

An EIS may provide a simple form of an adapter, where the adapter maps an API that is specific to the EIS to a reusable, standard API. Often, such an adapter

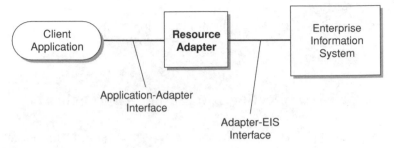

Figure 1.4   EIS Resource Adapter Approach to EAI

is developed as a library. When developed as a library, the application developer can use the same programming language to access the adapter that he or she uses to write the application, and the EIS requires no modifications. For example, a Java application developer can use a Java-based adapter—an adapter written in the Java programming language—to access an EIS that is based on some non-Java language or platform.

An EIS adapter may be developed as a C library. (See Figure 1.5.) A Java application uses a Java™ Native Interface (JNI) interface to access this C library or C-based resource adapter. The JNI is the native programming interface for Java, and it is part of the Java™ Development Kit (JDK). The JNI allows Java code that runs within a Java Virtual Machine to operate with applications and libraries written in other languages, such as C and C++. Programmers use the JNI to write native methods when they cannot write the entire application in Java. This is the case when a Java application needs to access an existing library or application written in another programming language. (Although the JNI was especially useful before the advent of the J2EE platform, many of its uses may now be replaced by the J2EE Connector architecture.)

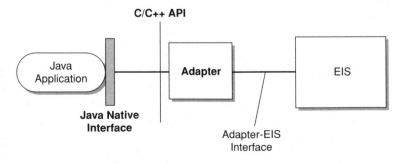

Figure 1.5   Using the Java Native Interface

The JNI interface to the resource adapter enables the Java application to communicate with the adapter's C library. Although this approach does work, it is complex to use. The Java application has to understand how to invoke methods through the JNI interface. This approach also provides none of the J2EE support for transactions, security, and scalability. The developer is exposed to the complexity of managing these system-level services and must do so through the complex JNI interface.

Another, more complex form of an EIS adapter might do its "adaptation" work across diverse component models, distributed computing platforms, and architectures. For example, an EIS may develop a distributed adapter that can communicate remotely with the EIS. This type of adapter exposes a client programming model based on a component model architecture.

Adapters use different levels of abstraction, and expose different APIs based on those abstractions, depending on the type of the EIS. For example, with certain types of EISs, an adapter may expose a remote function call API to the client application. If so, a client application uses this remote function call API to execute its interactions with the EIS.

An adapter for other types of EISs may expose a data-based programming model for the client application developer. When the adapter exposes this sort of programming model, a client application accesses EIS data using a data representation and access model specific to the EIS or relational data model.

It is also possible for an adapter to build on the API (the remote function call or data access API) exposed by the EIS. That is, a more advanced adapter may use the lower level abstraction layer exposed by the EIS to build a higher level business process or business object abstraction for client application developers.

1.5.2 Using Synchronous Adapters

An adapter can expose either a synchronous or an asynchronous mode of communication between the client applications and the EIS. Figure 1.6 illustrates using

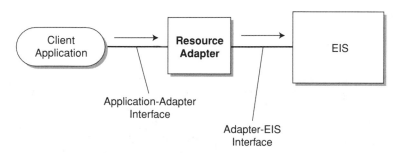

Figure 1.6 Using a Synchronous Adapter

adapters designed for synchronous communication. Adapters designed for this approach provide a synchronous request-reply communication model for use between an application and an EIS.

How might a synchronous adapter work? As an example, let's consider an adapter that defines an API that includes a remote function callable by an application. This remote function creates an accounts receivable item in the EIS. When an application wants to interact with the EIS to create an accounts receivable item, it invokes this remote function on the EIS. The application that initiated the call then waits until the function completes and returns its reply to the caller. The reply contains the results of the function's execution on the EIS. An interaction such as this is considered synchronous because the execution of the calling application waits synchronously during the time the function executes on the EIS.

One form of synchronous adapter allows bidirectional synchronous communication between an application and an EIS. This type of adapter enables an EIS to synchronously call an application.

1.5.3   Using Asynchronous Adapters

Asynchronous adapters provide another approach to application integration. Figure 1.7 provides a high-level view of this form of communication.

Let's use the same example of an adapter that exposes an API with a remote function that permits an application to interact with the EIS and create an accounts receivable item. This function is callable by an application.

Asynchronous Outbound Communication

Asynchronous Inbound Communication

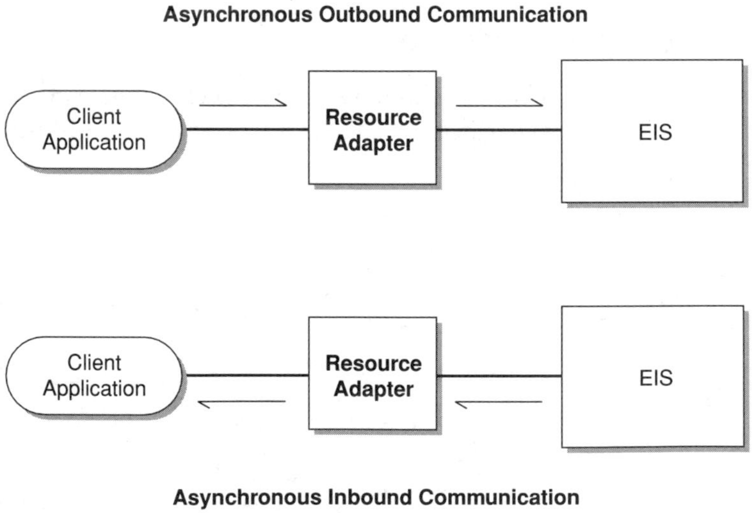

Figure 1.7   Using Asynchronous Adapters

With asynchronous communication, an application calls the remote function to create a new accounts receivable item in the EIS. The application makes the remote call, then immediately returns and continues its own processing. The remote function is sent to the EIS. The EIS handles the function and returns some reply information to the application as a separate asynchronous invocation. The resource adapter dispatches the asynchronous call from the EIS to the application.

The important point to remember is that the application does not suspend its own processing while the remote function executes on the EIS. Rather, the application continues its own work and receives notification at some later point of the results of its earlier remote function invocation. In addition, an EIS is able to asynchronously invoke or call an application.

1.5.4 Queue-Based Approach

Asynchronous message-based communication may also be used to integrate enterprise applications and EISs. There are two forms of asynchronous messaging: queue-based messaging and publish-subscribe messaging. A message broker may provide either one of these forms of messaging. Figure 1.8 illustrates queue-based communication.

In queue-based communication, which is also called point-to-point messaging, one application sends a message to a message queue. With queue-based communication, a queue that is independent from both the sender and receiver applications acts as a message buffer between the communicating applications. The sender application sends a message to this queue, and the receiver application receives its messages from the same queue.

1.5.5 Publish-Subscribe Approach

The publish-subscribe approach works differently from the queue-based approach. Figure 1.9 illustrates publish-subscribe messaging.

Figure 1.9 might be a stock quote service that publishes messages—updated stock prices—to subscribed portfolio applications. With publish-subscribe

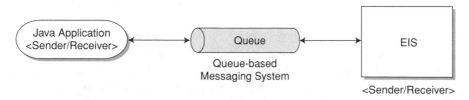

Figure 1.8 Using a Message Queue for EIS Integration

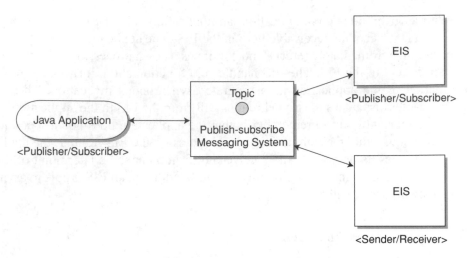

Figure 1.9   Using a Publish-Subscribe System for EIS Integration

messaging, there are message publishers, who produce messages, and message subscribers, who register their interest in particular messages. There is also a separate publish-subscribe facility that acts as the integration point—publishers publish messages to this facility and the facility delivers messages to subscribers.

Here's how publish-subscribe messaging works. A publisher application publishes messages on a specific topic, such as up-to-the-minute quotes on a specific stock symbol. Multiple applications can subscribe to this topic and receive the messages published by the publisher. The publish-subscribe facility takes the responsibility of delivering the published messages to the subscribing applications based on the subscribed topic.

When an application needs to use either queue-based or publish-subscribe messaging, it must also hook into a messaging system that provides these mechanisms. The application uses an API exposed by the messaging system to access the messaging services. The messaging system uses a messaging adapter, also called a provider, to implement the messaging API. Java™ Message Service (JMS) provides an API for enterprise messaging systems. Applications, called JMS clients, use the JMS API to access the messaging service and either a queue-based or publish-subscribe messaging system. (See Figure 1.10.) Refer to Chapter 6, Asynchronous Messaging, for more information on JMS.

Figure 1.11 illustrates using a message broker for EIS integration. Notice that an adapter enables an application to access the message broker. In this scenario, an adapter maps the application-level interface for the message broker to the underlying asynchronous messaging mechanisms supported by the message broker, plus the adapter maps the message formats supported by the message broker. (The underlying messaging mechanisms supported by the message broker may be a queue-

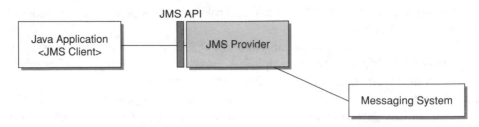

Figure 1.10 Using a JMS Provider

based or a publish-subscribe mechanism, for example.) Some adapters layer additional functionality between the application and the message broker. For example, they may add a message transformation capability—an adapter may transform application-specific messages to a format expected by the message broker. The message broker then converts the message to a format expected by the message receiver or subscriber.

When applications and EISs use a message broker for integration and message delivery, the applications and the EISs can act as both message producers and consumers. For example, a financial accounting application can subscribe to messages that carry information on financial transactions. An order management application may send a message through the message broker that updates an account payable in

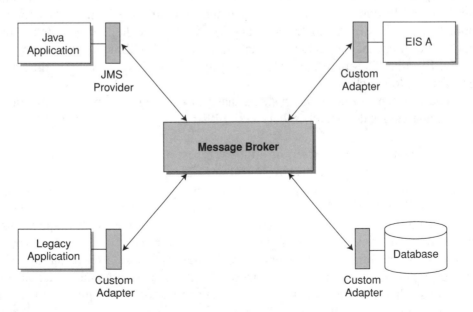

Figure 1.11 Using a Message Broker for EIS Integration

the accounting application. Most message broker vendors provide vendor-specific adapters for popular EISs.

When an application and an EIS communicate using asynchronous messaging, they are considered to be loosely coupled. A loosely coupled integration has advantages and disadvantages. With a loosely coupled integration between a target EIS and an application, the application can continue processing client requests without blocking on EIS performance or communication glitches. This improves scalability. However, application developers may find it difficult to program against an asynchronous messaging model. Also, these asynchronous messaging systems do not always support the propagation of security and transactional contexts.

A message broker may provide additional services for enterprise application integration. These additional services are message routing, transaction management, reliable message delivery, message priority and ordering, and message transformation. We discuss these topics further in Chapter 6.

1.5.6   Application Server-Based Integration

Figure 1.12 shows how an application server can be used for integration with existing enterprise applications and EISs.

An application server is a natural point for application integration because it provides a platform for development, deployment, and management of Web-based enterprise applications. Application servers are the platform of choice for applications that are developed using a multi-tier architecture.

A typical multi-tier application consists of three tiers: a client tier, a middle tier, and an EIS tier. The middle tier implements the business logic for an application. As part of its implementation of application business logic functionality, the middle tier might access data and functions associated with applications running on the EIS tier. The middle tier also serves up both static and dynamic presentation content to the client tier.

The EIS tier contains the systems that run existing enterprise applications and databases. As described earlier, these EISs can be custom or off-the-shelf applications.

The client tier is composed of different types of client applications. A client can be a Web browser-based HTML client or a peer application.

An application server supports a component-based model for developing applications. With this model, an application may be composed of different types of components, such as Web components or business components. The application server provides deployment and runtime support for these application components. In effect, an application server provides an extremely useful platform for the development of Web-based, transactional, secure, distributed, and scalable applications. This increases the usefulness of an application server environment for enterprise application integration.

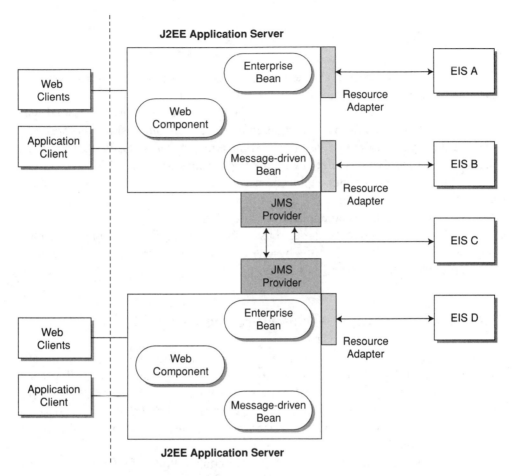

Figure 1.12 Application Server-Based Enterprise Application Integration

An application server provides a set of runtime services to its deployed components. These runtime services are hidden from the application components through a simplified application programming model. The services provided include

- Support for transactions
- Security
- Load balancing and failover
- Database access
- Asynchronous messaging
- Distributed communications

- Web protocols

- XML support

It is possible to develop and deploy applications on an application server such that the applications can connect and aggregate access to multiple heterogeneous EISs and existing enterprise applications. When applications are developed with this ability to access multiple heterogeneous EISs, Web and business components that are deployed on the middle tier (or application server) use adapters to access the data and functions associated with the applications on these EISs.

Application components deployed on the application servers use synchronous resource adapters to connect and access EISs. As explained earlier, this is tightly coupled integration between applications and EISs.

Application components can also use an adapter (or JMS provider) to a message broker to integrate with EISs based on asynchronous messaging. We explain this approach in greater detail in Chapter 6.

1.6 J2EE Connector Architecture and EAI

How does the J2EE Connector architecture fit in with the EAI scheme of things? To begin with, the Connector architecture is designed to simplify integrating J2EE components with EISs. The architecture makes it easier to connect J2EE components and applications to heterogeneous enterprise information systems (EISs). Examples of EISs include database systems, ERP systems, and mainframe transaction processing (TP).

How does the Connector architecture accomplish this? The Connector architecture defines a set of mechanisms, referred to as contracts, so that EISs can easily integrate with application servers and enterprise applications. These mechanisms are designed to be scalable, secure, and transactional. These contracts exist between the J2EE application servers and the EISs.

The Connector architecture also defines a client interface API to enable J2EE application components to access a multitude of heterogeneous EISs. This client API is called the Common Client Interface (CCI).

An EIS vendor who wants to participate in the Connector architecture must provide its half of the bargain—that it, the EIS vendor must support the Connector contracts. The EIS vendor can provide a standard resource adapter for its EIS, and this resource adapter can plug into any J2EE-compliant application server. (A resource adapter is a system-level software library that a Java application on the J2EE platform uses to connect to an EIS.) The resource adapter is the connection conduit between the enterprise application on the application server and the EIS.

Because the Connector architecture defines the resource adapter requirements, the EIS vendor is assured that his or her resource adapter will work with any J2EE-compliant application server. This means that the EIS vendor must only provide one standard resource adapter for all J2EE application servers and not a separate adapter for each application server.

Likewise, the application server vendor, by following the terms of the Connector contracts defined for an application server, only has to extend its product once to support the Connector architecture. By supporting the Connector architecture, the application server also supports multiple EIS resource adapters, regardless of the EIS vendor.

Application integration in a Web-based, e-business environment encompasses three layers: a business process layer, an integration layer, and an application server layer. Each layer, in turn, holds technologies that serve as the application server integration building blocks. (See Figure 1.13.)

The application server layer technologies, which are based on the J2EE platform and use the Connector architecture, enable an application integration project to link not only with existing enterprise systems but also with the Web and other, wireless applications.

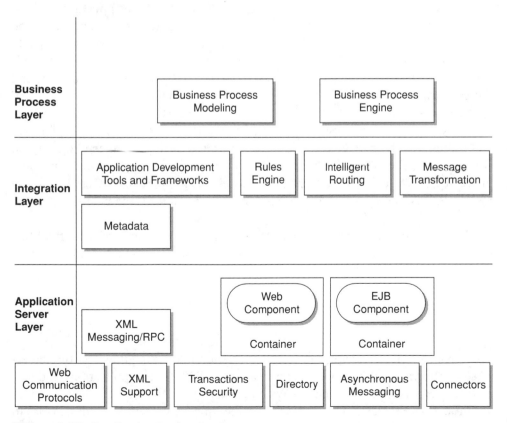

Figure 1.13 Application Integration Layers

A J2EE-based application server is at the bottom layer of this application integration platform. A J2EE application server provides value to the application integration platform through such services as

- **The J2EE component-container model**—This model includes the Enterprise JavaBeans (EJB) container and such components as enterprise beans and message-driven beans. It also includes the JavaServer Pages (JSP) and servlet components defined in the J2EE platform.

- **Java Message Service**—JMS provides support for asynchronous messaging.

- **A set of APIs that support transactions, security, and naming and directory services.**

- **A set of APIs that add support for XML messaging and Remote Procedure Calls (RPCs)**—(It is anticipated that this support will be in future versions of the J2EE platform specification.)

The application integration platform adds an integration layer on top of the J2EE-based application server. This integration layer provides support for application development tools and frameworks. These development tools and integration frameworks are based on the J2EE application programming model, and they rely on metadata for generating and providing services. The integration layer also adds support for such functionality as a rules engine, intelligent message routing, and message transformation, all on top of the base functionality provided by the J2EE application server.

Last, a business process layer serves as the top-most layer for the platform and represents an enterprise's unique way of doing business. Enterprises rely on software packages from different vendors to develop and manage their business processes. This business process layer exposes business process level abstraction by providing support for business process modeling and for the business process engine.

Figure 1.14 illustrates a typical application integration platform, with the J2EE platform and the J2EE Connector architecture together acting as building blocks for Web-driven application integration.

1.7   Conclusion

There is a definite trend among enterprises toward integrating their existing enterprise applications and information systems with Web-based applications and services. Enterprises must establish a Web presence and make their business services available to Web clients. However, at the same time, an enterprise cannot afford to

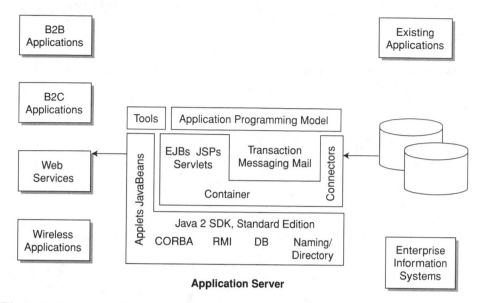

Figure 1.14 Application Integration on the J2EE Platform

discard its existing systems and applications, but must leverage these existing assets to be successful.

This chapter highlighted some of the tasks and challenges that face enterprises that are compelled to integrate their information systems and applications and then expose these applications and systems to the Web. It also showed how the J2EE platform and the J2EE Connector architecture serve as building blocks for Web-driven application integration. The J2EE platform and the Connector architecture, by providing standardized integration contracts, have enabled application servers to serve a key role in the Web-driven application integration process.

This Web-driven application integration is a process that closes the gap between existing applications and Web-based applications and services. Ultimately, Web service and wireless clients, in a B2C or B2B context, will be able to initiate business processes that act on critical information maintained in EISs.

In Chapter 2, we provide an overview of the Connector architecture and describe its role within the J2EE platform.

J2EE Connector Architecture Overview

THIS chapter provides a high-level overview of the J2EE Connector architecture. In addition to introducing the key concepts of the architecture, it describes the value that the Connector architecture adds to the J2EE platform.

The J2EE platform is a Java platform for developing and deploying Web-based, multi-user applications. These are distributed applications that require an environment that is secure, transactional, and scalable. The J2EE platform is the application architecture that is probably best suited for Web and network distributed environments.

The J2EE platform consists of several different technologies, some of which operate at the system level and some of which are more exposed to clients. These latter technologies include the Enterprise JavaBeans (EJB) architecture, JavaServer Pages™ (JSP™), and servlets. The EJB architecture defines a component model for enterprise applications, and it provides portability across application servers. JSP and servlets support dynamic HTML generation and session management for Web-based clients.

The other technologies and APIs of the J2EE platform operate closer to the system level. These technologies, such as JDBC, Java Message Service (JMS), Java™ Transaction Service (JTS) and Java™ Transaction API (JTA), among others, provide standard programming interfaces for Java applications to access enterprise infrastructure services.

2.1 What Is the J2EE Platform?

The J2EE platform is particularly suited for the development and deployment of enterprise Web-based applications that use the Java programming language. Its architecture provides both server- and client-side support for both enterprise and Web-based applications that run in multi-tiered environments.

Figure 2.1 shows the J2EE support for a typical multi-tier architecture.

Multi-tier applications usually are configured into three parts: a client tier, a middle tier, and an EIS tier. The client tier may include browser-based clients, peer enterprise applications, and Java-based client applications. The middle tier supports modules that provide application services to the client and that implement the application's business logic. Keep in mind that there can be more than one such middle tier. The enterprise information system (EIS) tier (sometimes referred to as the back-end tier) supports the enterprise information systems that manage and store enterprise critical data and functions. The Connector architecture integrates applications that are in the middle tier application server with the EIS tier.

For example, the J2EE architecture supports multi-tier applications that might be divided along the following lines:

- A Web browser-based client. Often, such a client encompasses the presentation logic.

- An application server with an EJB container and a Web container. The EJB container handles the business logic tier. The Web container, using servlets, JSPs, and so forth, provides services for the generation of dynamic and static content targeted for Web browser-based clients.

- A relational database or legacy system such as the EIS tier, connected to the middle tier via the Connector architecture.

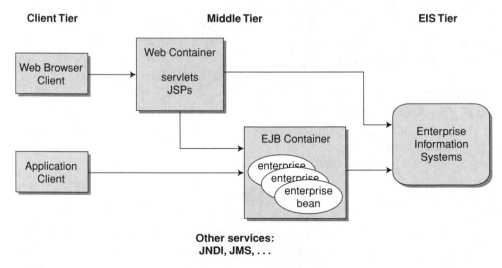

Figure 2.1   J2EE Support for Multi-tier Applications

The J2EE architecture is designed to support distributed application development. That is, in a J2EE multi-tier environment, each part of the application can run on a different platform or node. In fact, the middle tier itself is not restricted to one tier, but may be divided into sub-tiers and these sub-tiers distributed across nodes.

2.1.1   Components and Containers

Conceptually the J2EE architecture divides the programming environment into containers. A *container* is a standardized runtime environment that provides specific services to components. A *component* is an application-level software unit that is supported by a container. In the J2EE environment, a Web container provides standard Web-specific services, whereas an EJB container provides services to support enterprise bean components. For example, an EJB container provides such services as transaction management, security, multi-threading, distributed programming, and connection pooling. A Web container provides communication APIs and protocols and network services to facilitate sending and receiving requests and responses.

Keep in mind that all J2EE-compliant platforms, regardless of the vendor, are required to provide these services. Figure 2.2 illustrates the J2EE component types and their containers. It is a good road map to help you understand the discussion that follows.

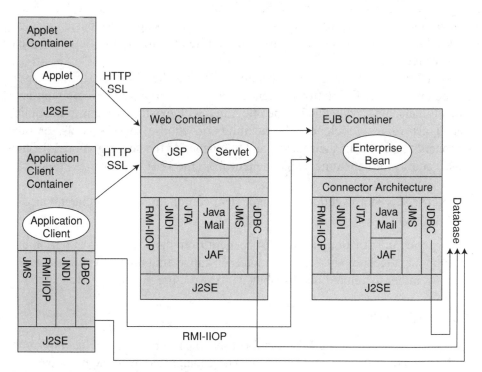

Figure 2.2   J2EE Components and Containers

The J2EE client tier supports a variety of client types. A client may be a Web browser using HTML pages, or it may use dynamic HTML generated with JSP technology. A client may be a Java applet or a standalone Java application. J2EE clients access the middle tier using standard Web communication protocols. In multi-tier environments, they never directly access the EIS tier.

The middle tier consists of the Web and EJB containers, plus other services, such as Java Naming and Directory Interface (JNDI), JMS, JavaMail, and so forth. The Web container provides the programming environment for developing and deploying servlets and JSPs. Typically, servlets and JSPs encompass an application's presentation logic and the logic that controls client interaction. Web components, when packaged together, comprise a Web application. The Web container, through servlets and JSPs, provides runtime support for receiving HTTP requests and composing HTTP responses to these requests. It ensures that results are returned to the requesting client.

The EJB container, which is also in the middle tier, provides the environment for developing and running enterprise bean components. It is often considered the backbone of the J2EE programming environment. Enterprise bean components are Java code that implement an enterprise's business processes and entities. They perform the application's business operations and encapsulate the business logic. The EJB container automatically handles transaction and life-cycle management for its enterprise bean components. In addition, the EJB container provides other services to its beans, such as lookup and security services, and standardized access via the Connector architecture to the EIS tier database or legacy system.

What are the advantages and benefits of using the J2EE platform? Among other benefits, the J2EE platform offers developers a simplified development environment that scales easily and can be integrated with existing systems and applications. It also gives developers the flexibility to choose servers, tools, or other components that best fit their needs, and to customize the security model for their needs. Vendors and customers alike benefit from the J2EE platform, as follows:

- Enterprise system vendors can implement compliant products that are also customizable.

- Corporate information technologists benefit from the advantages of portable component technology—they can focus on supporting business process requirements rather than handling distributed infrastructure integration problems.

2.1.2   J2EE Technologies

As we've already noted, the J2EE platform specifies technologies to support multi-tier, distributed application development. These supported technologies are divided into three categories: components, services, and communication.

Components are separate application modules—that is, separate application-level software units—that can be reused by other enterprise applications. (Technically speaking, a component is a reusable piece of software that encapsulates data and behavior, has a defined life-cycle model, and provides services to clients. Components can be packaged together to compose an application.) Generally these component technologies encompass the technologies used by developers to create the business logic and user interface portions of the application. The J2EE platform supports several different kinds of components, such as Enterprise Java-Bean (EJB) components, Web components (servlets and JSPs), and application clients, including applets. Typically, application clients and applets run on a client platform, whereas enterprise bean and Web components run on a server platform.

Enterprise service technologies encompass the APIs that provide access to existing enterprise services. These APIs pertain to database access, transactions, naming and directory services for lookup capabilities, and messaging services. The J2EE technology also enables communication between clients and servers. It also supports distribution protocols and mechanisms between multiple servers.

The J2EE platform also provides service technologies. These are the system-level services that support the other technologies and simplify application development. The principal services provided by the J2EE platform are naming, deployment, transaction, and security services.

The Java Naming and Directory Interface (JNDI) provides naming and directory functionality. It provides a means for an application to locate components that exist in a name space according to certain attributes. A J2EE application component uses the JNDI interfaces to look up and reference system-provided and user-defined objects in the component environment.

The J2EE deployment services allow users to customize components and applications when they are deployed in an operational environment. A deployment descriptor file is an XML document. Its elements declaratively describe how to assemble components and deploy the parts of the application into a specific environment. Users can customize the deployment descriptor for an application.

Transaction services are another important service of the J2EE platform. The J2EE platform manages transactions for an application. It provides for failure recovery and handles multi-user programming, thus ensuring that each transactional unit of work fully completes without interference from other processes. The platform provides the Java Transaction API (JTA) so that applications can use transactions.

Within the EJB container, transactions may be controlled completely by the container (container-managed transactions) or they may be handled by the enterprise bean itself (bean-managed transactions). With container-managed transactions, the EJB container handles all aspects of a transaction—starting the transaction, maintaining and propagating transaction context, and committing or rolling back the transaction—based on elements in the deployment descriptor.

When bean-managed transactions are used, the enterprise bean itself must manage these aspects of a transaction.

The J2EE platform also provides security services that ensure authorized access to resources. These security services control access through a two-step process of authentication and authorization. A principal, which is typically a user or another program, authenticates itself by providing a name and password, referred to as its authentication data. Once authenticated, a principal must have the correct authorizations to access a particular resource. The J2EE platform authorization is based on security roles, which are logical groupings of users defined for the application environment.

The JDBC API provides database-independent connectivity between the J2EE platform and a wide variety of relational databases. Using the JDBC API, an application can perform such functions as connect to a database server, manage transactions, execute stored procedures and SQL statements, and retrieve stored data.

The J2EE platform provides a messaging technology for asynchronous messaging. Java Message Service (JMS) is an API for using enterprise messaging systems. Such messages contain information describing specific business actions. JMS supports both point-to-point queue-based and publish-subscribe messaging.

JavaMail is an API for an electronic mail system. Its abstract classes and interfaces support various implementations of message stores, formats, and transports. JavaMail uses the JavaBeans Activation Framework (JAF) to integrate support for MIME data types into the Java platform. Applications do not use JAF directly.

The Remote Method Invocation (RMI) set of APIs allows developers to build distributed applications in the Java environment. RMI-IIOP is an implementation of the RMI API over the Internet Inter-ORB Protocol (IIOP). This implementation permits developers to write remote interfaces in Java. The remote interface can be converted to the Interface Definition Language (IDL) and then can be implemented in any other language that supports Object Management Group (OMG) protocols and includes an Object Request Broker (ORB) library. Thus RMI-IIOP provides interoperability with CORBA objects implemented in any language.

2.2   J2EE Connector Architecture Overview

The Connector architecture defines a standard architecture for connecting the J2EE platform to heterogeneous EISs. The architecture is based on the technologies that are defined and standardized as part of the J2EE platform. (The J2EE Connector architecture is a required part of version 1.3 of the J2EE platform.) It addresses the key issues and requirements of EIS integration by defining a set of scalable, secure, and transactional mechanisms that enable the integration of EISs with application servers and enterprise applications.

Prior to the existence of the Connector architecture, the Java platform had no standard architecture for integrating heterogeneous EISs. It was up to the individual EIS vendors and application server vendors to determine their own EIS integration approach. As a result, early EIS integration implementations used nonstandard, vendor-specific architectures.

The introduction of the Connector architecture has changed the situation for the better. By adhering to the Connector architecture, EIS vendors no longer need to customize their product for each application server. Application server vendors who conform to the J2EE Connector architecture do not need to add custom code when they add connectivity to a new EIS.

2.2.1 Connector Architecture Contracts

EIS vendors or third-party independent software vendors (ISVs) specializing in enterprise application integration use the Connector architecture to develop standard resource adapters for different EIS types. Because these resource adapters conform to the Connector architecture specifications, they can plug into any J2EE-compliant application server and provide connectivity among the EIS, the application server, and the enterprise application.

What advantages does the Connector architecture for standard resource adapters offer? For one, it makes application development faster and easier. An application server and resource adapter (and its underlying EIS) collaborate to keep all system-level mechanisms—transactions, security, and connection pooling—transparent from the application. As a result, an application developer focuses on the development of business and presentation logic for its application components and does not need to get involved in the system-level issues related to EIS integration. Removing the system-level issues improves the development cycle for enterprise applications that require connectivity with multiple EISs in a scalable, secure, and transactional manner.

To accomplish its goals, the Connector architecture defines two types of contracts (see Figure 2.3):

- A system-level contract between an application server and a resource adapter

- An application contract between an application component and a resource adapter

2.2.2 System-Level Contracts

The Connector architecture's system-level contracts define a "pluggability" standard between application servers and EISs. By adhering to the terms of these contracts when developing their components, an application server and an EIS know

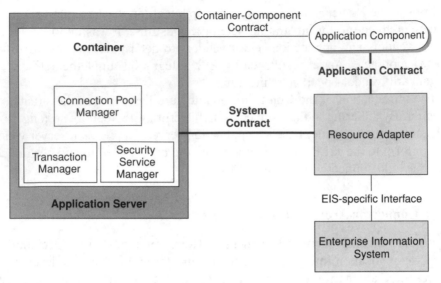

Figure 2.3   Connector Architecture: System and Application Contracts

that connecting will be a straightforward operation of plugging in the resource adapter.

The EIS vendor or resource adapter provider implements its side of the system-level contracts in a resource adapter. A resource adapter is a system library that is specific to the EIS and designed to provide connectivity to the EIS. The resource adapter is the component that plugs in to an application server. Keep in mind that a resource adapter is a library used within the address space of the application server.

You can think of an adapter as analogous to a JDBC driver. In fact, one example of a resource adapter is a JDBC driver that connects to a relational database (as specified in the JDBC specification). Other examples of resource adapters include an adapter that connects to an ERP system and one that connects to a mainframe transaction processing system.

Figure 2.3 shows that the system contracts sit between the application server and the EIS's resource adapter. In addition, notice the interface between a resource adapter and its particular EIS. This interface is specific to the type of the EIS, and it may be a native interface or some other type of interface. (Also note that the Connector architecture does not define this interface.)

The resource adapter abstracts the details of both the interface and communication between the underlying resource adapter library and the EIS system. Typically, the EIS and the resource adapter communicate over some EIS-specific protocol. A resource adapter can also use a native library as part of its implementation.

The application server is a J2EE-compliant server. The application server may host Web containers and EJB containers. Web containers, in turn, host JSPs and servlets, whereas EJB containers host enterprise beans. The application server also provides a set of services—including transaction management, security services, and connection pooling—that it implements in its own specific way. That is, the Connector architecture does not define how the server implements these services. The resource adapter, in turn, can rely on the set of system-level contracts to determine how it will plug in to an application server, and it must only implement the EIS side of the system contracts. The application server uses these system-level contracts with the resource adapter to manage transactions, security, and connection pooling.

Thus, from the application server point of view, the system contracts are considered a Service Provider Interface (SPI). An SPI provides a standard way for a vendor to extend a container to support connectivity to multiple EISs.

What are the contracts between the server and resource adapter that constitute the set of system-level contracts in the 1.0 version of the Connector architecture? Currently there are three contracts. (These contracts are expected to be extended in the 2.0 version of the Connector architecture to provide support for thread management and asynchronous communication with EISs.)

- **Connection management contract**—This contract enables an application server to pool connections to an underlying EIS, while at the same time it enables application components to connect to an EIS. Pooling connections is important to create a scalable application environment, particularly when large numbers of clients require access to the underlying EIS.

- **Transaction management contract**—This contract is between the transaction manager that is provided with the application server and an EIS that supports transactions. It gives an application server's transaction manager the ability to manage transactions across multiple EIS resource managers. (A *resource manager* provides access to a set of shared resources.) The contract also supports transactions that do not involve an external transaction manager; that is, local transactions that an EIS resource manager handles internally.

- **Security contract**—The security contract enables secure access to an EIS. It provides support for a secure application environment and protects the EIS-managed resources.

Note that the container component contract refers to contracts defined in various component model specifications. For example, the EJB specification specifies a contract between an enterprise bean and an EJB container.

2.2.3   Application Contract

The Connector architecture also defines an application-level contract between an application component and a resource adapter. In particular, this contract defines the client API that an application component uses for EIS access. The client API may be the Common Client Interface (CCI) or it may be an API specific to the particular type of resource adapter and the underlying EIS. JDBC is an example of a client API specific to one type of resource adapter, in this case, a relational database.

The CCI defines a common client API for accessing multiple heterogeneous EISs. It is well suited for enterprise application integration (EAI) and enterprise tool vendors. (See Chapter 7 for more information on the CCI.)

2.2.4   Packaging and Deployment

Because the Connector architecture emphasizes the pluggability of resource adapters in to application servers, it also provides a standard packaging model for resource adapters and a deployment model that enables such adapter pluggability. (See Chapter 11.)

A resource adapter provider is expected to develop a resource adapter according to the Connector architecture's packaging model. By adhering to this model, the server's deployment tools can easily deploy the packaged resource adapter in the application server's operational environment.

2.2.5   Why Use the Connector Architecture?

There are several reasons to use the Connector architecture. Principally, using the Connector architecture reduces the scope of integration and simplifies application development. It also makes it easier to use tools for EIS integration, and it avoids vendor lock in.

2.2.5.1   Scope of Integration

Of course, it is possible to accomplish EIS integration without using a standard architecture such as the Connector architecture. However, in such a situation, each application server vendor spends a significant effort to architect and implement its integration with each type of EIS. The application server vendor must repeat, to a great extent, the amount of effort—devising and implementing a new solution—for each type of EIS. The EIS vendor, too, must expend a significant amount of effort providing adapters to its EIS, and it must repeat this effort for each application server. As a result, the adapters and the application server's integration solutions are nonstandard, proprietary software, and they are both difficult to maintain and evolve.

Taking this one step further, suppose you have m number of application server vendors and n number of EIS vendors. The effort to integrate all these application servers with all EIS vendors, without using the Connector architecture, could be expressed by the formula m multiplied by n, or $(m * n)$. Given the growing number of application servers and EISs, it is easy to see that integration becomes a significant task.

The Connector architecture greatly reduces this level of effort. An application server vendor that uses the Connector architecture must only be extended once to support the system-level contracts. Likewise, an EIS vendor using the Connector architecture must only provide a single resource adapter that supports the Connector contracts. With one implementation effort, an application server can integrate with multiple EISs. Also, a single resource adapter for an EIS can plug in to multiple application servers. Thus the Connector architecture reduces the scope of the EIS integration effort to the sum of the number of application server vendors plus the number of EISs, or $m + n$. This represents a significant reduction in the scope of an integration effort. In addition, resource adapters are based on a standard architecture that includes a defined integration and application programming model.

2.2.5.2   Application Development

In addition to reducing the scope of integration, the Connector architecture simplifies application development. Because the application servers and resource adapters rely on the system contract to provide the transaction, security, and connection pooling services for EIS integration, the application component provider does not have to be concerned with these system-level details. The system details are actually kept hidden from the component provider because they are managed by the underlying platform. Instead, the application developer focuses on developing the business and application logic.

Application developers use the J2EE application programming model with its set of components to develop their applications and to integrate with EISs. The programming model and the components simplify application development.

2.2.5.3   Tools Integration

Up to this point we have looked at EIS integration from the point of view of the application server and an EIS. It is also important to consider EIS integration from the perspective of enterprise application development tools vendors and vendors of EAI frameworks. A similar scope of integration scale—that of $m * n$—applies to these vendors as it does for application server and EIS vendors.

An enterprise tools vendor provides tools to simplify the application programming model and reduce the effort required in EIS integration. An EAI vendor provides a framework to support integration across multiple EISs and enterprise applications. Both types of vendors must integrate their products across heterogeneous EISs.

Keep in mind that each EIS has its own specific client API. For example, SAP R/3 exposes its own client API, whereas CICS exposes a different client API. Typically, the tools vendor must adapt these different client APIs to a common layer API, and this is often a significant effort. The resulting adapted API, though it supports a common EIS application programming model, is also specific to the tools vendor. It's easy to see that the $m * n$ (where m represents the number of tools vendors and n represents the different EISs) integration problem quickly applies to tools vendors.

The Connector architecture's standard CCI, because it supports a common client API across heterogeneous EISs, provides a solution to tools vendors for this scope of integration problem. (Chapter 7, Common Client Interface, discusses the CCI in detail.) When a resource adapter supports the CCI, it is guaranteed that the adapter can be plugged in to any J2EE-compliant development tool and EAI framework, and that this plug-in can be achieved in a standard way. This narrows the scope of integration to m plus n ($m + n$) dimensions. Thus tool vendors need not adapt their API for a specific resource adapter. Instead, they can focus on their development tools.

2.3   Example Scenario

To illustrate how the Connector architecture helps enterprise environments integrate their disparate systems, we've developed a simple application scenario that is also broad enough to show how an enterprise might use the Connector architecture in different EAI scenarios. It's important to understand this application scenario starting with the high-level view that we present here, because we use this scenario in later chapters to describe design issues and as the basis for code examples. Keep in mind as you read through the application description that we've greatly simplified what in reality is a complex, real-world application. We did this because we wanted to highlight the important EAI concepts and not distract you with extraneous details.

Let's take the case of a fictitious company called ACI, Inc., a computer manufacturing firm that has decided to build a Web-enabled order processing system that supports business-to-business (B2B) interactions. ACI's primary goal is to have buyers place orders for its computers and software using the Web interface of the order processing system. At the same time, ACI wants the order processing system to handle XML-based B2B interactions with buyers and suppliers.

However, ACI has significant investments in its existing information systems and its legacy applications, and it is imperative that it continue to use these systems. As such, it is essential that ACI integrate this new order processing system with its existing EIS and legacy applications despite some serious challenges to this integration effort. What are those challenges?

To begin with, ACI's hardware division manages its manufacturing operations and inventory using an ERP system-based logistics application. The ERP system, now in operation for five years, required a significant investment to install and bring up to speed. Not only was there an investment in IT infrastructure and employee training, but virtually all of the business processes and manufacturing operations have been defined in terms of this ERP system. And, because ACI cannot afford to disrupt operations, the company is reluctant to replace this system. Thus ACI must find a way to integrate its existing ERP system with Web-based order processing.

ACI's software division procures its operating system and other bundled software from various software vendors. ACI developed an in-house inventory management system, which it uses to track these procured software products. This inventory management system is deployed on a mainframe system. ACI intends to keep this existing system and to integrate it with the Web-based order processing system, for the same reasons it wants to keep the ERP system.

Last, ACI must integrate its Web-based order processing system with its financial applications and its existing customer account databases.

Because of the features and perceived benefits of the J2EE platform, ACI has decided to integrate its heterogeneous EISs and enterprise applications on a J2EE-based application server.

2.3.1 Application Requirements

The order processing application has the following enterprise application integration requirements. (To keep the book focused, note that we only list application integration requirements rather than all system requirements.)

- **The application must integrate with ACI's existing EISs and other applications.** This includes its ERP system-based logistics application, the inventory management system, the financial application, and its customer accounts database.

- **The application must be scalable.** It especially must be able to process large numbers of concurrent Web transactions. Scalability is often limited by the number of concurrent connections from clients to an EIS. For example, our example order processing application needs to create connections to the one or more EISs it must access. However, the number of sessions or clients that can access an EIS is limited by the number of concurrent connections to the EIS. Because connections are costly—they hold resources such as sockets, memory, and file descriptors—a system's ability to create new connections is limited. Thus, to achieve application scalability, it is important to be able to reuse existing connections.

- **The application must be capable of managing transactions across integrated sets of EISs.** The order processing system should be able to initiate an operation across one or more EISs and be assured that the operation will not leave any EIS data in an inconsistent state. Keep in mind that EISs differ in their transactional capabilities. (Transactional capabilities refer to the support provided for atomic, isolated, consistent, and durable operations on data. We discuss transactions later.) For example, the example relational database supports a full set of transactional capabilities, whereas the ERP system's transactional support is limited to managing transactions internal to the ERP system. That is, the ERP's transactions cannot be combined with transactions that include other EISs. And, the inventory management system supports a limited set of transaction capabilities.

- **The application must not compromise the security of its EISs.** This includes no loss of data, no data inaccuracy, and no unauthorized access to the EIS. EISs also differ in their security mechanisms and policies. ACI's relational database supports user password-based sign-on. The mainframe-based applications do not require user sign-on. Instead, they perform application-specific authorization using access control lists.

- **The application's implementation must be portable.** ACI must be able to deploy the order management application on different hardware and software platforms.

- **The application should be developed using a component-based approach and designed to be extended to meet changing requirements.** It should support both loosely coupled and tightly coupled integration with EISs and existing enterprise applications.

2.3.2   Example Architecture

The order management application is a multi-tier, component-based application developed using the J2EE application programming model. It consists of the following tiers:

- **Web tier**—The Web tier consists of the Web container, which provides the runtime environment for Web applications. The container hosts the Web components—JSPs and servlets—providing the presentation logic.

- **Enterprise JavaBeans tier**—This tier hosts the EJB container and its enterprise bean components. The bean components provide application-specific business logic; these business components link Web components to the business-critical data residing in the EIS tier. The order management application includes entity beans, session beans, and message-driven beans.

• **EIS tier**—The EIS tier consists of enterprise information systems and legacy enterprise applications. The order management application uses enterprise beans to access the EIS tier using either Java Message Service or resource adapters defined according to the Connector architecture.

Figure 2.4 captures the major components of ACI's business as they relate to the order processing application.

ACI's order management application resides on a J2EE-compliant application server. The order management application interfaces with several subsystems both internal and external to ACI. Although we briefly mention these subsystems, we focus on those interfaces that use the Connector architecture contracts.

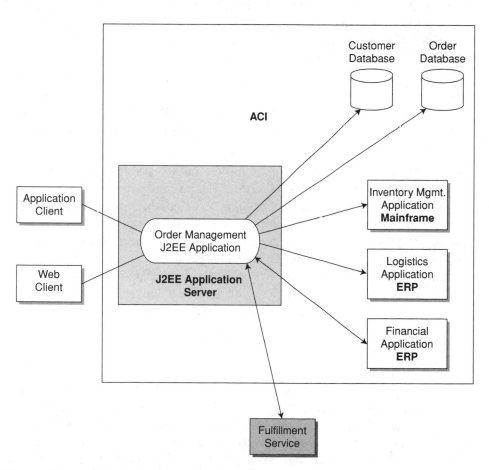

Figure 2.4   ACI Order Management System

2.3.2.1   Application Process

Orders for ACI's products come from buyers and from Web clients. Buyers use a procurement application to submit their product orders to ACI's order processing system. Web clients use a browser-based interface to initiate order processing. The order management application receives a purchase order in the form of an XML document or HTTP request, depending on how the communication between the client and the order processing application is structured.

Servlet and JSP components of the Web container within the J2EE application server receive and process HTTP requests. They pass these order requests to the enterprise bean components within the EJB container on the server. Enterprise bean components apply the appropriate order management business logic, according to ACI's business rules, to process the order.

The order management enterprise beans do such tasks as:

- **Check that the initiator of the order is in the Customer database.** This may include checking the validity of the customer's address, credit information, and so forth. The Customer database is a legacy database on a mainframe system that maintains information related to customer accounts. The interface between the Customer account database and the order management application uses the Connector architecture. A third-party ISV provides a resource adapter for this legacy database. This adapter is based on the Connector architecture and can be plugged in to any J2EE-compliant application server.

- **Check the inventory management application to establish the availability of any software products on the order.** The inventory management application resides on a mainframe system, and it manages the software product catalog and inventory. Performing this task could cause the Inventory management application to expedite its own orders for additional software products. Inventory is updated to reflect the pending order, and, at a later point, the shipped order. The inventory management application uses the Connector architecture to interface with the order management application. Because this application was developed in house, ACI's IT department has developed a resource adapter for accessing the inventory management application. The resource adapter is based on the Connector architecture specification.

- **Check the logistics application for hardware product availability.** The logistics application, which is part of an ERP system, maintains the hardware products bills of materials, build schedules, and purchasing data and lead times for parts. Depending on the current hardware availability, an order might generate a flurry of logistics application activity, including updating inventory to reflect the pending order. Later, the order management system notifies the logistics application to update the inventory balances. The ERP system vendor distributes a standard Connector architecture-based resource adapter for integrating with its logistics system, and the order management application uses this standard resource adapter to access the logistics application.

- **Interact with the financial application deployed on an ERP system to keep the financial records, such as accounts receivable, up to date**. The financial accounting application is integrated in a loosely coupled manner using asynchronous messaging. The order management application uses the Java Message Service (JMS) API to send and receive messages to the financial accounting application, which does its processing asynchronously.

- **Communicate with the Fulfillment Service Provider, an external application, to check shipping schedules and to ensure that the order is properly shipped to the customer.** This communication is accomplished using XML-based messaging.

- **Enter the order into the Order database.** The Order database is a relational database that keeps information about orders so that they can be tracked. After verifying account information, product availability, and the shipping schedule, the order management system creates a new order in the database with information about the product shipping schedule and pricing. Enterprise beans access the Order database using the JDBC API.

2.3.2.2 Roles

ACI's environment also illustrates the different Connector architecture-related roles. The resource adapter provider provides a resource adapter for an EIS. Because the adapter is specific to an EIS, the EIS vendor typically is the resource adapter provider, but a third party may serve as the provider.

The application server vendor, usually an OS or middleware vendor, provides the implementation of the J2EE-compliant application server. Often, the application server vendor is also a container provider, such as an EJB or Web container, and these containers provide additional system services to their components.

Yet another vendor supplied the JDBC driver that the order management application uses to connect to the order database. Finally, ACI's IT department developed their own adapter to their custom inventory management application.

Additional roles participate in the Connector environment. An application component provider, who is an expert in the application domain, produces the application components that access an EIS. This provider is expected to understand the enterprise's business and is not expected to be an expert at system-level programming.

An enterprise tools vendor provides tools that simplify application development for the application component provider. These tools simplify the integration of the applications with the respective EISs. (See Chapter 8, Tools and Frameworks, for more information on tools.) Some examples of typical tools include

- Data and function mining tools that allow providers to examine the scope and structure of EIS data and functions
- Analysis and design tools that simplify application design
- Code generation tools that generate Java classes for accessing EIS data and functions
- Deployment tools that simplify application deployment tasks, such as setting security and transaction requirements

The application assembler combines application components into sets of deployable modules, which the deployer uses to do the actual deployment of the application into the target operational environment. The operational environment encompasses all connected EISs and the application server. Deployment involves resolving all external application dependencies, and it is often done with the help of specific deployment tools. The deployer must ensure that all required connection factories are present in the operational environment and that the required resource adapters are also deployed. The deployer must also configure the EIS environment, especially with respect to security management.

Last, the system administrator configures and administers the enterprise infrastructure, including multiple containers and EISs. The system administrator and the deployer typically work closely together.

2.3.2.3 Application Interfaces with EISs

Figure 2.5 shows how the order management application interfaces with different EISs. Notice that most of the interfaces—to the customer database, the inventory management application, and the logistics application—are through resource adapters specific to the particular EIS. The interface to the order database uses a JDBC driver, whereas the interface to the financial application relies on a JMS provider.

2.4 Conclusion

This chapter provided a high-level overview of the Connector architecture and showed how the architecture fits with the overall J2EE platform. It also introduced the example application scenario and described the example's architecture. It is important to have a good grasp of this example because it is used to illustrate many of the architectural constructs discussed in the following chapters.

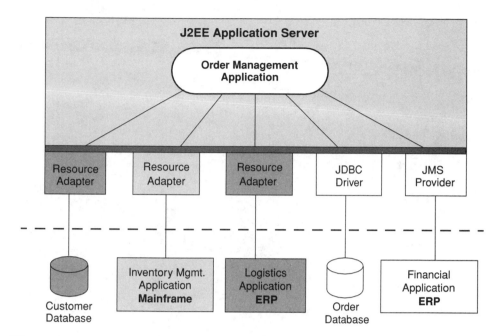

Figure 2.5   Interfaces Between Order Management Application and EISs

The next three chapters discuss the Connector architecture in more detail. We devote a separate chapter to each Connector contract—connection handling, transaction management, and security management—and discuss these contracts from an application developer's point of view. (Later chapters describe these same contracts from the point of view of an ISV.)

CHAPTER 3

Managing Connections

THIS chapter discusses how an application creates and uses connections to an underlying EIS. In particular, it focuses on the need for connection pooling and describes the different scenarios under which connection pooling is accomplished.

To provide some background and context, we begin by discussing the need for connection pooling. Enterprise applications that integrate with EISs run in either a two-tier or a multi-tier application environment. (Note that a two-tier environment is also called a nonmanaged environment, whereas a multi-tier environment is called a managed environment.) Figure 3.1 provides a simplified illustration of these two environments.

In a two-tier application environment, a client accesses an EIS that resides on a server. The client application creates a connection to an EIS. In this case, a resource adapter may provide connection pooling, or the client application may manage the connection itself.

In a multi-tier application environment, Web-based clients or applications use an application server residing on a middle tier to access EISs. The application server manages the connection pooling and provides this service to the applications deployed on the application server.

Applications require connections so that they can communicate to an underlying EIS. They use connections to access enterprise information system resources. A connection can be a database connection, a Java Message Service (JMS) connection, a SAP R/3 connection, and so forth. From an application's perspective, an application obtains a connection, uses it to access an EIS resource, then closes the connection. The application uses a connection factory to obtain a connection. Once it has obtained the connection, the application uses the connection to connect to the underlying EIS. When the application completes its work with the EIS, it closes the connection.

Why is there a need for connection pooling? Connection pooling is a way of managing connections. Because connections are expensive to create and destroy, it is imperative that they be pooled and managed properly. Proper connection pooling leads to better scalability and performance for enterprise applications.

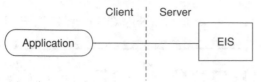

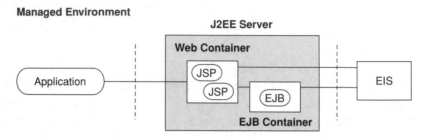

Figure 3.1 Managed and Nonmanaged Environments

Often many clients want concurrent access to the EISs at any one time. However, access to a particular EIS is limited by the number of concurrent physical connections that may be created to that EIS. The number of client sessions that can access the EIS is constrained by the EIS's physical connection limitation. An application server, by providing connection pooling, enables these connections to be shared among client sessions so that a larger number of concurrent sessions can access the EIS.

Web-based applications, in particular, have high scalability requirements. Note that the Connector architecture does not specify a particular mechanism or implementation for connection pooling by an application server. (Our example implementation presented later does demonstrate one possible approach to connection pooling.) Instead, an application server does its own implementation-specific connection pooling mechanism, but, by adhering to the Connector architecture, the mechanism is efficient, scalable, and extensible.

Prior to the advent of the J2EE Connector architecture, each application server implementation provided its own specific implementation of connection pooling. There were no standard requirements for what constituted connection pooling. As a result, it was not possible for EIS vendors to develop resource adapters that would work across all application servers and support connection pooling. Applications also could not depend on a standard support from the application server for connection pooling.

J2EE application servers that support the Connector architecture all provide standard support for connection pooling. At the same time, they keep this connection pooling support transparent to their applications. That is, the application server completely handles the connection pooling logic and applications do not have to get involved with this issue.

3.1   Connection Management Contract

The Connector architecture provides support for connection pooling and connection management through its connection management contract, one of the three principal contracts defined by the Connector architecture. The connection management contract is of most interest to application server vendors and resource adapter providers because they implement it. However, application developers will also benefit from understanding the application programming model based on the connection management contract.

The connection management contract is defined between an application server and a resource adapter. It provides support for an application server to implement its connection pooling facility. The contract enables an application server to pool its connections to an underlying EIS. It also enables individual application components to connect to an EIS.

The connection management contract defines the fundamentals for the management of connections between applications and underlying EISs. The application server uses the connection management contract to:

- Create new connections to an EIS.

- Configure connection factories in the JNDI namespace.

- Find the matching physical connection from an existing set of pooled connections.

The connection management contract provides a consistent application programming model for connection acquisition. This connection acquisition model is applicable to both managed and nonmanaged environments. More details on the connection acquisition model are given later in this chapter in the section "Application Programming Model." Chapter 12, Connection Management Contract, provides more information on the connection contract itself.

3.2   Connection Management Architecture

To understand how the connection management architecture works, let's look at Figure 3.2, which shows connection management for an application in a managed environment.

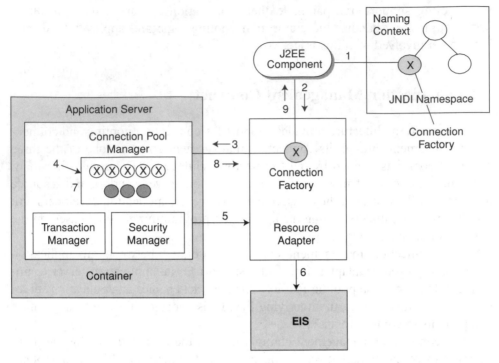

Figure 3.2   Connection Management

The resource adapter provides interfaces for an application component to create a connection to an EIS using a connection factory. An application component that wants to connect to an underlying EIS uses the services of the resource adapter.

Specific steps occur when an application component attempts to establish a connection to an EIS. However, prior to this, the deployer configures the JNDI namespace to include a connection factory. (This is marked as step 1 in Figure 3.2.) The connection factory carries the configuration information, specifically the EIS server and port number, required to create connections to the EIS. Briefly, here is what happens when an application component tries to establish a connection to an EIS.

1. The application component begins by doing a JNDI lookup of a connection factory from the JNDI namespace.

2. The application component, after successfully locating a connection factory, calls a method on the connection factory to create a connection to the EIS. It uses the connection factory to obtain a connection to the underlying EIS.

3. Before it creates the connection, the connection factory, which is provided by the resource adapter, delegates the connection request to the application server

using the connection management contract. The application server provides a connection pool, along with other services such as transaction management, security management, and error logging.

4. The application server, when it receives a request to create a connection, attempts to find a suitable existing connection in the application server's connection pool. The connections in the pool are called managed connections. A managed connection represents an actual physical connection to the underlying EIS. If the application server finds a matching connection in the pool, it uses that matching managed connection to satisfy the application's connection request.

5. If the application server cannot find a matching connection in the pool, then it uses the resource adapter to create a new physical connection—also represented by a managed connection—to the underlying EIS.

6. The resource adapter for the EIS creates a new managed connection by establishing a physical connection to the EIS. A resource adapter returns the newly created managed connection to the application server.

7. The application server adds the new managed connection to its connection pool. As part of this process, the application server creates an application-level connection handle for the managed connection. The application server returns this connection handle to the resource adapter, which in turn returns it to the application component.

8. The application component uses the connection handle returned by the resource adapter to access the EIS.

9. When the application component completes its work with the connection, it closes the connection handle.

What does all this mean to an application? Essentially, the connection management contract enables an application server to offer a number of important benefits to an application.

- It eliminates any dependencies of the application on the connection pooling and keeps the connection pooling transparent to an application. Because connection pooling is implemented independently from an application, the application need not have any knowledge of how the application server accomplishes connection pooling, nor does it have any dependencies on a particular connection pooling mechanism.

- It simplifies the application programming model for the management of connections. An application is not exposed to how the application server and resource adapter use the connection management contract.

- It enables the application server to provide different qualities of services related to EIS integration. Examples of services include transaction management, security management, and error logging and tracing support. An application server can also implement different levels of connection pooling using this connection management contract.

- It increases the scalability of an application. An application can now support a greater number of concurrent client sessions accessing EISs.

3.3   Application Programming Model

An application uses a standard application programming model when obtaining connections. The model is similar whether an application obtains the connection using an application server in a managed environment or whether it obtains the connection independent of the application server.

An application developer follows defined steps and relies on particular information to establish a connection to an underlying EIS. Before the developer can establish a connection, the necessary connection factory needs to be properly deployed and configured. The deployer is responsible for the deployment of a resource adapter and an application. The deployer also deploys and configures the connection factory. What is entailed in deploying and configuring a connection factory? The deployer configures the connection factory by providing configuration information—port number, server name, and so forth. This configuration information represents the information required by a resource adapter to create physical connections to an EIS. Once the connection factory is configured, the application can use the connection factory to create connections to the EIS. See Code Example 3.1.

Code Example 3.1   Establishing a Connection

```
package com.aci;
public class InventoryManagerEJB implements javax.ejb.SessionBean {
    private javax.resource.cci.ConnectionFactory cf;
    ...
    public int getQuantityAvailable(String productId)
            throws InventoryException {
        try {
            javax.resource.cci.Connection cx = getConnection();
            CheckInventoryCommand command =
                new CheckInventoryCommand(cx, cf.getRecordFactory());
```

```
            command.setProductId(productId);
            command.execute();
            // Close the connection.
            cx.close();
            return command.getProductQuantity();
        }
        catch (Exception e) {
            throw new InventoryException();
        }
        ...
    }

    public void removeFromInventory(String productId,
                            int quantity)
            throws InventoryException {
    }

    public Connection getConnection() {
        try {
            // Get a connection using the ConnectionFactory.
            Connection cx = cf.getConnection();
            return cx;
        }
        catch (ResourceException re) {
            throw new EJBException(re);
        }
    }

    private void initialize() {
        try {
            // Use JNDI interface to look up connection
            // factory instance.
            Context nc = new InitialContext();

            // Lookup ConnectionFactory from the JNDI namespace.
            cf = (ConnectionFactory)nc.lookup(
                "java:comp/env/eis/MainframeCxFactory");
        }
        catch (NamingException ne) {
            throw new EJBException(ne);
        }
    }
```

```
public void ejbCreate() throws RemoteException {
    initialize();
}

public void setSessionContext(SessionContext sc) {}
public void ejbRemove() throws RemoteException {}
public void ejbActivate() { /** Never Called **/ }
public void ejbPassivate() { /** Never Called **/ }
}
```

Code Example 3.1 uses the Connection and ConnectionFactory interfaces defined in the Common Client Interface. (See Chapter 7, Common Client Interface, for more information on the CCI.) When the application component needs to establish a connection, the developer uses the JNDI naming context to look up a ConnectionFactory instance.

Once the application component has a ConnectionFactory instance, the developer can obtain one or more connections to the EIS by invoking the factory's getConnection method. This method returns an application-level connection handle to the underlying physical connection. At this point, the developer may use the common client interface (CCI) application programming model to access the underlying EIS. See Chapter 12, Connection Management Contract, for details on a connection handle, and how an application server and resource adapter collaborate to manage connection pooling.

When the application component completes its work using the connection, the developer calls the close method on the connection handle.

3.4   Conclusion

We've seen in this chapter how an application can create connections to underlying EISs. In a managed environment, the application servers manage connection pooling, thus simplifying connection handling for an application. The connection pooling mechanism, because it is handled by the application server, remains transparent to the application.

The connection management contract results in a simplified application programming model. The contract also serves to increase the scalability of application integration with EISs.

Chapter 4 describes the transaction management contract, also from the point of view of an application developer.

Working with Transactions

THIS chapter discusses transactions and the transactional support provided by the Connector architecture. Transactional access to EISs is an important requirement for business applications. This chapter focuses on the transaction model for application developers.

The Connector architecture supports both local transactions and XA transactions (also called JTA or global transactions). JTA stands for Java™ Transaction API and is a Java mapping of the industry standard X/Open XA protocol. A local transaction is managed internal to a resource manager and does not require coordination by an external resource manager. An XA transaction, on the other hand, can span multiple resource managers. An XA transaction requires transaction coordination by an external transaction manager. A transaction manager uses a two-phase commit protocol to manage an XA transaction that spans multiple resource managers.

An application server uses a transaction manager to manage transactions. An application component can access multiple transactional resource managers.

The transaction management contract extends the connection management contract and provides support for management of both local and XA transactions. The transaction management contract is defined between an application server and a resource adapter (and its underlying EIS resource manager). This contract enables the application server to provide the infrastructure and runtime support for transaction management. An application component relies on the application server's transaction support for component level transaction demarcation. (See Figure 4.1.) Transaction demarcation refers to managing transaction boundaries.

Chapter 13, Transaction Management Contract, describes the transaction management contract in detail.

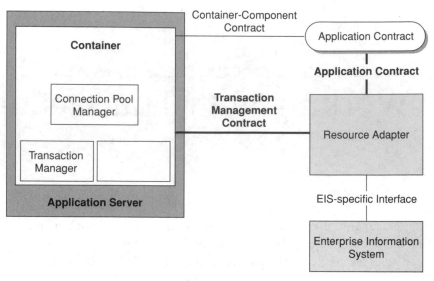

Figure 4.1   Transaction Management Contract

4.1   Introduction to Transactions

Transactions simplify the development of enterprise applications, which are typically distributed, multi-user applications. Transactions ensure data integrity because they enforce strict rules on an application's ability to access and update data. The J2EE platform, by supporting transactions, frees application developers from such complex issues as failure recovery and multi-user programming. The J2EE platform also does not limit transactions to a single database or single application server instance—global distributed transactions can simultaneously update multiple EISs across multiple server instances.

An application programmer divides the application's work into a series of units and treats each unit as a separate transaction. The underlying transaction management system ensures that each such unit of work, that is, each transaction, fully completes. This means the transaction is atomic. In addition, the transaction management system ensures that only one transaction manipulates the data at a time. If the transaction does not fully complete, the transaction management system rolls back the transaction, which means it completely undoes whatever work the transaction had performed.

It is important to understand certain terminology and functional roles that pertain to the transaction management contract, as specified in the Connector architecture. We use the terms transaction manager, application server, and resource manager. Here's how we define these terms.

- A *transaction manager* provides the services and management functions that are required to support transaction demarcation, transactional resource management, synchronization, and transaction context propagation. A transactional manager coordinates transactions across multiple resource managers. It also provides low-level services to facilitate the propagation of the transaction context across distributed systems. Often, the services of a transaction manager are not visible directly to the application components.

- An *application server*, as used in this book, is a generic term for a middle-tier component server that is compatible with the J2EE platform.

- A *resource manager* manages a set of shared EIS resources. A client requests access to a resource manager to use its managed resources. A transactional resource manager can participate in transactions that are externally controlled and coordinated by a transaction manager. In the context of the Connector architecture, a client of a resource manager is either a middle-tier application server or an application client. A resource manager is typically in a different address space or on a different machine from its clients. Database systems, mainframe TP systems, and ERP systems are all examples of resource managers.

4.1.1 Characteristics of Transactions

Data consistency is of utmost importance for business applications in an enterprise environment, and it is a transactional system that ensures data consistency. But what exactly is a transaction?

A *transaction* defines a unit of work, where that unit of work can have multiple sets of operations. Transactions refer to operations that access a resource manager, such as a database or an ERP system. A transactional application accesses an EIS within the context of a transaction. All transactions share the following characteristics, denoted by the acronym ACID:

- Atomicity

- Consistency

- Isolation

- Durability

Atomicity pertains to the operations of a transaction. Because a transaction often consists of more than a single operation, atomicity requires that all the operations of a transaction perform successfully for the transaction to be considered complete. If even a single operation cannot be performed, none of the transaction's operations may be performed.

Consistency refers to data consistency. A transaction must transition data from one consistent state to another. In addition, the transaction must preserve the data's semantic and physical integrity.

Isolation requires that a single transaction appears to be the only transaction currently manipulating the data. It is possible for other transactions to run concurrently, but a transaction should not see the intermediate data manipulation of other transactions until, and unless, they successfully complete and commit their work. Isolation prevents a transaction from obtaining an inconsistent view of the data. Data inconsistency could occur if the transaction were to see just a subset of another transaction's updates due to the interdependencies among these updates.

Isolation is related to transaction concurrency. Most transactional systems allow for different levels of isolation, and higher degrees of isolation limit the extent of concurrency. The highest level of isolation occurs when all transactions are serialized—each transaction runs to completion before the next transaction starts. Some applications require this level of isolation, but others may tolerate a reduced level of isolation for greater concurrency, particularly if they are only reading data and the accuracy of the data is not critical.

Durability means that updates made by committed transactions persist in the data store regardless of failure conditions. Durability guarantees that committed updates remain in the data store even if failures occur after the commit operation. In short, data can be recovered after a system or media failure.

4.1.2   Commit Protocols

As we've noted, transactions ensure data integrity by ensuring that a unit of work either fully completes, and is committed, or the work is fully rolled back. Committing a transaction means that the changes that the transactional work has made to the data are made durable.

The protocols of committing a transaction include supporting a one-phase commit process and, in a distributed transaction system, a two-phase commit process. Think of a typical transaction commit operation to a single resource manager as a one-phase commit protocol. The transaction commits the work that has been done to one, and only one, resource manager. Once it has been determined that the transaction has fully completed—all the ACID characteristics noted previously have been met—the changes are committed to the resource manager.

A two-phase commit protocol ensures that the transactional work correctly commits across multiple resource managers. The two-phase commit protocol essentially updates the multiple resource managers in two phases: first a prepare phase and then a commit phase. In the prepare phase, the transaction manager notifies each resource manager to prepare for the transaction commit. The resource managers indicate if they are prepared to commit. If all resource managers are prepared for the commit operation, the commit phase of the process occurs: the transaction manager notifies the resource managers to complete or commit the transaction. If even one resource manager is not prepared to commit, the transactional manager uses the commit phase to notify all of them to rollback the changes. In short, the two-phase commit protocol commits transactions across multiple resource managers.

4.1.3 Key Issues with Transactions

Developing business applications requiring transactions raises some key issues. To begin with, just about all enterprise environments have a multitude of users running the same applications. Many of the applications, even if concerned with different parts of an enterprise's business, may still access the same underlying data. In a production environment, literally hundreds of separate users may require concurrent access to the same pool of data. In this type of environment, it is essential that transactions achieve the ACID.

Usually, enterprise environments have many diverse back-end EISs. These different EISs often come with different transactional characteristics. Some EISs are transactional and support XA transactions, whereas other EISs are nontransactional or may just support local transactions. Business applications need to be capable of accessing all types of EISs, regardless of the EISs' transactional capabilities. This transactional variation adds to application complexity.

In addition, the transaction programming model cannot be overly complex. A too-complex model becomes a costly and major hindrance to application development and maintenance. If the model is too complex, businesses must employ developers who are business domain specialists and also skilled at system-level programming and transaction management. Because it is rare to find developers who can do both kinds of programming well, this usually means bringing in two sets of specialists. In short, a costly solution.

It is important to hide transaction management complexity. The J2EE platform provides a simple transaction programming model for application developers, plus it hides much of the complexity of transaction management. The Enterprise JavaBeans architecture, which is an integral part of the platform, handles the details of transaction management for an application.

The Connector architecture takes the J2EE platform even further. As we've just noted, transactional application components often must access multiple underlying resource managers. The diversity of these existing systems and applications is enormous. By providing a transaction management contract, the Connector architecture channels all access to multiple resource managers through standard interfaces. The Connector architecture enables a resource manager to plug in to a J2EE application server. Once plugged in, the resource manager can be accessed within transactions from applications developed and deployed on the J2EE server. In addition, the Connector architecture enables application developers to use the standard

J2EE programming model for transaction management and to access an underlying, diverse set of EISs. Thus the Connector architecture's transaction management contract ensures that the developer does not have to be conversant with the transaction management complexity of various transaction processing monitors and EISs.

4.2   Developing Transactional Applications

Traditionally an application developer was responsible for managing all aspects of a transaction. In addition to developing an application's business logic, the developer had to write code to explicitly start the transaction, then, depending on whether the transaction concluded successfully or not, the developer had to write code to commit or roll back the transaction. Applications that had more sophisticated transaction requirements might have required developers to suspend and resume the transaction.

The J2EE environment simplifies application development in terms of transactions. This section focuses on developing transactional applications within the J2EE environment.

4.2.1   Using the J2EE Platform

A transactional application on a J2EE platform comprises servlets and JSPs that access enterprise beans within a transaction. Each component in the transaction—the JSP, servlet, enterprise bean—may acquire a connection to a resource manager.

The J2EE platform supports both programmatic and declarative transaction demarcation. Programmatic transaction demarcation is typical of the traditional transaction management approach. In this approach, the application manages all aspects of the transaction. Declarative transaction demarcation is a style of transaction management that shifts transactional control from the application to the underlying application server and containers. The Enterprise JavaBeans architecture provides support for declarative transaction demarcation on the J2EE platform. An enterprise bean's container automatically starts and completes transactions for its application components.

For both kinds of transaction demarcation, the J2EE application server handles the necessary low-level transaction management protocols between the transaction manager and the resource managers. The J2EE application server also maintains the context for a transaction and may implement support for a distributed two-phase commit process.

When an application manages its own transactional aspects, the developer must write complex code that is system-level in detail and certainly very different from the application business logic. For example, in addition to business logic code, the developer must write code to explicitly start a transaction and commit the transaction's changes to the database (or roll back all changes if necessary). To do this properly, the developer must understand the mechanisms of the target EIS, in particular handling multiple processes and concurrency issues. Although this is often not the expertise of application developers, at times the developer wants this level of control over an application. Thus the EJB model of programmatic transaction demarcation allows developers to manage the application's transactions.

Declarative transaction demarcation, on the other hand, lets the developer declare transaction attributes separately from the application. Transaction attributes describe how to partition the application's work into separate transactional units. The J2EE application server then uses these attributes to apply its transaction management to the execution of the application.

4.2.2 Using Enterprise Beans

Enterprise beans play a major transaction management role in the J2EE platform. There are two types of transaction demarcation: bean-managed and container-managed transaction demarcation. Entity beans, which are enterprise beans designed for data access, use only container-managed transaction demarcation, whereas session beans may use bean-managed or container-managed demarcation.

An enterprise bean with bean-managed demarcation uses the methods of the JTA javax.transaction.UserTransaction interface to manage the transaction demarcation. The bean provider must set up the transaction context and write code to start and end the transaction.

With container-managed demarcation, the EJB container, instead of the bean provider, manages the transaction demarcation. For the container to do this, the developer first specifies a transaction attribute in the deployment descriptor for each method of an enterprise bean. (The developer does not write any explicit transaction begin and transaction commit code within the enterprise bean.) An attribute describes the transaction context for the associated method. The EJB container uses the transaction attributes to determine what it needs to do to manage transactions on these methods. For example, a particular method may have a transaction attribute requiring a new transaction context. When an application invokes that method, the container knows to begin a new transaction and commit the transaction when the method completes.

Application developers, whenever possible, should use container-managed demarcation and let the J2EE platform and the EJB container handle the complexities of transaction demarcation. By doing so, the developer does not have to write what is often complex transaction demarcation code. It is far simpler to declaratively define the transaction behavior of an enterprise bean rather than to programmatically define this behavior. Plus, the developer can change transaction behavior later without touching the code itself. All in all, an application is less prone to error if the EJB container handles the transactional aspects.

Using container-managed transaction demarcation is also not overly restrictive. Transaction attributes can be combined and used in a manner that makes it easy to compose multiple enterprise beans to perform tasks with specific transaction behavior.

An example scenario for both bean-managed and container-managed transaction demarcation is presented later in this chapter in the section "Sample Application Transaction Scenario."

4.2.3   Using JTA Transactions

It is recommended that Web components, such as JSPs and servlets, generally not engage in JTA transactions, but instead delegate such work to enterprise beans. However, Web components may use a JTA transaction to access an EIS.

A servlet or JSP uses JNDI to look up a javax.transaction.UserTransaction object, and then uses the UserTransaction interface to demarcate transactions. For example, a Web component might include the following code to demarcate transactions. (See Code Example 4.1.)

Code Example 4.1   Demarcating Transactions

```
Context ic = new InitialContext();
UserTransaction ut = (UserTransaction) ic.lookup
                    ("java:comp/UserTransaction");
// Start the transaction.
ut.begin();
// Perform transactional work here.
// End the transaction.
ut.commit();
```

Enterprise beans use one of two types of transaction demarcation: bean managed and container managed. With bean-managed transaction demarcation, an enterprise bean uses the javax.transaction.UserTransaction interface to explicitly demarcate the transaction's boundaries. (Bean-managed transaction demarcation is only available to session beans, whereas entity beans must use container-managed transaction demarcation.)

For example, a session bean with bean-managed transaction demarcation might include the following code to use JTA to demarcate a transaction. (See Code Example 4.2.)

Code Example 4.2 JTA and Bean-Managed Transaction Demarcation

```
UserTransaction ut = ejbContext.getUserTransaction();
// Start the transaction.
ut.begin();
// Perform transactional work here.
// End the transaction.
ut.commit();
```

When an enterprise bean uses container-managed transaction demarcation, the EJB container manages the transaction boundaries for the bean. The EJB container uses the transaction attribute associated with a bean's method to determine the degree of transaction management it must provide. Depending on the transaction attribute, the EJB container may begin a new JTA transaction or join the method to an existing JTA transaction.

To ensure the integrity and consistency of data, components should always access an EIS under the scope of a transaction. Accessing an EIS under the scope of a JTA transaction ensures that any updates are committed or rolled back, depending on the outcome of the JTA transaction. In addition, JTA allows multiple, simultaneous connections to an EIS, and it ensures that all updates made through these connections are atomic. Because the J2EE application server coordinates and propagates transactions between the server and the EIS, components need not include code to handle this coordination.

When the J2EE application server supports a transaction across multiple EISs, the application can access and perform updates on these EISs atomically from within a single JTA transaction. Code Example 4.3 illustrates how an application component might update two different databases in one JTA transaction.

Code Example 4.3 Using One JTA Transaction to Update Two Databases

```
InitialContext ic = new InitialContext("java:comp/env");
DataSource db1 = (DataSource) ic.lookup("OrdersDB");
DataSource db2 = (DataSource) ic.lookup("InventoryDB");
Connection con1 = db1.getConnection();
Connection con2 = db2.getConnection();

UserTransaction ut = ejbContext.getUserTransaction();
// Start the transaction.
ut.begin();
```

```
// Perform updates to OrdersDB using connection con1.
// Perform updates to InventoryDB using connection con2.
// End the transaction.
ut.commit();
```

4.2.4   Compensating Transactions

When an application component uses local transactions, it may be necessary to define a compensating transaction for each EIS access done under the scope of a local transaction. A *compensating transaction* is a transaction (or group of operations) that undoes the work of a previously committed transaction.

Compensating transactions are necessary when an application requires access to multiple EISs, but not all of the EISs support JTA transactions. In such a case, an application component needs to define a compensating transaction for each access to an EIS that is under the scope of a local transaction. If all EISs in a situation requiring access to multiple EISs do not support JTA, it is difficult to ensure the atomicity of the transaction. Compensating transactions are a means to group all the transactional work to multiple EISs in an atomic unit.

Take, for example, an application component that needs to perform an atomic operation to update three separate EISs. Two of the EISs support JDBC and JTA transactions, so the component knows that the transaction manager ensures the atomicity of these two updates. The third EIS is an ERP system that does not support JTA transactions. The application performs the transactional work to the ERP system under the scope of a local transaction and includes a compensating transaction to undo the local transaction, if necessary. Code Example 4.4 illustrates this.

Code Example 4.4   Using a Compensating Transaction

```
// Local transaction to update ERP system
updateERPSystem();
try {
    // JTA transaction to update 2 JDBC databases
    UserTransaction.begin();
    updateJDBCDatabase1();
    updateJDBCDatabase2();
    UserTransaction.commit();
}
catch (RollbackException ex) {
    // Compensating transaction
    undoUpdateERPSystem();
}
```

The `updateERPSystem` method performs the update to the ERP system under the scope of a local transaction, and the `updateJDBCDatabase1` and `updateJDBCDatabase2` methods update the two databases under the scope of a single JTA transaction. If a rollback occurs in the JTA transaction, the `undoUpdateERPSystem` method attempts to undo the work previously done by the `updateERPSystem` method.

Keep in mind that compensating transactions cannot always undo the effect of a committed transaction. For example, the compensating transaction may itself not commit for some reason, thus leaving the data in an inconsistent state. Or, because the JTA and local transactions are separate transactions, atomicity may be broken if the application server crashes after one transaction commit occurs but before the second transaction commits.

There is also the chance that another component may perform a concurrent access to the EIS updated with the local transaction and see inconsistent data. This might occur if the second access happens after the local transaction commit, but prior to a problem in the JTA transaction requiring the compensating transaction.

4.3   Transaction Levels

A resource adapter can be classified based on the level of transaction support it provides. These transaction support levels are as follows:

- **NoTransaction**—The resource adapter supports neither local nor XA transactions.

- **LocalTransaction**—The resource adapter supports local transactions only.

- **XATransaction**—The resource adapter supports both local and XA transactions.

Depending on a resource adapter's transactional capabilities and the requirements of its underlying EIS, a resource adapter can choose to support any one of the preceding transaction support levels. An application server provides support for resource adapters with all three levels of transaction support.

4.4   Sample Application Transaction Scenario

ACI's order management application illustrates common transaction scenarios. Recall that the order management application accesses several different EISs, including a Customer database, an Order database, an inventory management application, and a logistics application (see Figure 2.4). The resource adapters for each EIS offer a different transaction support level.

The resource adapter for the Customer account database, which is a nonrelational database, supports XATransactions. The JDBC driver for the Order database, which is a relational database, also supports XATransactions.

The OrderProcessor session bean performs access to both the Customer account database and the Order database. This bean uses container-managed transaction demarcation and is developed by the ACI IT staff. Because the bean uses container-managed transaction demarcation, the bean provider does not have to program the transaction management and security mechanisms required for connectivity to the Customer account database and the Order database. Instead, the EJB container and the application server handle these services.

The OrderProcessor session bean accesses both the Customer and Order databases within the same transaction. This scenario is illustrated in Figure 4.2.

Code Example 4.5 shows a business method that performs container-managed transaction demarcation. In this code snippet, the OrderProcessor session bean creates separate connections to the two databases. The transaction attribute for this method is set to Required. The EJB container takes the responsibility of invoking this method within a valid transaction context. For example, the EJB container may automatically start a transaction when this method is invoked.

The EJB container also automatically enlists the two connections with this transaction. All operations performed by OrderProcessorEJB on the two databases happen in the context of this transaction. The EJB container commits the transaction after this method is completed. Notice that the session bean code does not include any programmatic transaction demarcation. In this case, the EJB container takes the responsibility of transaction demarcation and management.

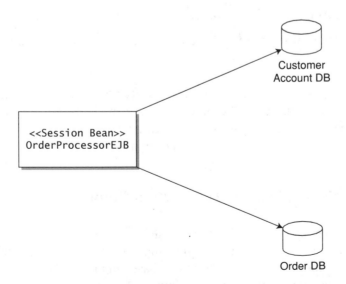

Figure 4.2   OrderProcessor session bean

Code Example 4.5   Container-Managed Transaction Demarcation

```
public class OrderProcessorEJB implements SessionBean {
    EJBContext ejbContext;
    ...
    public void checkCustomerAccount(PurchaseOrder po) {
        javax.sql.DataSource ds;
        javax.resource.cci.ConnectionFactory cf;
        java.sql.Connection cx1;
        javax.resource.cci.Connection cx2;

        try {
            Context nc = new InitialContext();
            // Get Connection to Order database
            ds = (javax.sql.DataSource)nc.lookup(
                    "java:comp/env/jdbc/OrderDB");
            cx1 = ds.getConnection();

            // Get Connection to CustomerAccount database
            cf = (ConnectionFactory)nc.lookup(
                    "java:comp/env/eis/CustomerAccountDB");
            cx2 = cf.getConnection();

            // Do operations on Order and CustomerAccount databases
            // using connections cx1 and cx2. The container
            // enlists cx1 and cx2 with the container managed
            // transaction

            // Close the Connections
            cx1.close();
            cx2.close();
        }
        catch (Exception e) {
            // ...
        }
    }
    // ...
}
```

Code Example 4.6 shows a business method that performs a bean-managed transaction involving two transactional resource managers. In this example, Or-derProcessorEJB uses the javax.transactionUserTransaction interface to demarcate a transaction. Behind the scenes, the EJB container enlists with the underlying transaction manager the two connections that are acquired by the OrderProcessorEJB. All updates to the Order and Customer databases between the `UserTransaction.begin` and `UserTransaction.commit` methods are performed within the transaction. The underlying transaction manager takes the responsibility for committing this transaction using a two-phase commit protocol.

Code Example 4.6   Bean-Managed Transaction Demarcation

```
public class OrderProcessorEJB implements javax.ejb.SessionBean {
    EJBContext ejbContext;
    // ...

    public void checkCustomerAccount(PurchaseOrder po) {
        javax.sql.DataSource ds;
        javax.resource.cci.ConnectionFactory cf;
        java.sql.Connection cx1;
        javax.resource.cci.Connection cx2;

        javax.transaction.UserTransaction ut;

        try {
            Context nc = new InitialContext();

            // Get Connection to Order database
            ds = (javax.sql.DataSource)nc.lookup(
                        "java:comp/env/jdbc/OrderDB");
            cx1 = ds.getConnection();

            // Get Connection to CustomerAccount database
            cf = (ConnectionFactory)nc.lookup(
                    "java:comp/env/eis/CustomerAccountDB");
            cx2 = cf.getConnection();

            // Start a transaction that includes Order and Account
            // databases
            ut = ejbContext.getUserTransaction();

            // Start the transaction
            ut.begin();
```

```
            // Do updates on Order and CustomerAccount databases
            // using connections cx1 and cx2. The container
            // enlists cx1 and cx2 with the transaction manager.

            // Commit the transaction
            ut.commit();

            // Close the connections
            cx1.close();
            cx2.close();
        }
        catch (Exception e) {
            //...
        }
    }
    //...
}
```

4.5 Conclusion

This chapter described the transactional concepts and the types of transactions supported by the Connector architecture. To guarantee the consistency and integrity of the data, we recommend that any access to an EIS be done under the scope of a transaction.

Chapter 5 shows you how the Connector architecture's security contract helps to manage and ensure EIS connectivity security.

Managing Security

SECURITY is an important requirement for all enterprise applications. The importance of security applications and systems is increasing as more businesses deploy distributed applications and conduct more of their operations over the Internet. Sensitive information routinely passes over Internet connections between user Web browsers and Web servers and containers. The same sensitive information passes between Web servers and application servers and between an application server and connected EISs.

It is critically important that an enterprise safeguard the integrity of its business information. Loss or inaccuracy of information or any unauthorized access to information can be extremely costly. At the same time, applications must be able to access EISs without creating security threats to the EIS resources.

Enterprise applications must clearly establish both the requirements and architecture for a secure EIS integration environment. Because the Connector architecture focuses on EIS integration for J2EE applications, it provides mechanisms and a set of standard APIs to support secure integration with EISs. It defines a security management contract that extends the J2EE security model to include support for secure connectivity to EISs. The J2EE security model defines the security that is applied to client access to the Web tier, and then from the Web tier to the EJB tier. (See Figure 5.1.)

The Connector security management contract allows support for different security mechanisms to protect an EIS against security threats such as unauthorized access and loss or inaccuracy of information. To begin with, the security management contract helps ensure that users (also referred to as principals) are who they say they are. The correct identification of principals is referred to as *authentication*. Once a user is authenticated, the security contract helps determine *authorization* and *access control* privileges. Authorization and access control determine whether a user is permitted to access a specific EIS resource. Authorization is typically performed in an EIS-specific manner.

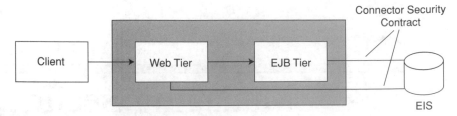

Figure 5.1   J2EE Security Model

The security contract also ensures the security of the communication links between an application server and an EIS. It accomplishes this by supporting protocols that provide authentication, integrity, and confidentiality services. The contract also provides for protecting communication by using a secure communication protocol, such as secure socket layer (SSL).

The security management contract is both security mechanism independent and technology independent. Because of this independence, application servers and EISs can support the security contract regardless of their own different levels of support for security technology and mechanisms. For example, the security contract supports an EIS or application server regardless of whether the EIS or application server uses basic user password-based authentication, a Kerberos-based end-to-end security environment, or just its own application server or EIS-specific security mechanism.

5.1   Security Concepts

A security contract is an agreement between a requestor (or caller) and a target service in which the access to the service requires authentication of the requestor's identity. In addition, the requestor may require proper authorization and access privileges to access this service. Optionally the communication between a requestor and the target services may be encrypted so that the communication is secure and protected.

5.1.1   Authentication

The term *authentication* refers to the security mechanism by which the requestor (or caller) and the service provider prove to one another that they are acting on behalf of specific users or systems. Authentication establishes the identities of the participating entities and proves that the entities are really instances of these identities. Authentication can be performed in one direction or it can be bidirectional. If bidirectional, it is called *mutual authentication*. If an entity participates in a call without establishing its identity or proving an identity, that entity is referred to as *unauthenticated*.

When calls are made from a client program run by a user, the caller identity is that of the user. A caller may also be an application component acting as an intermediary in a call chain that originated with some user. In that case, the identity may be associated with that of the user, and the component is considered to be impersonating the user. It is also possible for an application component to call another component using its own identity unrelated to that of its caller.

In a J2EE application, a user goes through a client container to interact with enterprise components in the Web or EJB tiers, and then subsequently to interact with enterprise resources in the EIS tier. These resources may be protected or unprotected. A protected resource includes authorization mechanisms that restrict access to some subset of nonanonymous, or known, identities. To access a protected resource, a user must present a credential such that its identity can be evaluated against the resource authorization policy.

When J2EE application components integrate with EISs, the components may use different security mechanisms and operate in different protection domains than the EIS resources. In such cases, either the calling container or the application component can manage authentication to the resource for the calling component. When the calling container manages authentication to the EIS resource, it is referred to as container-managed EIS sign-on. When the application component manages the authentication, it is called application-managed EIS sign-on. We describe these sign-on concepts in more detail later in this chapter.

5.1.2 Authorization

Authorization is a security mechanism through which it is verified whether the user (or requestor) has the authority to access the requested resource or service. Authorization mechanisms limit the interactions of users or systems with resources so that additional security constraints (such as confidentiality and integrity) may be enforced. An authorization mechanism allows only an authenticated caller to access resources.

The Java 2 platform, Standard Edition (J2SE) provides these authorization mechanisms, and they can be used to control access to code and resources based on identity properties, such as the location and signer of the calling code. The J2EE application programming model provides additional authorization mechanisms to limit access to called components based on who is using the calling code, rather than just the calling code's signer and location.

Although there are two basic approaches to defining access control rules—capabilities and permissions—the J2EE application programming model focuses on permissions. The permissions approach looks at who can do something. The capabilities approach focuses on what a caller can do. In the J2EE architecture, the deployer maps the permission model of the application (which has been supplied by the application assembler through the deployment descriptor) to the capabilities of users in the operational environment, thus establishing the container-enforced access control rules associated with a J2EE application.

5.1.3 Security Definitions

The following terms have been used in this chapter:

- **End User**—An end user is an entity, either a person or a service, that acts as a source of a request to an application.

- **Principal**—A principal is an entity that can be authenticated by an authentication mechanism. A principal is identified using a principal name and authenticated using authentication data. The content and format of the principal name and the authentication data depend on the authentication mechanism.

- **Security Attributes**—A principal has a set of security attributes associated with it. These security attributes are related to the authentication and authorization mechanisms. Examples are security permissions and credentials for a principal.

- **Credential**—A credential contains or references security information that can authenticate a principal to additional services. A principal acquires a credential upon authentication or from another principal that allows its credential to be used. The latter process is termed *principal delegation.* An X.509 certificate and a Kerberos service ticket are examples of credentials.

- **Initiating Principal**—The security principal representing the end user that interacts directly with the application. An end user can authenticate using either a Web client or an application client.

- **Caller Principal**—A principal that is associated with an application component instance during a method invocation. For example, an enterprise bean instance can call the `getCallerPrincipal` method to get the principal associated with the current security context.

- **Resource Principal**—A security principal under whose security context a connection to an EIS instance is established.

- **Security or Protection Domain**—A scope within which certain common security mechanisms and policies are established. An enterprise can contain more than one security domain. Thus an application server and an EIS can be in the same security domain or they can be in different security domains.

- **Security Context**—An object that encapsulates the shared state information regarding security between two entities.

In a managed multi-tiered application server-based environment, application components are deployed in Web or EJB containers. When a method gets invoked on a component, the principal associated with the component instance is termed a caller principal.

The relationship between an initiating principal and a caller principal depends on the principal delegation option for inter-container and inter-component calls. The relationship of a resource principal and its security attributes, such as its credentials and access privileges, to an initiating or caller principal depends on how the system administrator or deployer has set up the resource principal. We describe this in detail later in the chapter.

5.2   Security Model for EIS Connections

What does the security model look like from the perspective of an application component? Typically the application component requests that a connection be established under the security context of a resource principal. Once the connection is established, all invocations that the application component makes to the EIS instance occur under the security context of the resource principal.

The application component provider has two choices for the design of the EIS sign-on. The component provider uses an element in the deployment descriptor to indicate the component's sign-on approach. The two sign-on approaches are:

1. **Container-managed sign-on**—The application component lets the container take the responsibility of configuring and managing the EIS sign-on. The container determines the user name and password for establishing a connection to an EIS instance.

2. **Component-managed sign-on**—The application component code manages the EIS sign-on by including code that performs the sign-on process to an EIS.

Let's examine two examples that illustrate these two approaches.

5.2.1   Container-Managed Sign-On

With container-managed sign-on, the component developer designs the enterprise bean so that the container manages EIS sign-on. That is, the developer wants the application server and the deployer to be responsible for managing EIS sign-on. To indicate this, the developer sets the `res-auth` deployment descriptor element to `Container`.

The deployer sets up and configures the EIS sign-on security information. The deployer sets the name of the user that connects to the EIS instance and configures the authentication data, typically the user's password, needed to verify that the user is really who she says she is.

At this point, the component can establish a connection to the EIS instance without being concerned about security. The component invokes the `getConnection` method on the ConnectionFactory instance and does not need to pass any security-related parameters, as Code Example 5.1 shows.

Code Example 5.1   Container-Managed Sign-On

```
// Business Method in an application component
Context initctx = new InitialContext();

// perform JNDI lookup to obtain a connection factory
javax.resource.cci.ConnectionFactory cxf =
        (javax.resource.cci.ConnectionFactory)initctx.lookup(
            "java:comp/env/eis/MainframeCxFactory");

// Invoke factory to obtain a connection. The security
// information is not passed in the getConnection method
javax.resource.cci.Connection cx = cxf.getConnection();
...
```

5.2.2   Component-Managed Sign-On

In component-managed sign-on, the component developer includes code in the component to manage the EIS sign-on. When the developer takes this approach, he or she sets the deployment descriptor `res-auth` element to `Application`. This indicates that the component code is designed to perform programmatic sign-on to the EIS. The application component must pass explicit security information, typically the user's name and password, to the ConnectionFactory when invoking the `getConnection` method. This is illustrated in Code Example 5.2.

Code Example 5.2   Component-Managed Sign-On

```
// Method in an application component
Context initctx = new InitialContext();

// perform JNDI lookup to obtain a connection factory
javax.resource.cci.ConnectionFactory cxf =
        (javax.resource.cci.ConnectionFactory)initctx.lookup(
            "java:comp/env/eis/MainframeCxFactory");
```

```
// Invoke factory to obtain a connection
com.myeis.ConnectionSpecImpl properties = //..

// get a new ConnectionSpec
properties.setUserName("...");
properties.setPassword("...");
javax.resource.cci.Connection cx = cxf.getConnection(properties);
...
```

5.3   Understanding EIS Sign-On

Sign-on to an EIS happens when creating a new physical connection to the EIS. EIS sign-on typically requires the execution of one or more of the following steps:

- Determine a resource principal under whose security context the physical connection to the EIS will be established.

- Authenticate the resource principal if it has not already been authenticated.

- Establish a secure communication between the application server and the EIS. Once such a communication is established, additional security mechanisms, such as data confidentiality and data integrity, may be applied to the communication between the application server and the EIS.

- Provide access control for the EIS resources.

These steps are explained in the next sections.

5.3.1   Setting a Resource Principal

When an application component requests a connection from a resource adapter, the connection request is always made under the security context of a resource principal. The deployer sets the resource principal for the connection's security context using one of several approaches—configured identity, principal mapping, or caller impersonation.

In the *configured identity* approach, a resource principal has its own configured identity and security attributes, and these can be independent of the identity of the principal initiating the connection request. For example, in an application, the connections to an EIS are always established under the security context of a valid EIS user account, and this user account is always used regardless of the initiating or caller principal. That is, if the caller principal is A, the configured resource principals can be B and C on two different EIS instances. The three principals—A, B, and C—are independent entities.

Principal mapping is another approach to establishing a resource principal. With this approach, the container manages the mapping of the resource principal from the identity or security attributes of the initiating or caller principal. When this approach is used, the resource principal may not inherit identity or security attributes of the principal from which it is mapped. Instead, the resource principal gets its identity and security attributes based on the principal mapping. For example, if the caller principal has identity A, a mapped resource principal can be *mapping (A,EIS1)* and *mapping (A, EIS2)* on two different EIS instances.

Caller impersonation is a third approach. When a resource principal impersonates a caller principal, the caller's identity and credentials are delegated to the EIS instance. It is even possible for a caller principal to be a delegate of an initiating principal. When this occurs, the resource principal transitively impersonates the initiating principal.

5.3.2   Authenticating a Resource Principal

An application server and an EIS collaborate to ensure the proper authentication of a resource principal that establishes a connection to an underlying EIS. Although the Connector's security architecture is independent of any particular security mechanism, the architecture does identify two commonly supported authentication mechanisms:

- Basic user-password authentication mechanism specific to an EIS

- Kerberos version 5–based authentication mechanism

An application server should support these identified authentication mechanisms, and it may also support other authentication mechanisms for EIS sign-on.

5.3.3   Authorizing a Resource Principal

Once authentication is accomplished, the next step is authorization—ensuring that a principal has proper authorized access to the EIS resources. Authorization can be accomplished either at the EIS or at the application server. If an EIS performs authorization, it does so in its own EIS-specific manner. For example, an EIS may restrict certain users to executing only a subset of available functions.

The application server can also perform authorization checking. For example, the application server can authorize a principal to create a connection to an EIS only if the principal is authorized to do so. Application servers that use J2EE containers, such as EJB and servlet containers, can define their security authorization policies either programmatically or declaratively.

5.3.4   Establishing a Secure Communication

It is important that the communication between an application server and an EIS be secure. Whenever two separate entities communicate, there is always the risk of such security threats as data modification or loss of data.

Establishing a secure association counters such threats. A secure association is a shared security information that allows a component on the application server to communicate securely with an EIS. The establishment of a secure association can include several steps:

• The resource principal is authenticated to the EIS. This may also require mutual authentication.

• Communicating entities negotiate a quality of protection, such as confidentiality or integrity.

• A pair of communicating entities—an application server and an EIS instance—establish a shared security context using the credentials of the resource principal. The security context encapsulates shared state information, required so that communication between the application server and the EIS can be protected through integrity and confidentiality mechanisms. Examples of shared state information that is part of a security context are cryptographic keys and message sequence numbers.

A secure association between an application server and an EIS is always established by the resource adapter implementation. Note that a resource adapter library runs within the address space of the application server. A resource adapter can use any security mechanism to establish the secure association.

Once a secure association is established successfully, the connection is associated with the security context of the resource principal. Subsequently all application-level invocations to the EIS instance using the connection happen under the security context of the resource principal.

5.4   Managing Security

Various roles are involved in the development of an application and EIS integration. Each role has its own particular involvement with the security architecture and its own set of responsibilities. Here we examine how security management impacts the roles of application component provider, deployer, application server vendor, EIS vendor, resource adapter provider, and system administrator.

5.4.1   Role of the Application Component Provider

The application component provider does not have the burden of securing the application. Instead, the provider can focus on developing the application's business logic and integrating with EISs. He or she has only to declaratively specify the security requirements for the application in the deployment descriptor. Other roles, such as the application server vendor, resource adapter provider, and deployer, are responsible for satisfying the overall security requirements for applications and for managing the security environment.

The component provider can also manage security at the application level by using a simple programmatic interface. Using this interface, the provider can include code to allow access control decisions based on the method caller's security context (that is, the caller's principal and role). The component provider can also incorporate a programmatic sign-on to an EIS.

5.4.2   Role of the Deployer

The deployer specifies security policies that ensure an application component's secure access to the underlying EIS. Using tools specific to the environment, the deployer adapts an application's security requirements for connecting to an EIS to the actual security mechanisms that the application server and the EIS offer.

The deployer performs several tasks for each connection factory reference declared in the application component's deployment descriptor. To start, the deployer provides a connection factory with a specific security configuration, such as user name and password, for creating and managing connections to an EIS instance. The deployer also binds the connection factory reference to the connection factory instance registered in the JNDI namespace. This binding is done in the deployment descriptor. If security is to be managed by the container—when the `res-auth` deployment descriptor element is set to `Container`—the deployer also has to configure the necessary security information for EIS sign-on.

5.4.3   Role of the Application Server Vendor

The application server vendor provides an environment that ensures secure access to connected EISs. The environment includes specific security policies and mechanisms to support the security requirements of deployed application components and resource adapters. The vendor may also provide support for a single sign-on mechanism that spans the application server and its supported EISs.

Additionally the application server vendor provides the tools that the deployer uses to set up the security information for resource principals and EISs. The vendor also supplies tools to support the management and administration of a security domain. Security domain administration includes setting and maintaining the underlying authentication services and trusts between domains. These tools are almost always specific to the vendor's own technology and thus vary among application servers.

5.4.4   Other Roles

The EIS vendor, resource adapter provider, and system administrator also have roles in security management for EIS integration. The EIS vendor must provide a security infrastructure and environment that supports the security requirements of client applications. The EIS vendor may set up a separate security domain with its own security policies. Or, it may set up its security environment to be part of the enterprise-wide security domain.

The resource adapter provider implements the security management contract of the Connector architecture and provides a resource adapter that supports the security requirements of the underlying EIS. The resource adapter provider uses the deployment descriptor to specify the resource adapter's security capabilities and requirements.

Last, the system administrator coordinates security tasks with the administrators of the various EISs deployed in the operational environment. Some system administrator tasks are

- Setting up an operational environment based on the technology and requirements of the authentication service.

- Configuring user accounts for the application server and the EIS. This user account information is used to authenticate users who request to be connected to an EIS.

- Establishing password synchronization between the application server and an EIS. With password synchronization, the application server passes the user's password to the EIS when the EIS requires authentication. This ensures that the user's security information is the same on both the application server and the EIS.

5.5   Security Example

Here we examine how the Connector architecture security contract applies to the order management application introduced in Chapter 2. Recall that ACI's order management application integrates with two separate databases, a customer database residing on a mainframe and an order database, a relational DBMS. The order management application also interacted with an inventory management application, a logistics application, and a financial application.

From the security point of view, we are most interested in the order management application's relationship to the inventory management and logistics applications, as shown in Figure 5.2.

5.5.1 Security Environment

ACI has divided the management of its information systems into different departments. As a result, one IT department manages the mainframe inventory management application and a different IT department manages the ERP system logistics application. These two applications are also in different security domains. Each application system supports its own EIS-specific security policy and security technology and mechanisms. (See Figure 5.3.)

In our example, we assume that the mainframe inventory management application supports basic user-password authentication. We also assume that the ERP system supports a Kerberos-based security mechanism.

To handle security between the order management application and the inventory management application, the mainframe system administrator has created an inventory management account called OrderApplicationUser. This account is primarily set up for the order management application to use. The OrderApplication-User account is allowed access only to the business objects and functions that pertain to inventory management as required by the order management applica-

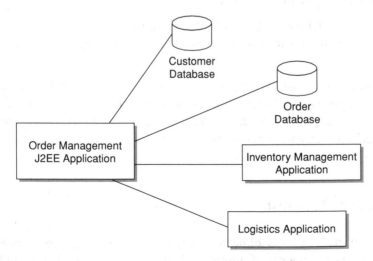

Figure 5.2 Order Management Application Architecture

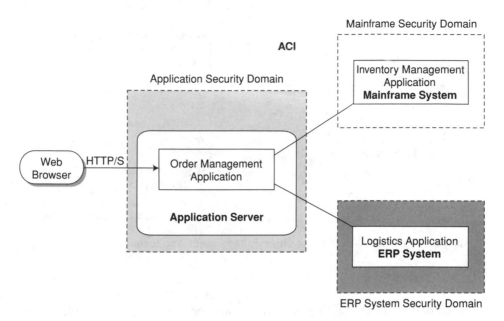

Figure 5.3   Example Security Environment

tion. The system administrator sets up the user password and specific access rights for this account.

A similar user account handles security between the order management application and the ERP logistics application. The ERP system administrator has configured an existing logistics application account called AppUser for the order management application to use. The system administrator also configures this account to use the Kerberos-based security mechanism of the ERP system.

The application server administrator, as part of the operational environment of the application server, configures access to an organization-wide LDAP-based directory service. This directory contains account information, including name, password, role, and access rights, for all the employees in the organization.

Not only are the inventory management and logistics applications physically separate from each other, they are also physically separate from the application server configuration for the order management application. This physical separation requires that a secure communication be established between the application server and the EISs. The resource adapter for each EIS assumes the responsibility for setting up the secure communication.

5.5.2   Example Deployment

The order management application consists of a set of enterprise beans responsible for connecting to and accessing the inventory management and logistics EISs.

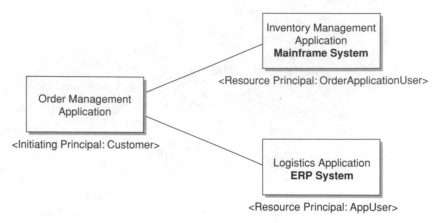

Figure 5.4   Principal Mapping for Order Management Application

These enterprise beans rely on container-managed sign-on. As a result, the EJB container assumes the responsibility for managing sign-on to both EISs, and it manages EIS sign-on based on the deployment configuration.

When deploying the order management application and the two resource adapters, the deployer configures the security information in the application server required to create connections to the inventory management and logistics applications. The deployer performs the principal mapping configuration as shown in Figure 5.4.

Principal mapping configuration ensures that all connections to the logistics application are established under the security context of the AppUser, the resource principal for the ERP system security domain. Similarly, all connections to the inventory management application are established under the security context of the OrderApplicationUser.

The application server handles the principal mapping for all authenticated initiating principals—that is, customers accessing the order management application—when the order management application connects to either the ERP system or the mainframe system. A customer accesses either EIS under the security context of the appropriate configured resource principal: OrderApplicationUser for the inventory management application and AppUser for the logistics application.

5.6   Conclusion

This chapter explained the support provided by the Connector architecture for secure EIS integration. It introduced and explained the relevant security concepts and terminology. It also described the types of sign-on to EISs—either component or container managed—and showed how each such sign-on is handled and the trade-offs of these different approaches.

Handling security involves the participation of different players or roles, and the chapter briefly described the responsibilities of these individuals. Last, it extended the order management application example to show how security might be handled within the Connector security management framework.

Chapter 6 focuses on communication between applications and EISs, particularly the Connector architecture's support for asynchronous communication.

Asynchronous Messaging

DIFFERENT forms of interaction modes are used for communication between applications and EISs. The 1.0 version of the Connector architecture provides support for synchronous communication with EISs. The 2.0 version of the Connector architecture adds support for asynchronous communication between applications and EISs. This chapter focuses on the support that the Connector architecture provides for asynchronous communication.

The chapter also describes the Java™ Message Service (JMS) in the context of the Connector architecture. For those readers not familiar with JMS, it includes a brief primer on JMS and explains its relationship with the Connector architecture and EIS integration. Scenarios illustrate this relationship.

It helps to understand synchronous communication to better understand asynchronous communication in relation to EIS integration. We begin with a short discussion of synchronous communication before we delve into the details of asynchronous communication.

6.1 Synchronous Communication

Synchronous communication between an application that is deployed and operational on an application server and an EIS follows a request-response interaction model. In this type of synchronous communication, an application initiates a request to the target EIS. The application then blocks its processing in the request invocation thread while it waits for a response from the EIS. The application continues its execution after it receives the response. Figure 6.1 shows this synchronous request-response model, though it does not show the involvement of a resource adapter and an application server in the synchronous invocation processing.

The 1.0 version of the Connector architecture supports a synchronous request-response interaction mode where an application component that is deployed and

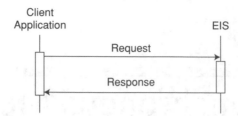

Figure 6.1 Synchronous Request-Response Model

operational on an application server initiates the synchronous request. The application server and the resource adapter for the underlying EIS manage transaction and security as part of the synchronous request-response interaction mode. They base this support on the 1.0 Connection architecture system contracts. The resource adapter takes the responsibility of propagating the security and transaction context to its underlying EIS using an EIS-specific communication protocol.

Keep in mind that the Connector architecture does not define any EIS-specific communication protocol. However, you should note that the 1.0 version of the CCI does provide support for two additional communication modes. These modes are:

- **SYNC_SEND**—The client application does a synchronous send to the target EIS.

- **SYNC_RECEIVE**—The client application does a synchronous receive from the target EIS.

Most EISs use the preceding synchronous request-reply interaction model. An EIS defines a remote function call-based API, which it exposes to applications that want to issue synchronous requests to the EIS. For example, an EIS might define an API that includes a remote function to create an account receivable item in the EIS. This remote function is callable by a client application. When an enterprise application deployed on an application server wants to interact with the EIS to create an account receivable item, it invokes this remote function on the EIS and waits until it receives a reply. The reply contains the results of the function's execution on the EIS. Such an interaction is considered synchronous because the invocation thread of the calling application waits synchronously during the time the function executes on the EIS. The invocation thread of the calling application continues when the remote function returns.

A synchronous mode of interaction leads to a tight coupling between an application deployed on an application server and an EIS. This tight coupling raises several issues that should be taken into consideration when integrating applications with EISs.

6.1.1   Issues to Consider

In a tightly coupled scenario, application performance may be closely tied to the performance of an EIS. Consider a scenario where an application that is deployed on an application server needs to access an EIS to process client-initiated requests. The application itself may be designed to handle multiple concurrent client requests. The application may employ either a multithreaded implementation or multiple application instances may be running on multiple application server processes on a cluster of nodes. When an application instance receives a client request, it synchronously invokes an EIS function. The invocation thread in the application process is then blocked from further processing until it receives a reply from the target EIS.

Suppose that the target EIS has a limited-load capacity. That is, unlike the application, the EIS is capable of handling only a limited number of concurrent requests at any particular instance. Although the application is capable of handling many more concurrent client requests, it may find when communicating synchronously with the EIS that the EIS may be unable to process the same number of concurrent requests. In addition, the same EIS may support a limited number of concurrent connections. This scenario is typical for EISs that offer limited scalability. In a tightly coupled synchronous integration, the application's response time and throughput for client requests may drop because the application threads must wait for synchronous invocations on the EIS to complete. Thus it's easy to see how synchronous communication tightly couples the application's response time to the performance and throughput of the target EIS. Even though the application is capable of scaling up and handling a large number of concurrent client requests, an EIS with a limited-load capacity may constrain the application's response time.

Asynchronous communication between an application and an EIS addresses this performance issue, which we explain later in this chapter in the section "Asynchronous Communication."

6.1.2   Dependency on Specific Middleware Mechanisms

In nonstandard integration platforms, synchronous remote function calls typically expose the underlying distribution and transaction management mechanisms. These mechanisms may be based on a middleware standard or they may be vendor specific.

When the synchronous communication API exposes these mechanisms and an application uses such an API, the application may become tightly coupled to the middleware mechanisms for transactions, distribution, and security. This tight coupling causes problems if the same application needs to integrate with other types of EISs. The application has been conducting its EIS communication in accordance with some vendor-specific mechanism, and it now faces the technical challenge of redesigning its communication model to handle a different middleware mechanism.

The Connector architecture addresses this problem by defining EIS-independent system contracts and an independent client API. The resource adapter abstracts its protocol and EIS-specific mechanisms on its implementation. These abstractions are not exposed to either the application or the container.

6.1.3 Dependency Between EIS and Application

The tight coupling that results from synchronous communication also raises issues in terms of the relationship between the application and the EIS. There may be too much dependency between the application and the EIS.

For example, the application's performance is impeded if communication fails between the application and the EIS. When such a communication failure occurs, such as if the EIS is down or otherwise unavailable, the application's synchronous request may return immediately with a reply indicating an error. When this happens, the application may need to retry the synchronous invocation that failed.

Or, the EIS may successfully execute the application's request but, because of a communication failure, the EIS may fail to send a reply to the application. To handle these situations, the application must include logic to time out the blocked request; otherwise, it will hang indefinitely waiting for a response. The logic must also include the ability to initiate a retry of the failed request. This situation creates a tight coupling between the application and the EIS.

These issues must be considered based on the requirements of your integration scenario and the capabilities of the target EIS.

6.2 Asynchronous Communication

With asynchronous communication, an application sends a request to an EIS. The application thread that sent the request (the request sender) continues its own processing—that is, the thread does not block—while the EIS handles the request asynchronously. The request sender does not have to wait for the EIS processing to complete and for the reply to come back. Instead, the thread returns after sending the message and it can continue processing client requests. Figure 6.2 shows this asynchronous interaction model.

In this book we focus on asynchronous message-based communication, of which there are two forms: queue-based communication and publish-subscribe messaging.

In queue-based communication, or point-to-point messaging, an application sends a message to a message queue. A message queue is independent from both the sender and receiver applications. The message queue acts as a message buffer between the communicating applications. The sender application sends a message to this queue, and the receiver application receives its messages from the queue. In

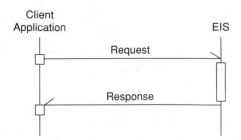

Figure 6.2   Asynchronous Communication

this form of communication, an application and an EIS can be senders and receivers relative to the message queue.

The publish-subscribe messaging mechanism operates differently from queue-based messaging. In this mechanism, a publisher application publishes messages on a specific topic. Multiple applications, called subscribers, can subscribe to this topic and receive the messages published by the publisher. The publish-subscribe facility takes responsibility for delivering the published messages to the subscribing applications based on the subscribed topic.

To put publish-subscribe messaging in more technical terms, a publishing application publishes its message to a well-known node, called a topic, within a content-based hierarchy. You can think of a publish-subscribe system as a message broker that gathers and distributes messages. The topic serves as the intermediary between message publishers and message subscribers.

Regardless whether queue-based or publish-subscribe messaging is used, a message represents structured data exchanged through asynchronous message-based communication. A message carries information used within a single enterprise's business processes or across the business processes of multiple enterprises. For example, a message can represent information required to invoke an EIS function. A message can also carry the results of this function invocation.

When asynchronous communication is used, an application and an EIS are said to be loosely coupled. With a loosely coupled integration between a target EIS and an application, an application thread can continue processing client requests without blocking on EIS performance or communication glitches. The application is not tightly coupled to the EIS or the communication delivery mechanism, as is the case with synchronous communication.

6.3   Connector Architecture 2.0 Message Handling

We explained earlier that the 1.0 version of the Connector architecture focuses on a synchronous request-response interaction mode between an application and EIS.

An application that is operational on an application server initiates a synchronous request and receives a synchronous response. This form of synchronous request-response communication is suitable for a majority of application integration scenarios that use an application server as an integration platform.

Additional interaction modes provided by the CCI, such as SYNC_SEND and SYNC_RECEIVE, provide support for additional integration scenarios. For example, a resource adapter can be developed for a message bus that supports asynchronous message-based communication. However, interactions between an application and this message bus that take place through the resource adapter are considered synchronous because they are supported by the SYNC_SEND and SYNC_RECEIVE interaction modes.

However, many EIS integration scenarios require loosely coupled asynchronous communication between the applications and the EISs. The 2.0 version of the Connector architecture addresses asynchronous integration with EISs, and this is an important feature of the architecture. The 2.0 version of the Connector architecture intends to support the following interaction modes:

- Asynchronous inbound communication

- Asynchronous outbound communication

- Synchronous inbound communication

- JMS-based communication

Keep in mind that, at the time this book went to press, the design details for this support had not yet been finalized.

6.3.1   Asynchronous Inbound Communication

An EIS initiates asynchronous inbound communication and targets the communication for an application that is deployed and operational on an application server. In this interaction mode, an EIS initiates an asynchronous request for the target application and a message-driven bean acts as a consumer of this asynchronous request. (See the section "Message-driven Bean" later in this chapter for more information on message-driven beans.)

Note that because this interaction mode does not involve a message queue, it cannot guarantee request delivery or reliable messaging.

The resource adapter and the application server take responsibility for dispatching the incoming request to the message-driven bean using a set of system contracts defined between the application server and the resource adapter. The Connector architecture 2.0 specification defines the system-level contracts for handling asynchronous inbound communication. (These contracts are extended from

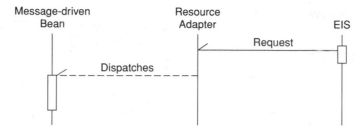

Figure 6.3   Asynchronous Inbound Communication

the system contracts defined in the 1.0 version of the Connector architecture.) Figure 6.3 shows this interaction mode.

6.3.2   Asynchronous Outbound Communication

In an asynchronous outbound communication mode, an application component on the application server sends an asynchronous request to the target EIS. A resource adapter for the underlying EIS takes responsibility for sending this request to the target EIS. The resource adapter uses the Connector-defined system contracts with the application server to dispatch this request to the target EIS. Figure 6.4 illustrates this interaction mode.

Similar to asynchronous inbound communication, this interaction mode also does not involve a message queue and thus cannot guarantee request delivery or reliable messaging.

6.3.3   Synchronous Inbound Communication

With synchronous inbound communication, an EIS initiates a synchronous request-response interaction with an application on the application server. Note that this mode is the opposite of the synchronous request-reply initiated by an application. In

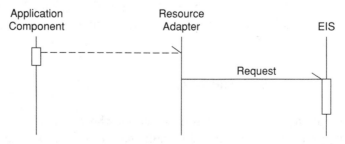

Figure 6.4   Asynchronous Outbound Communication

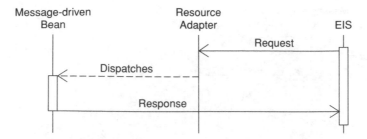

Figure 6.5   Synchronous Inbound Communication

synchronous inbound communication, a resource adapter and an application server use the Connector system contracts to dispatch the incoming synchronous request to an appropriate type of target application component. This incoming synchronous request may involve propagation of the transaction and security context. For example, an incoming request may lead the target application to participate in the EIS-initiated transaction. In such a case, it is not necessary that a message-driven bean be the target component.

Figure 6.5 illustrates the synchronous inbound communication mode.

6.3.4   JMS-based Communication

It is also possible for an application on the application server and an EIS to integrate using a JMS provider for either queue-based or publish-subscribe-based communication. In this mode, a JMS provider acts as a Connector architecture-based resource adapter—that is, it implements the extended set of system contracts specified in the 2.0 version of the Connector architecture—and uses a standard manner to plug in to an application server.

Currently there is no standard system-level pluggability contract that enables multiple JMS providers to plug in to an application server. A J2EE-based application server implements support for the JMS API by providing a JMS provider with the application server. Then Java applications use the JMS API to access the underlying enterprise messaging systems supported by the packaged JMS provider.

The section "Java Message Service" later in this chapter provides more details about this interaction mode.

6.4   Communication Trade-offs

Tightly coupled integration is typical in scenarios where an application that is deployed on an application server needs to aggregate its access to multiple EISs and perform transactions on these EISs. Usually, in this scenario, an application server acts as an EIS integration server.

For example, a J2EE-compliant application server in a tightly coupled EIS integration provides its platform and services layered on top of a synchronous interaction model with back-end EISs. When an application deployed on this application server receives a client request, it performs synchronous access to one or more EISs. The application server manages the connections to the target EISs and increases the scalability of deployed applications. In addition, the application can initiate transactions across multiple EISs. The application server may propagate the transaction and security context to the target EISs as part of the synchronous interactions.

In addition, many existing EISs and applications support a synchronous request-reply model of interaction. Although it is possible to adapt such synchronously modeled EISs to an asynchronous messaging model, such adaptation entails additional costs and infrastructure. The section "J2EE Platform and EAI" later in this chapter describes such loosely coupled integration in more detail.

You must decide whether or not your application uses synchronous communication and thus is tightly coupled with an EIS. It is best to make this decision after considering the following factors:

- **Ease of integration versus more services**—An asynchronous message-based communication using a queue or a publish-subscribe system provides more quality of services, such as message routing and reliable delivery, compared to the synchronous request-reply programming model. However, these additional services require a more advanced, and costly, programming model.

- **Type of application scenario**—A tightly coupled integration is more suitable in those application server-based integration scenarios where

  - An application needs to access one or more EISs synchronously for processing a client request.

  - An application can afford a tighter coupling with an EIS in terms of request processing and error handling.

  - An application initiates a transaction across multiple EISs as part of processing a client request.

- **Infrastructure requirements**—An asynchronous message-based integration requires an enterprise to invest in message brokers or message bus-based integration platforms. Currently such message brokers are not based on any standard architecture. Most message broker vendors provide vendor-specific adapters for popular EISs. These adapters are specific to a message broker product and require an in-depth knowledge of the message broker's proprietary APIs and message format. Such requirements add to the complexity of building these vendor-specific adapters and also lock you into using a particular vendor.

In addition, keep in mind that application server environments are becoming the standard for many enterprises. Such standardization increases the need for an enterprise application integration solution that is based on an application server environment and that supports EIS integration requirements for applications deployed on an application server. It appears to be more cost effective to invest in an EAI solution that integrates well with an application server environment than in one that does not integrate well.

6.5   Enterprise Messaging Technologies

Enterprise messaging systems, which are also called messaging-oriented middleware (MOM) products, provide support for asynchronous message-based communication.

Because asynchronous messaging is considered to be peer-to-peer communication, an application can act as both producer (or sender or publisher) and consumer (or receiver or subscriber) of an asynchronous message. In a typical scenario, an application connects and establishes a session with a messaging system using the system's API. For example, the JMS API is a standard Java API defined for enterprise messaging systems. Once the session is established, the application can produce and consume messages using the API defined by the underlying messaging system.

What sorts of services do these enterprise messaging systems provide? An enterprise messaging system may provide support for both publish-subscribe and queue-based messaging. In addition, a messaging system may provide the following services: message routing, transaction management, reliable message delivery, message priority and ordering, and message transformation.

- **Message routing**—A messaging system can process and route messages to one or multiple peer applications. The messaging system uses the routing information carried within a message. This information could include the names of the source and destination for a message, for example.

- **Transaction management**—A messaging system can act as a transactional resource manager. When the messaging system provides this service, a client application uses a transaction model to interact with the messaging system. For example, a client application can produce a set of messages and use a transaction to group the messages into a single atomic unit of work. When the transaction commits, the messaging system sends the set of messages as one unit. If the transaction rolls back, the messaging system discards the entire set of messages produced by the application within the rolled back transaction.

- **Reliable message delivery**—A messaging system can provide different levels of message delivery semantics, from making an attempt to deliver the message (called at-most-once delivery) to guaranteeing that the message is delivered (called exactly-once delivery). When a messaging system promises exactly-once delivery, the messaging system guarantees that it will do the following:

- Properly produce the message on behalf of the source application.

- Deliver the message reliably to the destination.

- Ensure that the message is properly consumed by the consumer application.

To accomplish exactly-once delivery and to support reliable message delivery, the messaging system uses a transacted persistent messaging facility. This facility ensures that committed messages are not lost if the messaging system suffers a failure of some kind. By contrast, with at-most-once delivery, an application sends a nonpersistent message. It's possible that this message can be lost. This can happen, for example, if the messaging system fails.

- **Message priority and ordering**—Some enterprise messaging systems permit applications to assign priorities to messages and to indicate a delivery order. An application can assign a higher or lower priority to its messages, so that the messaging system delivers higher priority messages ahead of lower priority ones. An application can also indicate that the messaging system should deliver the messages in serial order. The scope of serial ordering could be within a destination, and that destination could be a specific topic or queue based on the type of messaging system in use, or it could be across destinations, depending on the particular messaging system's capabilities. The messaging system can guarantee that it delivers messages serially in the order sent by the application.

- **Message transformation**—Some more advanced messaging systems support message transformation and use of rules engines. When a message flows through such a messaging system, the system transforms the message based on the system's configured set of rules and defined message schemas. For example, the messaging system could transform the format of a particular message to one that is better understood by the intended consumer. The message system first transforms the message, then routes the message to the appropriate consumer applications. It is also possible for an enterprise messaging system to integrate with a message repository that provides a messaging client with information on message schemas, metadata for message transformations, and a set of configured rules.

6.6 Java Message Service

The Java Message Service (JMS) is a standard Java API defined for enterprise messaging systems. It is meant to be a common messaging API that can be used across different types of messaging systems. A Java application uses the JMS API to connect to an enterprise messaging system. Once connected, the application uses the facilities of the underlying enterprise messaging system (through the API) to create messages and to communicate asynchronously with one or more peer applications.

The JMS specification includes the concepts of a client, API, provider, and messaging system, as illustrated in Figure 6.6.

6.6.1   JMS Overview

A JMS provider implements the JMS API for an enterprise messaging system and provides access to the services provided by the underlying message system. Vendors who provide application servers also include a JMS provider implementation as part of an application server. Currently, a JMS provider is plugged in to an application server in a vendor-specific manner. The Connector architecture 2.0 version defines a standard for plugging a JMS provider in to an application server. This standard means that a JMS provider can be treated similarly to a resource adapter in terms of the system-level contracts that are based on the Connector architecture 2.0 version. However, a JMS provider will have a JMS API as a client API for its underlying enterprise messaging system.

A client application, which we call a JMS client, uses the JMS API to access the asynchronous messaging facilities provided by the enterprise messaging system. Because JMS supports peer-to-peer messaging, both source (or producer) and destination (or consumer) applications act as clients to the JMS provider. Note that a client application can be an application client or some J2EE component. The section "Message-driven Bean" later in this chapter discusses the message-driven bean that acts as a message consumer based on the EJB component model.

A JMS domain identifies the type of asynchronous message-based communication that a JMS provider and an underlying enterprise messaging system support. The two domain types are queue-based point-to-point or publish-subscribe. The application programming model for a Java application that uses the JMS API differs depending on the type of domain that the application uses. For example, a Java application uses the queue-based interfaces QueueConnectionFactory and

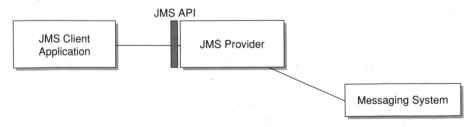

Figure 6.6   JMS API and JMS Provider

MessageQueue, among other queue-based interfaces, to interact with a point-to-point domain. (The JMS specification defines these interfaces.)

6.6.2   JMS Interfaces

This section is intended to be a brief primer on the JMS API specification. For more complete information, you should refer to the online version of the JMS API specification. (Refer to the Preface for the URL to this specification.)

A Java application uses the JMS interfaces as part of its application programming model to access the messaging facilities that the JMS provider and the underlying enterprise messaging system provide. Here we briefly present the JMS interfaces for facilities common to both queue and publish-subscribe messaging domains. Later, we show how to use these interfaces in different application scenarios.

6.6.2.1   JMS Common Facilities

The JMS API specifies a set of Java interfaces that are part of the common facilities in the javax.jms package. You should refer to the JMS specification for more details on these interfaces.

- **The Destination interface**—Encapsulates the representation of a destination address. An application sends or publishes a message to a destination. Examples of destinations are message queues or topics (see the next section, "JMS Publish-Subscribe Model"). A destination is configured as an administered object in the JNDI namespace.

- **The ConnectionFactory interface**—Represents a factory of connections to an enterprise messaging system. When instantiated, a ConnectionFactory instance is first configured with the configuration required for creating connections to the messaging system. It is then registered in the JNDI namespace. An application looks up a ConnectionFactory instance and uses it to create a connection to the enterprise messaging system. In this sense, the JMS programming model is similar to the Connector architecture-based application programming model.

- **The Connection interface**—Represents an active connection to an enterprise messaging system. Once a connection is established, a Java application can use the messaging facilities of the connected messaging system.

- **The Session interface**—Represents a single-threaded context for producing and consuming messages. Note that a Session instance can be specified as transacted. A transacted session enables an application to use a transaction model for producing and consuming messages.

- **The JMSMessage interface**—Encapsulates the representation of a message. Each JMS message is composed of header (a set of standard fields) and body sections. The JMS specification lists the standard header fields, which can include destination of the message, delivery mode, message identifier, timestamp, and priority. In addition to the standard fields, a message header can contain application-specific and JMS provider-specified fields. The data in the message body can be described by one of these types: StreamMessage, MapMessage, TextMessage, ObjectMessage, or BytesMessage.

- **The MessageProducer interface**—Is used by a Java application to send messages to a destination. If a Java application creates a MessageProducer without supplying a destination, it must pass a destination as input to each message sent.

- **The MessageConsumer interface**—Is used by a Java application to receive messages from a destination. A Java application can receive messages synchronously by using the synchronous receive option, or it can have a JMS provider deliver the message asynchronously through a MessageListener. A Java application can configure a message selector to filter the messages that are delivered to a consumer.

In addition to these interfaces, JMS specifies the Java interfaces that extend the common interfaces for supporting both publish-subscribe and queue-based point-to-point messaging domains.

6.6.2.2   JMS Publish-Subscribe Model

The JMS API enables a Java application (acting as a JMS client) to interface with a publish-subscribe message facility. A JMS client can publish messages to a topic. As noted previously, a topic gathers and distributes messages that are addressed to it. An example of a topic is a stock quote provider for a specific ticker symbol or a node representing purchase order acknowledgments. A messaging system arranges topics in a hierarchy and associates access control lists (ACLs) with these topics. The ACL associated with a topic controls whether or not a particular JMS client is authorized to subscribe to that topic.

A topic represents a form of association between the publisher and subscriber. One or more JMS clients act as subscribers to a specific topic. Publishers publish messages to this topic. The publish-subscribe messaging facility, in turn, delivers these published messages to the subscribers. Throughout the process, publishers and subscribers remain independent of each other. Figure 6.7 shows the JMS publish-subscribe model.

When a subscriber subscribes to a topic, that subscription can be durable or nondurable. A *nondurable subscription* lasts only during the lifetime of the subscriber. When a subscriber uses a nondurable subscription on a topic, then, when that subscribing JMS client is inactive, the subscriber misses messages that the

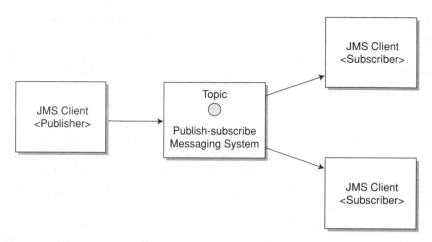

Figure 6.7   JMS Publish-Subscribe Model

publisher has sent to this topic. However, the JMS publish-subscribe facility retains messages for an inactive subscriber if the subscriber created a *durable subscription* on a topic. The requirements of an application dictate the use of durable versus nondurable subscriptions.

JMS extends the common Java interfaces (these were discussed in the section "JMS Common Facilities") so that they support the publish-subscribe messaging facility. These publish-subscribe interfaces are as follows:

- **The Topic interface**—Encapsulates a provider-specific identity or address for a destination in a publish-subscribe messaging domain. A JMS client publishes and subscribes to a specific topic.

- **The TopicConnectionFactory interface**—Acts as a factory for connections to a JMS publish-subscribe messaging system.

- **The TopicConnection interface**—Represents an active connection to a JMS publish-subscribe messaging system. A JMS client uses a TopicConnection instance to create one or more TopicSession instances.

- **The TopicSession interface**—Represents a single-threaded context for a JMS client so that the client can publish and receive messages. A JMS client uses a TopicSession instance to create TopicPublisher and TopicSubscriber instances.

- **The TopicPublisher interface**—Is used by a JMS client to publish messages on a topic.

- **The TopicSubscriber interface**—Is used by a JMS client to receive messages that have been published to a specific topic. By default, a TopicSubscriber represents a nondurable subscription. When a subscription is nondurable it means that a JMS client can only receive messages when the client is active. A JMS client can create a durable TopicSubscriber so that it registers its intention to receive messages published even when the client was inactive.

6.6.2.3   JMS Queue-based Model

JMS also supports a queue-based model using point-to-point messaging. With JMS queue-based messaging, a JMS client, acting as a sender, sends messages to a specific message queue. The message queue, in turn, delivers the message to the receiver application. The JMS message queue facility provides the point-to-point communication between two applications.

Figure 6.8 shows the JMS queue-based model. The diagram shows two JMS clients. The sender acts as a JMS client and sends a message to a message queue. Note that a messaging system provides a message queue, and the message queue is a pre-configured resource that is statically created. The receiver is a JMS client that consumes the message and optionally acknowledges its receipt.

JMS extends the common Java interfaces (discussed earlier in "JMS Common Facilities") to support the point-to-point queue-based messaging facility. These queue-based interfaces are as follows:

- **The Queue interface**—Encapsulates a provider-specific identity or address for a destination in a queue-based messaging system. A JMS client sends and receives messages to and from a queue. Typically, queues are long-lived static resources that are created and deleted by the messaging system administrator.

- **The QueueConnectionFactory interface**—Acts as a factory for connections to a JMS queue-based messaging system.

- **The QueueConnection interface**—Represents an active connection to a JMS queue-based messaging system. A JMS client uses a QueueConnection to create one or more QueueSession instances.

- **The QueueSession interface**—Represents a single-threaded context for a JMS client to send and receive messages to and from a specific queue. A JMS client uses a QueueSession instance to create QueueSender and QueueReceiver instances.

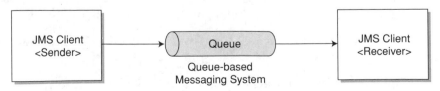

Figure 6.8   JMS Queue-based Messaging Model

- **The QueueReceiver interface**—Is used by a JMS client to receive messages that have been delivered to a queue.

- **The QueueSender interface**—Is used by a JMS client to send messages to a queue.

6.7 JMS and EAI

In a typical EAI configuration based on asynchronous messaging, a message broker provides support for asynchronous messaging using publish-subscribe or queue-based mechanisms, message routing, and transformation.

Multiple enterprise applications and EISs use adapters to plug in to these message brokers. These adapters are specific to each EIS and enterprise application and developed for a specific message broker product. A J2EE application—that is, an application deployed and operational on a J2EE application server—can access this message broker using a standard JMS provider.

Because these applications and EISs can act as both message producers and consumers, their integration appears as a hub-and-spoke model with a message broker as the hub. For example, a financial accounting application can subscribe to messages that carry information on financial transactions. A message broker delivers messages from applications and EISs to the financial accounting application. (See Figure 6.9.)

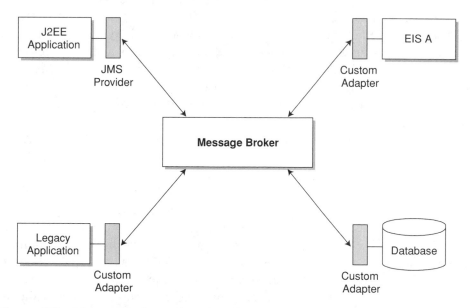

Figure 6.9 Message Broker Hub-and-Spoke Model

A custom adapter adapts an EIS or enterprise application into the message broker. An adapter may also layer additional functionality in the form of message transformation and support for higher level business process abstractions. As a result of this adaptation, the EIS can integrate with other applications that use the services of the message broker. Most message broker vendors provide their own vendor-specific adapters for popular EISs. Development of these adapters requires an in-depth knowledge of the message broker's proprietary APIs and its message formats. Requiring such knowledge adds to the complexity of building custom adapters.

A message broker vendor may provide a JMS provider such that a JMS client can access the services of a message broker for EAI purposes. A JMS provider for a message broker enables Java applications to access the message broker using the JMS API. The JMS provider maps the JMS API to the underlying messaging facilities—queue-based or publish-subscribe asynchronous messaging—and the message formats supported by the message broker. A JMS provider, through this mapping, becomes more of a JMS-based adapter for the underlying message broker.

6.8   J2EE Platform and EAI

The J2EE 1.3 platform requires that application server vendors support the JMS API. Earlier versions of the J2EE platform only recommended that JMS be supported. However, the majority of application server vendors had already supported the JMS API because of its importance for asynchronous messaging.

JMS combined with the Enterprise JavaBeans 2.0 architecture message-driven beans together provide support for loosely coupled asynchronous integration scenarios using a J2EE application server. With JMS and message-driven beans, J2EE components—whether they are servlets or enterprise beans—may act as message producers. The EJB 2.0 specification defines a *message-driven bean* as an enterprise bean component type that acts as a message consumer for JMS messages.

A J2EE-based application server can act as an enterprise application integration server, and it can use asynchronous messaging and the Connector architecture to integrate applications and EISs. J2EE components act as both message producers and consumers relative to EISs and existing applications. The JMS provider in the application server takes the responsibility for delivering and routing messages across message producers and consumers. Application components need only drive the business processes and message transformations. In this environment, communication among application components can be either synchronous or asynchronous. EISs and existing applications plug in to the application server using either synchronous resource adapters or a loosely coupled asynchronous resource adapter.

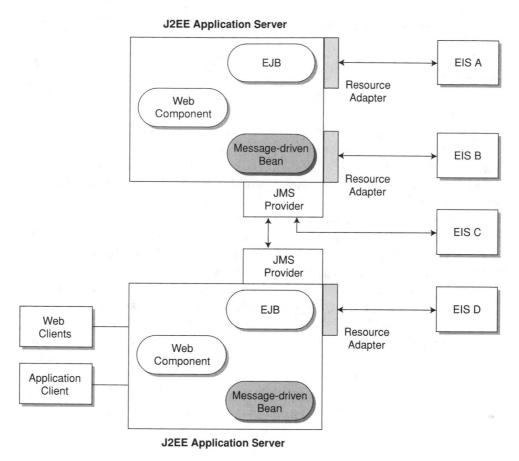

Figure 6.10 J2EE Application Server Integration Approach

Figure 6.10 shows the integration server approach based on a J2EE application server.

This approach differs from a message broker hub-and-spoke model, which is based on a proprietary message broker and custom adapters. Here, a J2EE-based integration server is built on the standard J2EE platform and APIs. Resource adapters are based on the standard J2EE Connector architecture. Application development is simplified because integrated applications and business processes can be developed using the standard J2EE application programming model.

This model also simplifies development of Web applications and services that integrate with multiple EISs and existing applications. In short, this approach captures the key advantages of the standard J2EE platform—simplified application development, a standard component model, support for tools, no vendor lock-in, and simplified connectivity to EISs and relational database—and applies these advantages to EAI.

6.9   Message-driven Bean

The EJB 2.0 specification defines a new type of enterprise bean called a message-driven bean. A message-driven bean extends the EJB architecture model to support consumers of asynchronous messages, thus enabling EJB-based applications to integrate with JMS.

The EJB model for message-driven beans differs from that for session and entity beans. The EJB model for session and entity beans indicates that an EJB client views an entity or session bean as a server-side component with home and remote interfaces. An EJB client can synchronously invoke session beans and entity beans. When the EJB client makes such an invocation, the EJB container dispatches a synchronous invocation to the appropriate EJB instance.

A message-driven bean acts as a consumer of asynchronous messages. It implements business logic that is driven by the receipt and consumption of asynchronous messages. A client accesses a message-driven bean by sending an asynchronous message to a JMS destination, either a queue or topic. When the EJB container receives the JMS message, it invokes the linked message-driven bean. (See Figure 6.11.)

Contrary to session and entity beans, a message-driven bean does not have a remote or local interface. A JMS client views a message-driven bean through its associated JMS destination.

A JMS client acting as a message producer uses the JMS API to send or publish a message to a JMS destination. The client does not directly know that a message-driven bean may be the message consumer for a message sent to a specific JMS destination.

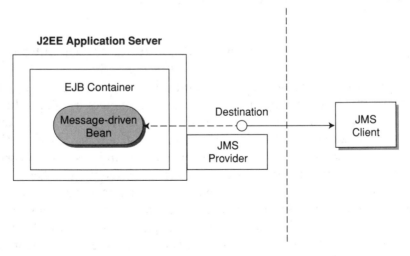

Figure 6.11 Message-driven Bean

EXAMPLE **105**

When a JMS client sends a message to a JMS destination, the EJB container creates an instance of the message-driven bean class that is specified as the message consumer for that destination. The message-driven bean instance receives the message and handles it based on its implementation. For example, a message-driven bean might handle the received message by invoking other entity beans and driving some business logic.

A message-driven bean instance does not maintain any conversational state on behalf of any client. In that sense, a message-driven bean is conceptually similar to a stateless session bean. An EJB container can pool multiple instances of a message-driven bean class and use these instances to handle concurrent processing of multiple asynchronous messages.

6.10 Example

As you recall, the order management application presented in Chapter 2 in "Example Scenario" uses JMS to integrate in a loosely coupled manner with the financial applications on the ERP system. Here, we use this example to explain how you can use asynchronous message-based communication, in the form of JMS and message-driven beans, to integrate Java applications with existing applications.

Our example shows how the order management and financial accounting applications use a message queue to perform an asynchronous point-to-point, message-based communication. Keep in mind that the financial application may also be integrated using a synchronous communication approach, depending on the application integration scenario. (See Figure 6.12.)

Code Example 6.1 shows the order management application code that produces a message targeted for the financial accounting application on the ERP system. The message carries certain information, such as account receivable information, that indicates to the financial system how to account for an order processing transaction.

Figure 6.12 Using Asynchronous Point-to-Point Messaging

Code Example 6.1   Session Bean as a Message Producer

```
public class OrderManagementBean implements SessionBean {

    private javax.jms.QueueConnectionFactory factory;
    private Context ctx;
    // ...

    public void updateFinancialAccounts(PurchaseOrder po) {
        javax.jms.QueueConnection qcx;
        javax.jms.QueueSession qs;
        try {
            // Obtain the initial JNDI naming context
            Context context = new InitialContext();

            // Get a QueueConnectionFactory
            javax.jms.QueueConnectionFactory qcf =
                (QueueConnectionFactory) context.lookup
                ("java.comp/env/jms/FinAccountQueueFactory");

            // Lookup a queue configured in the JNDI context
            // for component's environment
            javax.jms.Queue queue = (Queue)context.lookup(
                "java.comp/env/jms/FinAccountQueue");

            qcx = qcf.createQueueConnection();
            qs = qcx.createQueueSession
                (true, Session.AUTO_ACKNOWLEDGE);

            // Create a message producer
            javax.jms.QueueSender sender = qs.createSender(queue);

            // Create ObjectMessage that carries PurchaseOrder.
            // This message enables the financial application
            // to receive PurchaseOrder and accounting information
            // for the financial transaction.
            javax.jms.ObjectMessage msg = qs.createObjectMessage();
            msg.setObject(po);

            // Send the message with Purchase order
            qcx.start();
            sender.send(msg);
```

EXAMPLE **107**

```
            qs.close();
            qcx.close();
        }
        catch (javax.jms.JMSException je) {
            // ...
        }
        catch (NamingException ne) {
            // ...
        }
    }
    // ... Additional methods not shown
}
```

As background to the example, bear in mind that, because of the EJB 2.0 specification of the programming model and deployment descriptor, the enterprise bean code refers to a connection factory using a logical name called resource manager connection factory reference. This reference is a special entry in an enterprise bean's environment. The deployer binds the resource manager connection factory reference to the actual connection factory configured in the container.

At the start of the code snippet, OrderManagementBean looks up a Queue-ConnectionFactory, which is the resource manager connection factory for Queue-Connection. The lookup operation uses the name FinAccountQueueFactory, which is a logical name declared in the java:comp/env/jms JNDI subcontext.

After the bean obtains the QueueConnectionFactory, it looks up a JMS Queue using JNDI. The environment entry jms/FinAccountQueue is the resource environment reference name that refers to this JMS queue, and that name was assigned by the OrderManagementBean provider. A resource environment reference allows an enterprise bean to refer to an administered resource, such as a JMS Destination, using a logical name.

Now, the bean uses the QueueConnectionFactory to create a QueueConnection to the JMS provider. It then uses the QueueConnection to create a QueueSession. Using the QueueSession, the bean creates a QueueSender.

At this point, the bean starts the QueueConnection so that the QueueConnection can begin delivering messages to its message consumers. Finally, the Order-ManagementBean creates an ObjectMessage to send the PurchaseOrder to the message consumers for this message queue. The QueueSender.send method sends the message to the message queue.

The financial application in this asynchronous communication scenario acts as a message consumer. It receives the purchase order and updates the financial accounts related to this order processing transaction. Because the financial application

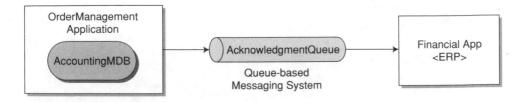

Figure 6.13 Queue-based Messaging System

is an existing application and is not Java-based, it must adapt into the message queue system through a custom adapter. A custom adapter enables the financial application to receive messages through message queues.

After updating the financial accounts for the order processing transaction, the financial application sends a message that acknowledges the completion of the financial accounting transaction. In this case, the financial application acts as a message producer and sends the message to a configured message queue. This queue is configured to manage the financial accounting system's acknowledgment messages.

As noted previously, message-driven beans enable EJB-based applications to consume asynchronous messages. An EIS or legacy application can act as a message producer and send messages to a JMS destination (Queue or Topic) associated with a message-driven bean. The message-driven bean consumes these messages. (See Figure 6.13.)

Code Example 6.2 shows how the order management application provides a message-driven bean called AccountingMDB that consumes acknowledgment messages. This message-driven bean acts as a message listener for the messages sent on the message queue that handles the financial accounting acknowledgment messages. From the perspective of the financial application, the message-driven bean is hidden behind this message queue.

Code Example 6.2 Message-driven Bean as Message Consumer

```
public class AccountingMDB implements javax.ejb.MessageDrivenBean,
                                javax.jms.MessageListener {
    // ...
    // Not shown: Constructor, ejbCreate, ejbRemove,
    // setMessageDrivenContext

    public void onMessage(Message message) {
        try {
```

```
        ObjectMessage objectMessage = (ObjectMessage)message;
        AccountingAck ack = (AccountingAck)message.getObject();
        // process the financial application acknowledgment
    }
    catch (Exception e) {
        // ...
    }
  }
}
```

The AccountingMDB implements two interfaces: javax.ejb.MessageDriven-Bean and javax.jms.MessageListener. AccountingMDB defines an `onMessage` method that takes a single parameter of the type javax.jms.Message. In addition, the bean class includes `ejbCreate` and `ejbRemove` methods to handle calls related to the life cycle of a message-driven bean.

6.11   Conclusion

In this chapter, we explained how asynchronous messaging can be used for enterprise application integration. We described the key differences between synchronous and asynchronous communication and introduced JMS with a brief primer.

JMS API currently provides support for asynchronous messaging in the J2EE platform. JMS can be used together with the 1.0 version of the Connector architecture to support different types of integration scenarios, both loosely coupled and tightly coupled. The 2.0 version of the Connector architecture adds support for asynchronous integration between J2EE applications and EISs. This enables the Connector architecture to support asynchronous integration scenarios.

Chapter 7 describes the CCI API provided by the Connector architecture.

Common Client Interface

THE Connector architecture provides a common client interface for different types of EISs. This interface, called the Common Client Interface (CCI), is an application contract (a set of APIs) between application components and the resource adapter. This chapter describes the interfaces and methods of the CCI.

Two types of contracts exist between application components and a resource adapter: system contracts and an application contract (also referred to as a client interface). See Figure 7.1. Because the system contracts are independent from the application contract, a resource adapter may implement its own API that is specific for its EIS. Although a resource adapter must support the system contracts, the same adapter may choose to support its own, or even some other, EIS-specific client API instead of the CCI.

Because a resource adapter—the software component that enables J2EE platform components, such as enterprise beans, JSPs, and servlets, to access and interact with an underlying resource manager—is specific to its EIS, there is typically a different resource adapter for each type of database or EIS. The CCI provides an API that is common across heterogeneous EISs. As a result, enterprise application integration (EAI) vendors do not have to adapt their products to each specific EIS client API. An EAI vendor can use the CCI as a standard way to plug in resource adapters for heterogeneous EISs. A vendor builds an application integration framework using the CCI, and this framework provides a higher level functionality to the underlying EISs.

The CCI client API relies on simple remote function calls. It provides sufficient functionality that applications can create and manage connections to an EIS, execute an interaction, and access data records.

In addition, the CCI is also designed to be "toolable." By "toolable" we mean that the CCI leverages the JavaBeans architecture and the Java Collection framework so that development tools can incorporate the CCI into their architecture. In this case, the CCI functions as a plug-in contract for an application development

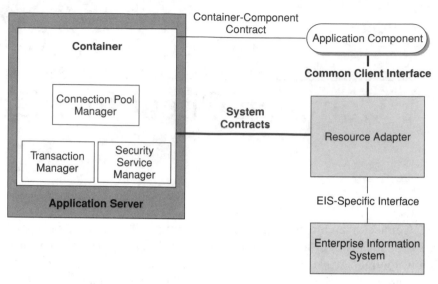

Figure 7.1   Application and System Contracts

tool that simplifies application development by supplying additional functionality over a resource adapter.

7.1   Overview of the CCI

The Connector architecture CCI defines a set of interfaces and classes whose methods allow a client to perform typical EIS connection, remote function execution, and data access operations. These interfaces and classes, which are all found in the javax.resource.cci package, divide functionally into four categories: connection, interaction, data, and metadata.

Clients or application components use the *connection interfaces* to represent connections, specifically a connection factory and an application-level connection. *Interaction interfaces* enable a component to execute or drive an interaction with an EIS instance. Application components use the *data interfaces* to represent the data structures that are involved in an interaction with an EIS instance. Last, the *metadata interfaces* provide meta information about a resource adapter implementation and an EIS connection. Two additional classes provide error information.

Figure 7.2 shows the classes and interfaces of the CCI and their relationships to each other. The sections that follow discuss each of the interfaces. We also include sample code to illustrate how an enterprise bean might use these various interfaces. (If you are not familiar with UML diagrams and symbols, see Figure 1 in the Preface for an explanation.)

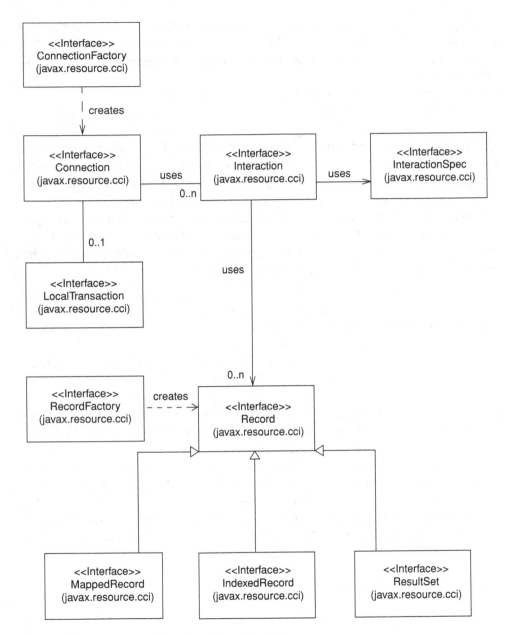

Figure 7.2   Common Client Interface Class Diagram

A client or application component that uses the CCI to interact with an underlying EIS does so in a prescribed manner. The component must establish a connection to the EIS's resource manager to perform any interactions with the EIS. The component establishes this connection using the ConnectionFactory methods.

The Connection instance represents a connection handle to the EIS, and it is used for subsequent interactions with the EIS. (Refer to Chapter 12, Connection Management Contract, to see how a ManagedConnection represents the actual physical connection.)

Once the component has obtained a Connection instance, it can use that instance for any number of interactions with the EIS. These interactions are represented by Interaction instances.

The component performs its interactions with the EIS, such as executing a stored procedure or remote function, using an Interaction object. The application component uses an InteractionSpec object to specify properties related to the target interaction on the EIS. When the application component reads data from the EIS (such as from database tables) or writes to those tables, it does so using a particular type of Record, for example, a MappedRecord, IndexedRecord, or ResultSet. Just as the component uses the ConnectionFactory to create Connection instances, it uses a RecordFactory to create Record instances.

7.2   CCI Programming Example

Before we delve into the details of each of the interfaces, let's look at a simple example—a session bean that uses the CCI interface and a sample resource adapter to access a relational database. (The sample resource adapter in this example can be found with the J2EE SDK.) Although our example application component is a session bean, our discussion focuses on the connector-specific code within the session bean, rather than the enterprise bean-specific code.

Our session bean component first looks up the relational database's resource adapter and its ConnectionFactory. We do the look up in the session bean's setSessionContext method, using the JNDI Context.lookup method. We use the lookup method to obtain three pieces of information: the user's name, password, and a reference to the resource adapter's ConnectionFactory. (See Code Example 7.1.)

Code Example 7.1   Using the lookup Method

```
public void setSessionContext (SessionContext sc) {
    try
        this.sc = sc;
        Context ic = new InitialContext();
        user = (String) ic.lookup("java:comp/env/user");
        password = (String) ic.lookup("java:comp/env/password");
        cf = (ConnectionFactory) ic.lookup("java:comp/env/CCIEIS");
...
```

The session bean uses the resource adapter's ConnectionFactory to obtain a connection to the database. (Later in the example, when the bean needs to create record objects, it uses the same ConnectionFactory object to obtain references to the adapter's RecordFactory.) When requesting the connection, the bean must identify itself for security purposes, and it does so using the name and password values. The bean does not pass these values directly to the ConnectionFactory. Instead, the bean creates an instance of a ConnectionSpec object to hold these values and passes that object to the ConnectionFactory's `getConnection` method. The `getConnection` method returns a connection to the database. (See Code Example 7.2.)

Code Example 7.2   Getting a Connection

```
Connection con = null;
try {
    ConnectionSpec cSpec = new CciConnectionSpec(user, password);
    con = cf.getConnection(cSpec);
    ...
```

Now that the session bean has obtained the connection to the database, it can invoke functions to access and update the database. For example, suppose the bean wants to add a record or row to one of the database's tables. To accomplish this, the bean might invoke a database stored procedure to add the record. Because the stored procedure (or other method that accesses the EIS) must be invoked using the Interaction interface's `execute` method, the bean first creates an Interaction object. It does so by invoking the Connection object's `createInteraction` method. The bean also instantiates an InteractionSpec object so that it can pass such properties as the schema, catalog, and function names to the `execute` method. (The schema and catalog pertain to the database, whereas the function name is the name of the procedure to be invoked.) The bean then sets up these property values, as shown in Code Example 7.3.

Code Example 7.3   Setting Up InteractionSpec Values

```
    ...
    Interaction ix = con.createInteraction();
    CciInteractionSpec iSpec = new CciInteractionSpec();
    iSpec.setSchema(user);
    iSpec.setCatalog(null);
    iSpec.setFunctionName("AddRecord");
    ...
```

The bean might also have to set up two Record objects—one is an input record to pass parameters to `AddRecord` and the other is an output record to hold the returned results, if there are any. Our example bean gets a reference to a RecordFactory from the ConnectionFactory object, and then uses the RecordFactory's `createIndexedRecord` method to create an IndexedRecord object which it designates as the input record.

An input record maps the input parameters passed to a stored procedure. Keep in mind that a stored procedure's input parameters may be solely for input (called IN parameters) or they may hold output or returned values as well (in which case they are referred to as INOUT parameters). An output record maps equivalent output parameters of the stored procedure, referred to as the OUT and INOUT parameters.

The bean sets up the input record by using the Record object's `add` method to insert the input values into the record. Once the input record is properly defined, the bean uses the Interaction object's `execute` method to invoke the `AddRecord` stored procedure, which inserts the new record or row into the table. (See Code Example 7.4.)

Code Example 7.4   Using the execute Method

```
...
    RecordFactory rf = cf.getRecordFactory();
    IndexedRecord iRec = rf.createIndexedRecord("InputRecord");
    boolean flag = iRec.add(name);
    flag = iRec.add(new Integer(qty));
    ix.execute(iSpec, iRec);
...
```

In a similar manner, the session bean might invoke a database stored procedure to read all the records from a particular database table. It would still create an input record and pass it as a parameter to the `execute` method even if it did not need to pass input parameters to the function. The bean merely creates the input record but does not set any values into the record. When the bean executes the stored procedure, the results would be returned to an output record, as shown in Code Example 7.5.

Code Example 7.5   Using execute to Return an Output Record

```
...
    iSpec.setFunctionName("ReadRecords");
    RecordFactory rf = cf.getRecordFactory();
```

```
IndexedRecord iRec = rf.createIndexedRecord("InputRecord");
Record oRec = ix.execute(iSpec, iRec);
Iterator iterator = ((IndexedRecord)oRec).iterator();
while (iterator.hasNext()) {
    //read in data from each entry
}
...
```

Notice that the `execute` method returns an OutputRecord. In our example, the bean casts the OutputRecord to an IndexedRecord type. Because an IndexedRecord holds its elements in an ordered, indexed list based on java.util.List, the bean uses a Java Iterator to access the elements of the list.

You may have noticed in this example that the session bean did not include any transaction code. That is because the bean used container-managed transaction demarcation rather than bean-managed transaction demarcation. Simply put, the bean allowed the EJB container to handle the transaction demarcation, rather than including code to handle the transaction itself.

The CCI defines a LocalTransaction interface that may be used by an enterprise bean to manage local transactions on an underlying resource manager. An enterprise bean manages a local transaction when the bean uses bean-managed transaction demarcation. We recommend that enterprise beans use container-managed transaction demarcation.

If we want to use a local transaction, we could rewrite the session bean in the previous example and have it use the methods of the LocalTransaction interface to do transaction management. In this case, the session bean would first explicitly create the transaction context by calling the Connection object's `getLocalTransaction` method. The method returns a LocalTransaction instance to the component. The bean then starts the transaction using the LocalTransaction object's `begin` method, proceeds to do its transactional work—invoking the stored procedure to insert the new record into the database table—and finally commits the transaction by calling the LocalTransaction object's `commit` method. Here's how the code might look for a session bean using a local transaction to insert a database record. (See Code Example 7.6.)

Code Example 7.6 Inserting a Database Record Within a Local Transaction

```
...
    iSpec.setFunctionName("AddRecord");
    RecordFactory rf = cf.getRecordFactory();
    IndexedRecord iRec = rf.createIndexedRecord("InputRecord");
```

```
boolean flag = iRec.add(name);
flag = iRec.add(new Integer(qty));
javax.resource.cci.LocalTransaction transaction =
        con.getLocalTransaction();
transaction.begin();
ix.execute(iSpec, iRec);
transaction.commit();
...
```

This example was meant to give you an overview of how to code with the CCI API. The next sections discuss the CCI interfaces and methods in greater detail.

7.3 Connection Interfaces

The CCI API provides four connection interfaces.

- **ConnectionFactory**—Provides an application component with a Connection instance to an EIS.

- **Connection**—Represents an application-level connection handle to the underlying EIS.

- **ConnectionSpec**—Provides a means for an application component to pass connection request-specific properties to the ConnectionFactory when making a connection request.

- **LocalTransaction**—Used for application-level local transaction demarcation. Keep in mind that a local transaction is managed totally internal to a resource manager, with no involvement of an external transaction manager.

7.3.1 ConnectionFactory Interface

The ConnectionFactory interface provides an application component with an interface for getting a connection to an EIS instance. An application component uses JNDI APIs to first look up a ConnectionFactory instance from the JNDI namespace. Then, it uses the ConnectionFactory instance to obtain a connection to the EIS instance. The ConnectionFactory interface defines the following `public` methods. (See Code Example 7.7.)

Code Example 7.7 ConnectionFactory Interface

```
package javax.resource.cci;
public interface ConnectionFactory
        extends java.io.Serializable, javax.resource.Referenceable {
    public Connection getConnection() throws ResourceException;
    public Connection getConnection(ConnectionSpec properties)
            throws ResourceException;
    public ResourceAdapterMetaData getMetaData()
            throws ResourceException;
}
```

The principal methods of the ConnectionFactory are the getConnection methods. The two getConnection methods both obtain a connection to an EIS instance, which they return as a Connection object. An application component uses getConnection with no parameters when it requires the container to manage the EIS sign-on. Because the container manages the sign-on, the application component does not need to pass any security information to the ConnectionFactory. It is recommended that applications obtain a connection using this form of the getConnection method, thus letting the container handle the EIS sign-on.

A component uses the second form of the getConnection method when it manages the EIS sign-on (referred to as component-managed sign-on). A component that manages EIS sign-on needs to pass security information and connection parameters to the Connection factory. The parameters and security information are passed through the ConnectionSpec object, shown as the properties parameter.

This ConnectionSpec properties object contains only client-specific properties, such as user name, password, and language, rather than information related to the EIS target configuration.

7.3.2 ConnectionSpec Interface

An application component uses the ConnectionSpec interface to pass properties specific for a connection request to the getConnection method.

The ConnectionSpec interface defines two standard properties relevant for a connection: UserName and Password. A resource adapter that implements the ConnectionSpec interface can add its own additional properties.

Because it is intended that the ConnectionSpec interface be implemented as a JavaBean, applications use access (getter) and mutation (setter) methods to access the individual properties. For example, a ConnectionSpec implementation class would include `setUserName` and `setPassword` methods, in addition to `getUserName` and `getPassword` methods.

7.3.3   Connection Interface

The Connection interface is a representation of an application-level connection handle. An application component uses this connection handle to access an EIS instance. (Note that the Connection instance represents a logical connection to an EIS; it is a ManagedConnection instance that represents the actual physical connection. See Chapter 12, Connection Management Contract, for more information on the ManagedConnection interface.)

A component needs to obtain a connection before it can initiate any interactions with the EIS. However, once it obtains a Connection object, it can use the same object for any number of EIS interactions. (We have already shown how an application component gets a Connection instance by calling the ConnectionFactory `getConnection` method.)

Code Example 7.8 shows the methods defined by the Connection interface.

Code Example 7.8   Connection Interface

```
package javax.resource.cci;
public interface Connection {
    public Interaction createInteraction() throws ResourceException;
    public ConnectionMetaData getMetaData()
        throws ResourceException;
    public ResultSetInfo getResultSetInfo()
        throws ResourceException;
    public LocalTransaction getLocalTransaction()
        throws ResourceException;
    public void close() throws ResourceException;
}
```

Most application components typically use the `createInteraction` and `close` methods. Before an application component can begin some interaction with an EIS instance, it must first create a new Interaction instance. The component does this by invoking the Connection instance's `createInteraction` method. This method creates a new Interaction instance, and this instance is associated with the Connection instance. When a component has completed its work with the EIS, it should invoke the `close` method to close the connection to the EIS.

Application components that are interested in managing their own local transactions, such as enterprise bean components that use bean-managed transaction demarcation (and thus include code to handle transactions), will use the `get-LocalTransaction` method. The `getLocalTransaction` method creates a new LocalTransaction object. The LocalTransaction object provides the context for the transaction, and it enables the component to demarcate resource manager local transactions. (See the next section, "LocalTransaction Interface," for more information on using the LocalTransaction interface.)

The Connection interface also defines methods that return EIS information. The `getMetaData` method returns meta information about the EIS instance currently associated with the Connection instance. The `getResultSetInfo` method returns meta information on the result set functionality supported by the connected EIS instance.

7.3.4 LocalTransaction Interface

The LocalTransaction interface defines a transaction demarcation interface for transactions that are local to a resource manager. These are transactions that are managed internal to the EIS resource manager with no assistance or coordination from an external transaction manager. This interface is part of the javax.resource.cci package, and it is meant to be used for application-level local transaction demarcation. It differs from the system contract-level LocalTransaction interface, which is defined in the javax.resource.spi package, and which is used by the container for local transaction management. (See Chapter 4, Working with Transactions, for a more complete discussion of transactions.)

A resource adapter that supplies a CCI implementation is not required to implement the LocalTransaction interface. When the LocalTransaction interface is supported, an application component obtains a LocalTransaction instance using the Connection interface `getLocalTransaction` method. The component uses the LocalTransaction instance to demarcate a resource manager local transaction on the underlying EIS instance. Keep in mind that the local transaction is associated with the Connection instance.

The LocalTransaction interface defines the following methods. (See Code Example 7.9.)

Code Example 7.9   LocalTransaction Interface Methods

```
package javax.resource.cci;
public interface LocalTransaction {
    public void begin() throws ResourceException;
    public void commit() throws ResourceException;
    public void rollback() throws ResourceException;
}
```

A component that includes code to manage its own transaction first obtains a reference to a local transaction using its Connection instance's `getLocalTransaction` method. The component then uses the LocalTransaction methods to start and complete its transaction. Before invoking transactional code (that is, code that accesses or updates the EIS) the component must start the transaction. It does so using the `begin` method. The `begin` method starts a local transaction on an EIS instance.

The component then performs its transactional work, such as modifying data held by the EIS. When this work completes, the component can either commit the changes, or it can roll back whatever changes occurred and restore the EIS data to the state it was in prior to the start of the transaction. The `commit` method commits the current local transaction and releases all locks held by the underlying EIS instance. The `rollback` method undoes the current local transaction.

7.4   Interaction Interfaces

The CCI API defines two interfaces for interactions between an application component and the EIS. An application uses these interfaces to execute operations on the underlying EIS. The two interfaces are

- **Interaction**—Provides a means for an application component to execute EIS functions, such as stored procedures.

- **InteractionSpec**—Holds properties pertaining to an application component's interaction with an EIS. For example, a property might specify the target EIS function.

An application component uses the methods of the Interaction interface to execute EIS functions. For example, if the underlying EIS is a relational database, a component might instantiate an Interaction instance to execute the database's stored procedures. Along with an Interaction instance, a component uses an InteractionSpec to pass properties for driving the interaction with the EIS. For example, the InteractionSpec object might hold the name of the EIS function, such as the stored procedure function, along with database schema and catalog information, such as the identity of the user, and so forth.

7.4.1   Interaction Interface

The Interaction interface defines methods that enable an application component to execute EIS functions. An application component must create an instance of the Interaction interface from a Connection instance. The Interaction instance is associated with the Connection instance for as long as the component interacts with the EIS.

The Interaction interface is defined as shown in Code Example 7.10.

Code Example 7.10 Interaction Interface

```
package javax.resource.cci;
public interface javax.resource.cci.Interaction {
    public Connection getConnection();
    public void close() throws ResourceException;
    public boolean execute (InteractionSpec ispec, Record input,
            Record output) throws ResourceException;
    public Record execute (InteractionSpec ispec, Record input)
            throws ResourceException;
}
```

The `execute` methods are the important methods of the Interaction interface. Both variants of the method execute a specified EIS function on behalf of the application component. One form of the `execute` method has three input parameters: an InteractionSpec instance, an input record, and an output record. The other form has two input parameters: an InteractionSpec instance and an input record, and this form returns an output record.

When you use the CCI `execute` method to invoke some EIS function, such as invoking a stored procedure, you first must set up an InteractionSpec instance, as it is this object which holds the information identifying the EIS function to be invoked. You also may need to create instances of input and output records. You create an instance of an input record if you're passing a parameter to the EIS function. If the EIS function you're executing returns data, you may also need to create an output record instance. These input and output records are instances of the supported Record types, which are IndexedRecord, MappedRecord, or ResultSet. The next section, "Data Representation Interfaces," discusses these record types in more detail.

Although a component creates an Interaction instance from a Connection instance, it can use the Interaction interface's `getConnection` method to check the Connection object to which the Interaction instance is associated. When the component has completed its processing work with the EIS—it has executed all the EIS functions it intended to execute—it should use the `close` method to close the Interaction instance and allow the resource adapter to release resources held for the instance. Note that closing the Interaction instance does not affect the Connection instance.

7.4.2   InteractionSpec Interface

The InteractionSpec interface defines and holds the properties that drive a component's interaction with an EIS instance. An application component must use both the InteractionSpec and the Interaction instances together to access an EIS function.

The CCI defines a set of standard properties for an InteractionSpec. The implementation of the InteractionSpec, which is either a derived interface or an implementation class, should only support a standard property if that property applies to the underlying EIS supported by this CCI implementation. The CCI provides the definition of the InteractionSpec interface shown in Code Example 7.11.

Code Example 7.11 InteractionSpec Interface

```
package javax.resource.cci;
public interface InteractionSpec
          extends java.io.Serializable {
    public static final int SYNC_SEND = 0:
    public static final int SYNC_SEND_RECEIVE = 1:
    public static final int SYNC_RECEIVE = 2:
}
```

The CCI's standard properties include `FunctionName` and an `Interaction-Verb`. `FunctionName` is a string that represents the name of the EIS function. `InteractionVerb` is an integer that represents the mode of the interaction with the EIS. Execution of an interaction can encompass either a send or receive operation without a synchronous response, or it can send and receive synchronously. By default, an interaction sends and receives synchronously. (Note that the Java Message Service supports asynchronous message delivery. See Chapter 6, Asynchronous Messaging, for more information.) The InteractionSpec implementation can go further than the CCI and can support additional properties specific to a CCI implementation.

The InteractionSpec interface defines several other standard properties, but these may not be supported by all implementations. The ExecutionTimeout property is an integer that specifies (in milliseconds) how long an Interaction instance waits for an EIS to perform the requested function. It also defines standard properties that pertain only to ResultSet. (See "Data Representation Interfaces.")

Because InteractionSpec implementations are JavaBeans, they must follow standard JavaBeans requirements. They must define getter and setter methods for each of their properties and also extend the Serializable interface. They also may implement their properties as bound or constrained properties.

For example, our sample resource adapter might define a CciInteractionSpec implementation class for the InteractionSpec interface. This particular implementation class chooses to define three properties, two of which are applicable only to the underlying EIS (`Schema` and `Catalog`), plus the required `FunctionName` property. It must also define getter and setter methods for each of these properties because the properties are `private` and cannot be directly accessed by application components. Thus our example CciInteractionSpec might look as shown in Code Example 7.12.

Code Example 7.12 Implementation of an InteractionSpec Interface

```
public class CciInteractionSpec implements InteractionSpec
                    extends java.io.Serializable {
    private String Schema;
    private String Catalog;
    private String FunctionName;
    ...
    public String getSchema();
    public void setSchema(String schema);
    public String getCatalog();
    public void setCatalog(String catalog);
    public String getFunctionName();
    public void setFunctionName(String function);
    ...
}
```

Later, an application component, before invoking an EIS function called `UpdateOrder`, might set the CciInteractionSpec properties as follows:

```
CciInteractionSpec iSpec = new CciInteractionSpec();
iSpec.setSchema ("User");
iSpec.setCatalog (null);
iSpec.setFunctionName ("UpdateOrder");
```

7.5   Data Representation Interfaces

Records encapsulate the information that passes between an application component and an EIS. The following five interfaces pertain to data representation:

- **Record**—The Record interface is the base interface for the different kinds of records. Records may be MappedRecord, IndexedRecord, or ResultSet, and they each extend from the base Record interface.

- **RecordFactory**—Creates a Record instance.

- **IndexedRecord**—Represents a Record based on the java.util.List interface.

- **MappedRecord**—Represents a Record based on the java.util.Map interface.

- **ResultSet**—Represents tabular data.

The Record interface is the base interface for structuring input and output record data to the Interaction interface's execute methods. It defines methods for getting and setting record identification and descriptive information, such as name and format. These methods are used by tool developers.

A resource adapter for an EIS extends the base Record interface to support different record types. The Record interface may be extended to support these three types:

- **javax.resource.cci.IndexedRecord**—An IndexedRecord is an ordered and indexed collection. It extends both Record and java.util.List interfaces.

- **javax.resource.cci.MappedRecord**—A MappedRecord is a key-value pair-based collection. It extends both Record and java.util.Map interfaces.

- **javax.resource.cci.ResultSet**—A ResultSet represents tabular data. It is the extension of both the Record and java.sql.ResultSet interfaces.

Code Example 7.13 shows the definition of the Record interface.

Code Example 7.13 Record Interface

```
package javax.resource.cci;
public interface Record
          extends java.lang.Cloneable {
    public String getRecordName();
    public void setRecordName(String name);
    public void setRecordShortDescription(String description);
    public String getRecordShortDescription();
    public boolean equals(Object other);
    public int hashCode();
    public Object clone() throws CloneNotSupportedException;
}
```

An application component uses the RecordFactory interface to create Mapped-Record or IndexedRecord instances. (See Code Example 7.14.)

Code Example 7.14 RecordFactory Interface

```
package javax.resource.cci;
public interface RecordFactory {
    public MappedRecord createMappedRecord(String recordName)
            throws ResourceException;
    public IndexedRecord createIndexedRecord(String recordName)
            throws ResourceException;
}
```

The component passes the record name to be created to both these methods. For example, a record name can be a pointer to a specific record found in the EIS's metadata repository.

The MappedRecord interface represents a key-value map-based collection of record elements. It extends both the Record and java.util.Map interfaces, as follows:

```
package javax.resource.cci;
public interface MappedRecord extends Record, java.util.Map {}
```

The IndexedRecord interface represents an ordered collection of record elements based on the java.util.List interface. This interface allows a component to access record elements by their integer index (position in the list) and search for elements in the list.

```
package javax.resource.cci;
public interface IndexedRecord extends Record, java.util.List {}
```

The ResultSet interface represents a JDBC result set, that is, tabular data. The Interaction interface's execute method can return a ResultSet instance. The CCI ResultSet interface is based on the JDBC ResultSet interface. It extends the Record and java.sql.ResultSet interfaces as follows:

```
package javax.resource.cci;
public interface ResultSet extends Record, java.sql.ResultSet {}
```

7.6   Metadata Interfaces

The CCI defines two interfaces that pertain to meta information. The ConnectionMetaData interface provides basic meta information about an EIS connection.

The other interface, ResourceAdapterMetaData, focuses on a resource adapter implementation.

An application component that has already established a connection to an EIS instance, through a Connection instance, uses the methods of the Connection-MetaData interface to retrieve information about that connected EIS instance. The component gets a ConnectionMetaData instance by invoking the Connection's getMetaData method. (See Code Example 7.15.)

Code Example 7.15 ConnectionMetaData Interface

```
package javax.resource.cci;
public interface ConnectionMetaData {
    public String getEISProductName() throws ResourceException;
    public String getEISProductVersion() throws ResourceException;
    public String getUserName() throws ResourceException;
}
```

The first two methods, getEISProductName and getEISProductVersion, return information about the EIS instance. The getUserName method returns the user name for the active connection. This is the user name that is known to the EIS, and it corresponds to the name of the resource principal that established the EIS connection. (Refer to Chapter 5, Managing Security, for more information about resource principals.)

The ResourceAdapterMetaData interface provides information about the capabilities of a resource adapter implementation. A component uses the ConnectionFactory's getMetaData method to obtain a ResourceAdapterMetaData instance. Keep in mind that a component can get information about a resource adapter for an EIS without having to first establish a connection to the EIS. Typically, tools vendors use these methods.

The ResourceAdapterMetaData interface defines the methods shown in Code Example 7.16.

Code Example 7.16 ResourceAdapterMetaData Interface

```
package javax.resource.cci;
public interface ResourceAdapterMetaData {
    public String getAdapterVersion();
    public String getAdapterVendorName();
    public String getAdapterName();
    public String getAdapterShortDescription();
```

```
        public String getSpecVersion();
        public String[] getInteractionSpecsSupported();
        public boolean supportsExecuteWithInputAndOutputRecord();
        public boolean supportsExecuteWithInputRecordOnly();
        public boolean supportsLocalTransactionDemarcation();
    }
```

The interface defines methods that return version and other identifying information about the resource adapter. Another method returns various Interaction-Spec implementations supported by this adapter. The last three methods return information about how the Interaction implementation handles its `execute` method(s) and whether it supports local transaction demarcation.

7.7 Exception Interfaces

The CCI defines two exception interfaces: ResourceException and ResourceWarning. ResourceException serves as the root interface of the CCI exception hierarchy. When thrown, it provides both an error code and a string describing the error. These error codes and messages are specific to the resource adapter. ResourceException also provides a link to another exception, particularly if ResourceException is thrown due to a lower level problem.

ResourceWarning provides information on any warnings that occur related to interactions with an EIS. A ResourceWarning is tied to the Interaction instance. An application component calls the Interaction interface's `getWarning` method to access the first warning returned from the EIS. The component can access additional warnings, if any occurred, because they are linked to the first warning.

7.8 Code Examples

The following code snippets summarize the CCI APIs that might be used by application components. Refer to Chapter 8, Tools and Frameworks, to see how tools vendors build value-added functionality over the CCI.

7.8.1 Obtaining a Connection

You obtain a Connection instance to an EIS instance after looking up a ConnectionFactory instance from the JNDI namespace. In this example, the component obtaining the connection instance lets the EJB container manage the EIS sign-on. The code first establishes a JNDI naming context. It then uses the Context's lookup method to find the ConnectionFactory instance for the particular EIS. Last, the component calls the getConnection method on the ConnectionFactory to obtain the new connection to the EIS.

```
...
javax.naming.Context nc = new InitialContext();
javax.resource.cci.ConnectionFactory cf =
    (ConnectionFactory)nc.lookup
    ("java:comp/env/eis/ConnectionFactory");
javax.resource.cci.Connection cx = cf.getConnection();
...
```

Once the component has established the connection, it can create an Interaction instance by invoking the Connection object's createInteraction method, as follows:

```
javax.resource.cci.Interaction ix = cx.createInteraction();
```

7.8.2   Using an InteractionSpec Object

You can create a new instance of an InteractionSpec implementation class or you can use the JNDI APIs to look up a pre-configured InteractionSpec instance in the JNDI namespace. Here's an example of what the code to do this might look like. Note that you must substitute the specific EIS function name as the parameter in the call to setFunctionName.

```
...
com.wombat.cci.InteractionSpecImpl ixSpec = // ...

ixSpec.setFunctionName("<EIS_SPECIFIC_FUNCTION_NAME>");
ixSpec.setInteractionVerb(InteractionSpec.SYNC_SEND_RECEIVE);
...
```

7.8.3   Using a Generic Record

In this section, we show you how to create and use two generic CCI records: a MappedRecord and an IndexedRecord. You create a generic record instance using a RecordFactory.

```
javax.resource.cci.RecordFactory rf = // ... get a RecordFactory
```

You use a RecordFactory's createMappedRecord method to create a generic MappedRecord. You use the name of the record, as stored in a metadata repository for a specific EIS, as a pointer to the meta information for the particular record type. Note that the metadata repository stores record meta information.

```
javax.resource.cci.RecordFactory rf = // ... get a RecordFactory
javax.resource.cci.MappedRecord input =
    rf.createMappedRecord("<NAME_OF_RECORD>");
```

In this example, the code uses the created MappedRecord as input for an interaction. Because it is input, you populate the generic MappedRecord instance with input values. In this code snippet, the component adds values based on the meta information it has accessed from the metadata repository.

```
...
input.put("<key: element1>", new String("<VALUE>"));
input.put("<key: element2>", ...);
...
```

Next, you invoke the RecordFactory's `createIndexedRecord` method to create a generic IndexedRecord. The IndexedRecord is used to hold output values returned by the execution of the interaction with the EIS.

```
javax.resource.cci.IndexedRecord output =
        rf.createIndexedRecord("<NAME_OF_RECORD>");
```

At this point, the component is ready to execute the interaction with the EIS. To do this, it invokes the Interaction object's `execute` method:

```
boolean ret = ix.execute(ixSpec, input, output);
```

When the execution completes, the component can extract data from the output IndexedRecord. In this example, the component uses a Java Iterator to extract the data.

```
...
java.util.Iterator iterator = output.iterator();
while (iterator.hasNext()) {
    // Get a record element and extract value
}
```

7.8.4   Using a ResultSet

When using a ResultSet, it is recommended that you first set the requirements for the ResultSet that will be returned by the execution of an Interaction. However, setting the requirements is optional. If they are not explicitly set, the CCI implementation uses default values for the ResultSet. The following code snippet shows how to set the ResultSet requirements:

```
com.wombat.cci.InteractionSpecImpl ixSpec =
        // .. get an InteractionSpec;

ixSpec.setFetchSize(20);
ixSpec.setResultSetType(ResultSet.TYPE_SCROLL_INSENSITIVE);
...
```

Now you are ready to execute an Interaction object that returns a ResultSet. Do this execution as follows:

```
javax.resource.cci.ResultSet rs =
        (javax.resource.cci.ResultSet) ix.execute(ixSpec, input);
```

You now must extract the data from the ResultSet, which you do by iterating over the ResultSet. In this example, we position the cursor on the first row of the ResultSet and then iterate forward through the ResultSet contents. The getXXX methods indicate methods that retrieve column values.

```
...
rs.beforeFirst();
while (rs.next()) {
    // get the column values for the current row using getXXX method
}
```

You are not restricted to iterating over a ResultSet from the first row through the last row. It is just as easy to iterate over a ResultSet from the last row through the first row. The next code snippet shows a backward iteration through the ResultSet:

```
...
rs.afterLast();
while (rs.previous()) {
    // get the column values for the current row using getXXX method
}
```

For more information on ResultSet, refer to the JDBC references listed in the Preface.

7.8.5 Using a Custom Record

You can use the base Record interface to represent an EIS-specific custom record, and then use the CCI methods for this custom record.

To illustrate, we have included an example in which we define an interface called CustomerRecord that supports a simple JavaBeans-based getter and setter method design pattern for its field values. We also define a PurchaseOrderRecord, which is another custom record. A development tool generates the implementation classes for these custom records. (Refer to Chapter 8, Tools and Frameworks, for more details on using development tools.) For example, our CustomerRecord interface might be defined as follows:

```
public interface CustomerRecord extends javax.resource.cci.Record,
        javax.resource.cci.Streamable {

    public void setName(String name);
    public void setId(String custId);
    public void setAddress(String address);

    public String getName();
    public String getId();
    public String getAddress();
}
```

Our example creates an empty instance of the CustomerRecord. This instance holds output generated from the execution of an interaction.

The Interaction object expects a purchase order record as input. A purchase order is represented by the PurchaseOrderRecord, which is another example of a custom record. The component creates a new PurchaseOrderRecord instance for input to the interaction. It also sets properties on this instance, as follows:

```
...
PurchaseOrderRecord purchaseOrder = // ... create an instance
purchaseOrder.setProductName("...");
purchaseOrder.setQuantity("...");
// ...
```

Now, the component is ready to execute the interaction. The interaction populates the output CustomerRecord instance.

```
...
// Execute the Interaction
boolean ret = ix.execute(ixSpec, purchaseOrder, customer);
```

```
// Check the CustomerRecord
System.out.println( customer.getName() + ":" +
        customer.getId() + ":" +
            customer.getAddress());
...
```

7.9   Conclusion

This chapter provided an in-depth view of the CCI, particularly focusing on the interfaces and classes of the CCI. It described how application developers might use the CCI methods defined in these interfaces and classes to perform data access operations on that EIS. The chapter showed how an application component uses the CCI API to establish EIS connections and to execute interactions with an EIS. It also explained how to use the CCI's data representation interfaces to represent the various data structures potentially returned from an EIS.

Chapter 8 shows how tools vendors can add functionality over the CCI.

CHAPTER 8

Tools and Frameworks

TOOLS and frameworks play an important role in EIS integration, particularly in handling the differences in EISs. You have certainly seen by now that EISs are heterogeneous in nature. EISs differ in their client APIs, their applications programming models, and their transaction and security support. This heterogeneity is a major challenge in EIS integration.

Tools are particularly important when developing products that focus on enterprise application integration. Tools provide support for end-to-end application development and deployment, and they simplify EIS integration.

For several reasons, developers find it difficult to use client APIs that lack tool support. In some cases, the client API may be tied to a programming model that is specific to one EIS. Developers must familiarize themselves with that particular EIS and its API. Or, the API may not use object-oriented abstractions, but instead require remote calls to access business functions on an ERP system. Developers must learn the protocols for accessing the ERP system's business functions. Or, the client API may also expose system-level concepts, requiring developers to become proficient in areas outside their expertise. For example, the API might expose the developer to transaction management and security issues.

Many developers are also accustomed to models that make extensive use of visual or graphical tools for application composition and development, such as the JavaBeans component model. These developers may have a difficult time using an API that does not support these graphical development tools, and they may resort to hand-coding both data and function access.

To provide a solution to this issue, the Connector architecture defines a Common Client Interface (CCI) that provides support for application development tools and EAI frameworks. The CCI is targeted toward tools and EAI framework vendors. The CCI provides a means for tools vendors to develop their products free from the complexity of EIS integration. Tools vendors can layer their products on top of the CCI or any other system contract. The CCI or system contract insulates the vendors from the details of managing transactions, security, and connection pooling. The application server and resource adapter handle these details according to the contract specifications.

8.1   Types of Tools

Both the J2EE programming model and the Connector architecture encourage and promote the use of tools to simplify development during the system integration phase. Although different vendors provide the actual tools, it is often possible to link multiple tools so that developers have an end-to-end development environment. Vendor tools provide such functionality as metadata extraction, analysis and design, code generation, integrated debugging and runtime management, XML support, business process modeling, and application assembly and deployment.

- **Metadata extraction and visualization**—Metadata includes such information as input and output records for a function, function names, interaction specifications, and type mapping. A tool often groups metadata for a specific EIS based on the functional characteristics and business-level abstractions that the EIS exposes. For example, a tool might group all EIS functions for a financial accounting application with an associated set of accounting records. A developer uses these tools to visualize the metadata for both data records and EIS functions, analyze the requirements of application integration, select appropriate records and functions, and develop applications that invoke EIS functions.

- **Analysis and design**—A developer may start with a use case analysis of application integration scenarios and then develop an analysis and design model for the application under development. This process includes an analysis of EIS specific metadata and importing that data into the model. The majority of analysis and design tools provide support for the J2EE application programming model. For example, a tool can be used to model entity and session beans and to generate implementation artifacts.

- **Code generation**—Tools provide support for the generation of object-based abstractions that simplify application development. These abstractions hide the complexity of programming against a low EIS-specific client API or CCI by exposing a high-level JavaBeans-based abstraction for developers to use. Generated abstractions based on JavaBeans offer a simple and consistent application programming model. Depending on the type of abstraction—either data or function oriented—and the programming model, an abstraction may be called a business object, a command bean, a data access object, or a record bean. Some tools go a step further and generate enterprise beans, JSPs, and servlet components that may abstract access to EIS functions or may aggregate access across multiple EISs.

- **Integrated debugging and runtime management**—Tools may provide support for debugging integrated applications. They may also help manage a running application by supporting error logging and error tracing.

- **XML support**—A new class of tools has recently emerged that supports XML for inter-enterprise messaging and Web services. These tools support the transformation of data formatted specifically for an EIS to an XML representation. Such tools may also support a "push-button" generation of Web services facades over EIS-specific abstractions. For example, an enterprise bean component that aggregates access to multiple EISs and defines a set of business methods can be transformed by a tool to a Web service. The tool generates a wrapper that serves as a Web services facade.

- **Business process modeling**—Tools may layer business process modeling on the top of an EIS integration framework. These tools expose business process abstractions and enable business domain-specific applications to be modeled using such abstractions.

- **Application assembly and deployment**—Tools provide support for assembling component-based applications. These assembled applications can then be packaged and deployed across multiple tiers. Deployment tools provide wizards that simplify the numerous steps of the deployment process.

8.2 Connector Architecture Tools Support

The CCI defines a standard client API for application components. The CCI enables application components and EAI frameworks to drive interactions across heterogeneous EISs using a common client API.

EAI vendors who are developing EAI frameworks rely on the Connector architecture's CCI and vendor-specific metadata repository. The tool vendor provides an application integration framework that sits on top of the functionality provided by resource adapters from different EISs. The vendor uses the CCI as a standard way to plug in different resource adapters with the integration framework. That is, the framework uses the standard CCI interfaces to drive its interactions with the connected EISs through their resource adapters.

The vendor's development tool might also use a metadata repository, which maintains meta information about functions on an EIS system, to drive its CCI-based interactions with an EIS. The repository contains type mapping information and information about the data structures used for invocation parameters. See Figure 8.1.

How does a development tool that adds functionality to a resource adapter fit within this framework? The tool uses the CCI as a plug-in contract to the resource adapter. The tool generates Java classes that are based on the meta information it extracts from a metadata repository. These classes encapsulate CCI-based interactions, and they also expose a simple application programming model (based on the JavaBeans framework) to application developers. An application component can use these generated Java classes to access the EIS.

Keep in mind that an application development tool can also compose or generate an application component that in turn uses the generated Java classes to access the EIS. Figure 8.2 illustrates this approach.

8.3   EIS Access Objects

A component can access data and functions in an enterprise information system in several ways, either directly by using the corresponding client API or indirectly by abstracting the complexity and low-level details of an enterprise information system access API into higher level *access objects*.

Access objects may be referred to by different names, depending on whether an access object is data or function oriented and the exposed programming model of abstractions. An access object may be called a command bean, a data access object, or a custom record. Different types of access objects differ in form, scope, and structure.

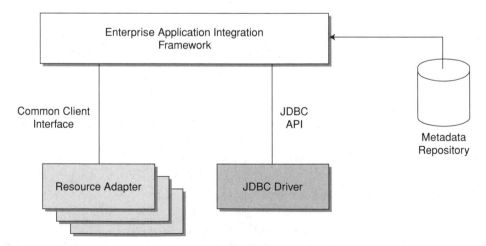

Figure 8.1   EAI Framework

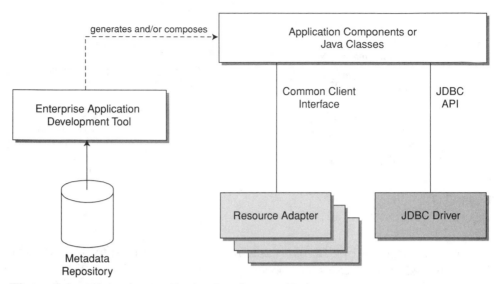

Figure 8.2 Enterprise Application Development Tool

The advantages to using EIS access objects are as follows:

- An access object can adapt the low-level programming API used for accessing EIS data and/or functions to an easy-to-use API that can be designed to be consistent across various types of enterprise information systems. For example, an access object may follow a design pattern that maps EIS function parameters to setter methods and EIS return values to getter methods. The application component provider uses a function by first calling the appropriate setter methods, then calling the method corresponding to the EIS function, and finally calling the getter methods to retrieve the results.

- A clear separation of concern between access objects and components enables a component to be adapted to different EIS resources. For example, a component can use an access object to adapt its persistent state management to a different database schema or to a different type of database.

- By supporting the JavaBeans model, access objects can be made composable. This simplifies the application development effort because components can be composed out of access objects or can be linked with generated access objects using application development tools.

Because access objects primarily provide a programming technique to simplify application development, the Connector architecture recommends that application component providers consider using them anywhere they need to access

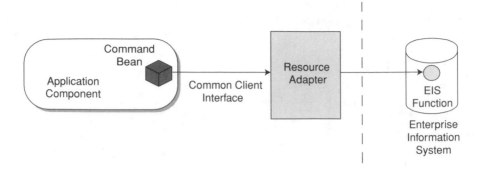

Figure 8.3   Command Bean

data or functions in an EIS. In some cases, tools may be available to generate such access objects. In other cases, component providers must hand-code these access objects.

8.3.1   Command Bean

A command bean abstracts access to an EIS function or to a stored procedure. Generally, a tool generates a command bean.

Figure 8.3 illustrates how a command bean works with an application component. The command bean interfaces with the resource adapter for an EIS.

Code Example 8.1 shows the code for a command bean that accesses an EIS to check inventory levels.

Code Example 8.1   Command Bean Code

```
import javax.resource.cci.*;
    import javax.resource.*;

    public class CheckInventoryCommand extends
        com.example.tool.Command {
            private MappedRecord input;
            private MappedRecord output;
            private RecordFactory rf;

    public CheckInventoryCommand(Connection cx,
                                 RecordFactory rf) {
        super(cx);
        this.rf = rf;
    }
```

```
    public void setProductId(String productId)
            throws CommandException {
        try {
            if (input == null) {
                input = rf.createMappedRecord("PRODUCT_INFO_RECORD");
            }
            input.put("PRODUCT_ID", productId);
        }
        catch(ResourceException re) {
            throw new CommandException(re);
        }
    }

    public int getProductQuantity() throws CommandException {
        if (output == null) {
            throw new CommandException("Command not executed");
        }
        Integer quantity = (Integer)output.get("PRODUCT_QUANTITY");
        return quantity.intValue();
    }

    public void execute() throws CommandException {
        try {
            InteractionSpecImpl ixSpec = new InteractionSpecImpl();
            ixSpec.setFunctionName("GET_PRODUCT_QUANTITY");
            ixSpec.setInteractionVerb(
                InteractionSpec.SYNC_SEND_RECEIVE);

            output = rf.createMappedRecord("PRODUCT_INVENTORY_RECORD");

            Interaction ix = cx.createInteraction();
            ix.execute(ixSpec, input, output);
        }
        catch(ResourceException re) {
          throw new CommandException(re);
        }
    }
}
```

A command bean such as `CheckInventoryCommand` hides the low-level aspects of programming access to a particular type of EIS function to which the command bean is associated. Without a command bean, programming access to the EIS function is through the EIS's client-side API or the CCI. With a command bean, an application component accesses the EIS by programming to the interface exposed by the command bean. This relieves the application component of having to know how to program to the EIS's specific API.

Code Example 8.2 shows the use model for a command bean. It is easy to see in this example how simple it is to use a command bean. The InventoryManagerEJB enterprise bean code invokes a setter method, `setProductId`, to set the input parameter, `productId`, to the command bean. It then executes the command by invoking the `command.execute` method and calls the `command.getProductQuantity` method to get the output parameters.

Code Example 8.2   Using a Command Bean

```
public class InventoryManagerEJB implements SessionBean {
    private javax.resource.cci.ConnectionFactory cf;

    public int getQuantityAvailable(String productId)
            throws InventoryException {
        try {
            Connection cx = getConnection();
            CheckInventoryCommand command =
                new CheckInventoryCommand(cx, cf.getRecordFactory());
            command.setProductId(productId);
            command.execute();
            cx.close();
            return command.getProductQuantity();
        }
        catch (Exception e) {
            throw new InventoryException();
        }
    }
    //..
}
```

8.3.2   Record

A *record* is the Java representation of a data structure. It is used as input or output to an EIS function. A record has both development-time and runtime aspects to it.

An implementation of a record can be either a custom implementation or a generic implementation.

- *A custom record implementation* is generated at development time by a tool. The tool bases its generation of a custom record implementation on the metadata it accesses from a metadata repository, and the custom record implementation includes type mapping and data representation. A custom record implementation does not need to access the metadata repository at runtime. (See Figure 8.4.)

- *A generic record implementation* uses a metadata repository at runtime for its meta information. For example, a generic record may access type mapping information from the repository at runtime.

The metadata used in a record representation and type mapping may be available in a metadata repository in one of the following forms:

- Meta information expressed in an EIS-specific format. For example, an ERP system has its own descriptive format for its meta information.

- Data formatted according to the programming language that has been used for writing the target EIS function, for example, COBOL structures used by CICS transaction programs.

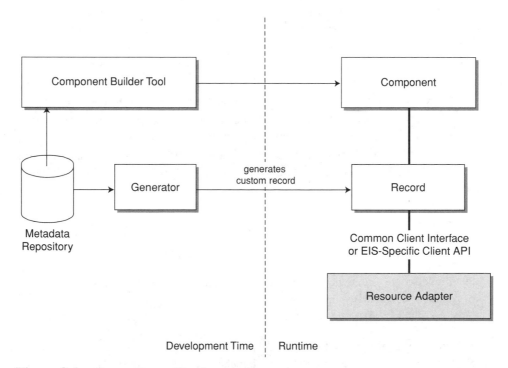

Figure 8.4   Custom Record Implementation

- Standard representation of data structures as required for EIS functions. The standard representation is aggregated in a metadata repository based on the meta information extracted from multiple EISs.

Code Example 8.3 is an example of a custom record generated by a tool. In this example, the CustomerRecord interface extends the Record interface to represent an EIS-specific custom record. CustomerRecord supports a simple getter and setter design pattern for its field values. A development tool generates the implementation class of the CustomerRecord interface.

Code Example 8.3   Generating a Custom Record

```
public interface CustomerRecord extends javax.resource.cci.Record,
            javax.resource.cci.Streamable {

    public void setName(String name);
    public void setId(String custId);
    public void setAddress(String address);

    public String getName();
    public String getId();
    public String getAddress();
}
```

Code Example 8.4 shows how an application component might use two custom records—PurchaseOrderRecord and CustomerRecord. The application component uses setter and getter methods to access properties for both CustomerRecord and PurchaseOrderRecord. This JavaBeans-based design pattern simplifies application development and abstracts the complexity of the underlying client API or CCI.

Code Example 8.4   Using a Custom Record

```
CustomerRecord customer = // ... create an instance

PurchaseOrderRecord purchaseOrder = // ... create an instance
purchaseOrder.setProductName("...");
purchaseOrder.setQuantity("...");

// Execute the Interaction
boolean ret = ix.execute(ixSpec, purchaseOrder, customer);
```

```
// Check the CustomerRecord
System.out.println( customer.getName() + ":" +
        customer.getId() + ":" +
    customer.getAddress());
```

8.3.3   Data Access Object

A data access object encapsulates access to persistent data, such as data that is stored in an EIS or database. Data access objects have the advantage of providing a consistent API across different types of EISs or databases. A data access object is typically generated by a tool. (See Figure 8.5.)

Code Example 8.5 shows a data access object that provides access to all products in a product catalog. In this example, ProductCatalogDAO is a data access object generated by a tool. This data access object abstracts the use of CCI and provides a simple interface for getting products in the product catalog. The ProductCatalogDAO extends a DAO base class that may be specific to a tool or EAI framework.

An important benefit of a data access object is that it decouples the user of a data access object from the APIs and mechanisms used for accessing the underlying database or EIS. For example, if the ProductCatalogDAO class uses a different client API to implement access to the database, the programming model for the user of this DAO does not get impacted. Also, provided that the interface to the DAO remains the same, changes to the schema or function specification in the underlying EIS also do not impact the code of a user component. Using DAOs means that application component code is easier to maintain and simpler to understand.

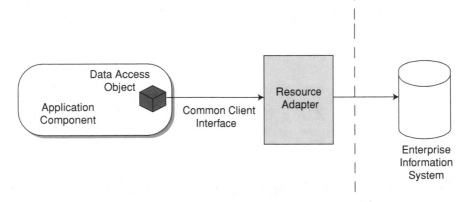

Figure 8.5   Data Access Object

Code Example 8.5 Example of a Data Access Object

```
public class ProductCatalogDAO extends com.example.tool.DAO {
    private RecordFactory rf;

    public ProductCatalogDAO(Connection cx, RecordFactory rf) {
        super(cx);
        this.rf = rf;
    }

    public Collection getAllProducts() throws DAOException {
        try {
            MappedRecord input =
                    rf.createMappedRecord("PRODUCT_INPUT_RECORD");
            input.put("ORDER-ID", "*");

            IndexedRecord output =
                    rf.createIndexedRecord("PRODUCT_INFO_RECORD");

            InteractionSpecImpl ixSpec = new InteractionSpecImpl();
            ixSpec.setFunctionName("GET_PRODUCTS");
            ixSpec.setInteractionVerb(
                    InteractionSpec.SYNC_SEND_RECEIVE);
            Interaction ix = cx.createInteraction();
            ix.execute(ixSpec, input, output);

            java.util.Iterator iterator = output.iterator();
            while (iterator.hasNext()) {
                // Get a record element and extract value
                // Add element to the collection
            }
            // Return Collection
        }
        catch(ResourceException re) {
            ...
        }
    }
}
```

Code Example 8.6 shows how an application component might use the `ProductCatalogDAO` data access object. The application component first instantiates the ProductCatalogDAO object. Then it invokes a getter method to get the list of products in the product catalog.

Code Example 8.6 Using a Data Access Object

```
public Collection getAllProducts() {
    try {
        Connection cx = getConnection();
        ProductCatalogDAO dao =
                new ProductCatalogDAO(cx, cf.getRecordFactory());
        Collection products = dao.getAllProducts();
        cx.close();
        return products;
    }
    catch (Exception e) {
        //... Handle Exception
    }
}
```

An access object can aggregate access to other access objects, thus providing a higher level of abstraction and functionality. For example, a PurchaseOrder aggregate access object can access a purchase order business function using a command bean and can also use a data access object to maintain persistent attributes of the purchase order. An aggregate access object can also encapsulate logic to process multiple access objects in a specific order. Such aggregate access objects are generated by tools.

8.4 Guidelines for Access Objects

Here are some guidelines to follow in developing access objects:

- An access object should not make assumptions about the environment in which it will be deployed and used.

- An access object should be designed to be usable by different types of components. For example, if an access object follows the set-execute-get design pattern described previously, its programming model should be consistent across both enterprise beans and JSP pages.

- An access object should not define declarative transaction or security requirements of its own. It should follow the transaction and security management model of the component that uses it.

- All programming restrictions that apply to a component apply to the set of access objects associated with it. For example, an enterprise bean is not allowed to start new threads, to terminate a running thread, or to use any thread synchronization primitives. Therefore, access objects associated with an enterprise bean should conform to the same restrictions as the enterprise bean.

8.5 EJB 2.0 Container-Managed Persistence

The Connector architecture has been designed to work closely with the EJB architecture specifications. As such, the Connector architecture is affected by the changes to container-managed persistence (CMP) that have been made with the EJB 2.0 specification. Here we provide an overview of the EJB 2.0 CMP implementation and in particular show how these changes relate to the Connector architecture.

The EJB 2.0 specification defines a CMP contract for the management of persistent state and relationships for the entity beans. Resource adapters based on the Connector architecture can use the EJB 2.0 CMP contract for their APIs to the underlying database. (For a complete specification of CMP, refer to the EJB 2.0 specification.)

According to the EJB CMP programming model, a bean provider develops a set of entity beans for an application and specifies the relationships between these beans. For each entity bean, the bean provider specifies an abstract persistence schema that defines a set of methods for accessing the container-managed fields and relationships for the entity bean. The bean provider specifies this persistence schema in the deployment descriptor.

The deployer uses container-provided tools to determine how persistent fields and relationships are mapped to the underlying persistence mechanism, such as a database accessed through a resource adapter. The deployer also uses tools to generate additional classes and interfaces that enable the container to manage the persistent fields and relationships of the entity beans at runtime.

CMP enables entity beans to be logically independent of the underlying persistence mechanism, and this has several advantages. Container-provided tools can use the CCI or JDBC to provide access to the underlying data store. A CMP-based entity bean can be deployed across different containers and persistent data stores without any significant changes to the entity bean class or its client view. CMP also leads to a simple programming mode for managing persistence for entity beans. The bean provider does not write any persistence mechanism-related calls in the entity bean class. The bean provider implements only the business logic methods and relies on the container-provided tools to generate the implementation code for persistent state management.

An entity bean with CMP consists of three parts: its implementation class, an interface that defines its client-view methods, and a home interface that defines create, remove, home, and finder methods. The abstract persistence schema consists of a set of properties, with each property representing a field or relationship that is part of the persistent state of the entity bean. The entity bean defines a set of accessor (setter and getters) methods for these persistent fields and relationships.

The code snippet in Code Example 8.7 shows an OrderBean entity bean class.

Code Example 8.7   Entity Bean with CMP

```
// Entity Bean class
public abstract class OrderBean implements javax.ejb.EntityBean {
    // Getters and setters for CMP fields
    public abstract int getOrderStatus();
    public abstract void setOrderStatus(int orderStatus);

    public abstract Date getOrderDate();
    public abstract void setOrderDate(Date date);

    // Getters and setters for relationship fields
    public abstract Customer getCustomer();
    public abstract void setCustomer(Customer customer);

    // Business methods
    public void someBusinessMethod(...) {
        // Implementation of business method here ...
        // This method uses setter and getter method to
        // access persistent state
    }
    ...
}
```

Note that the OrderBean entity bean implementation has no database access calls. Instead, the container manages the bean's persistence at runtime. The bean provider codes all access to persistent data using the setter and getter methods defined for the container-managed persistent and relationship fields.

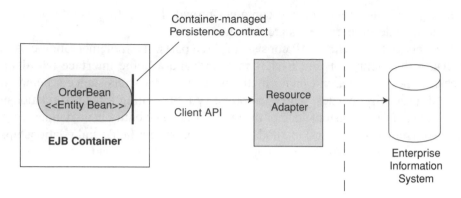

Figure 8.6   Using Connector Architecture for CMP

The deployer uses container-provided tools to map the abstract persistence schema of an entity bean to the physical schema required by the underlying persistence mechanism. A tool uses the entity bean's deployment descriptor, which contains the specification of container-managed fields and relationships for the bean, to perform this mapping. This tool generates the concrete implementation class for each entity bean abstract class provided by the bean provider.

The concrete implementation class contains the actual code that implements the setter and getter methods for these container-managed fields and relationships based on the underlying persistence mechanism. A concrete implementation class manages the relationships between the entity beans and manages the access to the persistent state. It can manage persistence by using the client interface exposed by a resource adapter for the underlying EIS. Figure 8.6 illustrates this.

8.6   Conclusion

We've seen in this chapter how tools vendors can use the Connector architecture CCI to insulate their products from the low-level, system details of an EIS and such system services as security, transaction management, and connection pooling. This chapter also discussed the different types of access objects available to application components. It provided code samples to illustrate each of these access objects and also showed how an application component might use such objects.

Chapter 9 discusses XML and how it is used in the Connector architecture to represent data and facilitate messaging.

XML and the Connector Architecture

$\mathbf{X}$ML, or eXtensible Markup Language, was developed by the World Wide Web Consortium (W3C). XML is to data what the Java programming language is to computer languages—XML is a platform-independent way of representing data. XML provides such benefits as portability, extensibility, validation support, wide support, and readability.

XML is becoming a key technology for enterprise application and business-to-business integrations. In fact, XML is becoming the strategic instrument for defining corporate data across application domains. It also serves as a foundation for the next generation of Web service technologies.

Java and the J2EE platform provide a set of APIs that make it easier to use XML. These APIs help with such tasks as parsing, transforming, representing, and sending XML entities. In addition, the J2EE platform and the Connector architecture together offer the infrastructure that allows developers to build scalable XML-based Web services. The combination of XML-formatted data and applications written using Java and J2EE provides a powerful solution for corporate, Web-enabled, computing environments.

9.1 Enterprise Application Integration and XML

Using XML and J2EE technologies together makes it easier to integrate the many disparate applications present in a typical enterprise environment into one cohesive system. Much of this integration involves the distribution of data among the various applications.

The J2EE platform supplies the connectivity to the middleware services, such as databases, messaging systems, object request brokers, Web servers, and application servers. The J2EE platform also provides tools for developing enterprise applications. With XML, developers have a way of representing Java object data and transmitting that data across Java and non-Java middleware. XML also provides a way of standardizing and structuring data.

XML is emerging as the standard medium for exchanging data between enterprise applications. As such, it has become a key technology in both enterprise application integration and business-to-business (B2B) applications. Enterprises gain several key benefits by using XML in enterprise application integration and B2B situations, including portability, extensibility, validation support, technology support, and readability.

- **Portability**—XML is based on an open standard. A company that uses XML is not locked into a particular product or vendor.

- **Extensibility**—XML defines a meta language that can be used to define document formats specific to an enterprise's purpose. For example, XML technology permits a company to define a document format specific to a particular application. Currently a variety of industries are defining document formats applicable to their specific industry domains. (See "Defining Document Types and Formats" later in this chapter.)

- **Validation support**—Combining XML with Java for Web-based applications in the enterprise facilitates electronic data exchange and application integration. Automated exchange of data, such as in an e-commerce environment, requires the ability to validate data format and ensure content correctness. XML provides direct support for validating document content and structure. Enterprises can define what constitutes a valid XML document, and a standard XML parser can validate the document content by ensuring that all required fields are correctly included in the document.

- **Wide technology support**—Many technologies and products support XML today. For example, XML parsers are available to process XML documents and convert them into data structures useful for programming. Transformation of XML documents into different formats is also well supported. In particular, the Java and J2EE platforms provide several APIs to simplify XML manipulation and handling. (These are discussed in "Java Technologies Supporting XML" later in this chapter.)

- **Readability**—Because XML documents are text documents, people can read them with no trouble if they find this necessary. This feature makes XML invaluable in terms of debugging considerations, especially when compared to data kept in binary format. For example, suppose you have two companies, A and B, that engage in a business-to-business transaction. If company A sends an invalid document to company B, it is much easier to locate the error in a text document than in a binary data file. In addition, people can potentially process XML documents manually in situations when automated processing is not appropriate.

9.2   Overview of XML Concepts

XML is a text-based markup language designed to deliver structured documents or content over the Web. *Markup* is a set of tags and other codes that are used to describe the contents of text. XML uses a form of structured markup called generalized markup that a variety of applications can interpret.

XML itself specifies neither tags nor semantics, nor does it specify the relationships between tags. Instead, it provides a facility that lets you define a set of tags and the structural relationships between them. Thus XML is a language for defining sets of tags or markup languages for different purposes. In addition, because XML enforces a strict set of rules, any standard XML parser can handle each of these special-purpose XML formats.

Applications that process XML documents define and apply semantics to the tags. Or, an XML document can have a stylesheet associated with it. Stylesheets contain rules describing how an application should interpret the markup embedded in the text. XML makes it is easy to generate high quality print and online renditions of a document. In fact, the same text marked up with XML can use different stylesheets—one stylesheet might determine its printed look, whereas another stylesheet controls how it displays on a browser.

In addition, XML markup tags specify the structure of a text document. By embedding XML markup tags into text, you enable the text to be read and understood by a computer. Each piece of text has a label and a notation. Not only can the computer format the text, it can also store and process the document according to the notation regarding the types of text in the document. It can even search for a particular type of text.

A significant strength of XML is that it enables text to be passed and used among different applications and different platforms. This characteristic of XML has helped it to become a very popular technology in recent years. In particular, enterprises are increasingly using XML to exchange data between applications. This use extends to exchanging XML documents within an enterprise and, more and more, to exchanging XML documents between companies and across platforms.

To use XML effectively, you should understand the following concepts:

- **XML syntax**—There is a set of rules for forming XML tags and defining XML documents.

- **Document Type Definitions, or DTDs**—DTDs define the elements, attributes, and rules for the XML tags used by a particular document or set of documents.

- **eXtensible Style Language, or XSL**—XSL is a language for defining style sheets for XML content.

- **XML APIs that allow applications to process XML documents, such as JAXP, SAX, and DOM**—SAX, or Simple API for XML, is a standard interface for event-based XML parsing. The DOM (Document Object Model) interface provides a set of objects to represent XML documents. It allows applications to dynamically access and update the content, structure, and style of XML documents.

We discuss these concepts in more detail throughout this chapter.

9.3   Defining Document Types and Formats

Valid XML documents, which are structured text documents, must be "well formed." A well-formed document is one in which its markup syntax correctly adheres to XML parser rules. An XML document is also valid when its content conforms to the rules specified in a Document Type Definition, or DTD. There is also an emerging standard, called XML schema, that supports the expression of these DTD rules.

The DTD specifies the rules for the structure of a particular document or set of documents. That is, the DTD describes the elements and structure of a valid XML document. The DTD rules may be included within the XML document itself. Or, the DTD can be a separate document that may be associated with one or more XML documents.

For example, you might use an XML document to represent a customer order. The document must contain the order number, plus customer-related information and information about the items ordered. You can set up the DTD to specify these requirements. Applications that process this customer order use the DTD to validate the XML customer order document for structural errors.

The structure of an XML document is formed using markups. As noted earlier, markups are tags that describe the contents of documents. An XML tag is merely a label applied to a piece of data. The label tells you what the tagged data means; however, it does not tell you how to display or present the data. (You use a script or a stylesheet to determine how to present the XML data.)

Code Example 9.1 shows a fragment of an XML document:

Code Example 9.1   XML Sample Document

```
<purchase-order priority="Urgent">
    <item>
        <item-id>493</item-id>
        <type>Book</type>
```

```
        <name>EAI Overview</name>
        <price>39.95</price>
    </item>
</purchase-order>
```

Each markup tag has a start and end tag. The start and end tags, together with the data they enclose, form an element. For example, one of the elements in Code Example 9.1 is `<price>39.95</price>`. This element has `<price>` as the start tag and `</price>` as the end tag, and together they enclose the data `39.95`.

Attributes are another key concept of XML. Elements may have attributes, and these attributes provide additional information about that element. Attributes are name-value pairs that occur within an element's start and end tags, appearing immediately after the element name.

The element `purchase-order` in Code Example 9.1 has the attribute `priority`:

```
<purchase-order priority="Urgent">
```

Notice that the `priority` attribute is followed by an equals sign (=), then the attribute value within double quotes (`"Urgent"`). If an element has multiple attributes, these attribute name-value pairs are separated by commas.

9.4   Java Technologies Supporting XML

Both XML and the Java programming language were designed for the Web environment. As a result, there is a natural synergy in the two technologies—they work well together, particularly for Web-based applications.

By using XML and Java together, developers get the maximum benefits of portable data and code. XML documents are portable because they must adhere to a set of rules known to every XML parser. Most platforms will have an XML parser available that can parse and use data contained in the XML document.

Likewise, the Java programming language has been designed to be a completely portable language that runs without modification on any platform. Several Java technologies directly support XML processing. These APIs make it easier to handle and manipulate XML entities in Java applications. These technologies are all developed under the Java Community Process, with industry-wide participation. This section briefly describes these technologies.

9.4.1 Java API for XML Processing (JAXP)

The Java API for XML Processing (JAXP) includes several Java APIs for parsing and manipulating XML documents. JAXP is part of the J2EE 1.3 platform. JAXP itself includes several technologies, as follows:

- Simple API for XML Parsing (SAX)

- Document Object Model (DOM)

- XSL Transformation (XSLT)

9.4.1.1 Simple API for XML Parsing

The Simple API for XML Parsing, commonly referred to as SAX, is a public domain API developed by the members of the XML-DEV mailing list. The SAX parser processes an XML document using an event-driven paradigm. Here is how SAX works.

An application developer first defines a number of callback handlers. Callback handlers are methods that the SAX parser invokes at various times as it processes a document. The application developer embeds in the callback handlers business logic for processing particular XML data. For example, in the code snippets (Code Examples 9.2 and 9.3) that follow, the SAX parser calls a callback handler that has been implemented with two callback methods. It calls the startElement method when it encounters a start tag. Similarly, the SAX parser calls the endElement method when it encounters an end tag.

Code Example 9.2 shows how to use the SAX API and JAXP. Notice how the example uses the API to create a default handler and then a new instance of a SAX parser factory. The example then uses the factory's newSAXParser method to obtain a reference to a SAX parser. Finally, it invokes the parser's parse method on its XML document, mycontent.xml. The callback handler is defined in the MyHandlerImpl class.

Code Example 9.2 Defining a SAX Callback Handler

```
DefaultHandler handler = new MyHandlerImpl();
SAXParserFactory factory = SAXParserFactory.newInstance();
SAXParser parser = factory.newSAXParser();
parser.parse("http://myserver/mycontent.xml", handler);
```

The MyHandlerImpl class provides the implementation of the callback handler in this example. (See Code Example 9.3.) The MyHandlerImpl class implements the logic for the callbacks from the SAX parser. That is, it includes the implementations of the `startElement` and `endElement` callback handler methods. In our example, the callback handlers merely print a message when a start tag or an end tag is encountered:

Code Example 9.3 Using a SAX Callback Handler

```
public class MyHandlerImpl extends DefaultHandler {
    public void startElement(String uri, String name,
                             String qName, Attributes attr)
        throws SAXException {
        System.out.println("Start of element: " + name);
    }
    public void endElement(String uri, String name, String qName)
        throws SAXException {
        System.out.println("End of element: " + name);
    }
}
```

9.4.1.2 Document Object Model (DOM)

The Document Object Model (DOM) was developed by the World Wide Web Consortium. DOM consists of a core specification and several optional specifications. Its Java interfaces are all defined in the org.w3c.dom package. Keep in mind that JAXP 1.1 requires support for only the DOM Level 2 core specification; JAXP does not require support for the optional specifications.

DOM represents an XML document as a tree model. It defines APIs to traverse and manipulate the nodes of the tree. Nodes are the basic building blocks in the DOM standard. Nodes represent elements, text, declarations, and other entities of an XML document. The DOM API defines methods for

- **Obtaining node information**—An application can use the methods provided by the DOM API to obtain information about a node. For example, there are methods to obtain the type, name, and value of the node.

- **Node navigation**—The DOM API also defines methods that enable navigation among nodes. Using these methods, an application can navigate from a node to its parent, children, or siblings.

- **Node maintenance**—DOM provides a set of methods to insert, remove, or replace nodes on the tree.

For example, you can create a DOM tree from a document by using the DocumentBuilder object's `parse` method. The method parses a specified XML document and builds a tree structure, modeling its elements and other entities. Code Example 9.4 shows how to create a DOM tree:

Code Example 9.4 Creating a DOM Tree

```
DocumentBuilderFactory factory =
    DocumentBuilderFactory.newInstance();
DocumentBuilder builder = factory.newDocumentBuilder();
Document doc = builder.parse("http://myserver/mycontent.xml");
```

Similar to the SAX parser, the code first creates a new instance of a DocumentBuilderFactory, then uses the factory to instantiate a new DocumentBuilder object. It can then invoke the DocumentBuilder object's `parse` method on the particular XML document.

9.4.1.3 XSL Transformation

The XML Stylesheet Language (XSL), and its related XSL Transformation (XSLT) standard, specify the formatting of an XML document. An XML document may have one or more different XSL stylesheets associated with it. The stylesheet specification determines the format in which the XML document can be displayed or printed. The stylesheet's related XSLT standard defines the mechanism to transform an XML document into a specific format. For example, an application can use XSLT and an XML stylesheet to convert an XML document into an HTML document for displaying in a Web browser.

Besides using XSLT to determine presentation format, developers are using XSLT more and more to convert one XML document to another XML document. This is particularly useful in enterprise application integration (EAI) and business-to-business (B2B) integration scenarios.

Although various efforts are underway to define standard XML schemas for different business domains, this degree of standardization is not yet a reality. Today most companies still use their own custom XML schemas for business documents. Because each company's XML schema is different, one company cannot simply exchange its business documents with another company. To exchange XML business documents between different companies, it is necessary to convert documents from one schema to another. In cases such as this, companies can either use XSLT to perform the conversion or they can write their own code to perform the conversion manually. It is easier to define a stylesheet and use XSLT to perform conversions between XML schemas than to write code to perform the conversion. This is particularly true when two documents contain the same information but have minor structural differences.

XSLT is also useful in enterprise application integration. If an enterprise has XML as the common data format, XSLT can be used to transform data to the format required by different applications within the enterprise.

Code Example 9.5 shows how to use JAXP and XSLT to transform an XML document. The example code first sets up two URLs—one to reference the stylesheet for the document and the other URL to reference the source document itself. Then the code creates a new instance of a TransformerFactory and uses the factory to create a transformer instance, passing it the stylesheet URL. Last, the code invokes the transformer instance's `transform` method to perform the actual transformation of the source XML document to a new XML document, based on the instructions in the stylesheet.

Code Example 9.5   Using XSLT to Transform an XML Document

```
String stylesheetURL = "http://myserver/mystylesheet.xml";
String sourceURL = "http://myserver/mycontent.xml";
TransformerFactory factory = TransformerFactory.newInstance();
Transformer transformer =
        factory.newTransformer(new StreamSource(stylesheetURL));
// Transform source xml to system output
transformer.transform(new StreamSource(sourceURL),
                    new StreamSource(System.out));
```

Code Example 9.6 shows the contents of an XSL stylesheet that converts occurrences of the customer tags <customer> to client tags <client>.

Code Example 9.6   XSL Stylesheet

```
<?xml version="1.0"?>
<xsl:stylesheet xmlns:xsl="http://www.w3.org/1999/XSL/Transform"
    version="1.0">
    <xsl:template match="customer">
        <client><xsl:apply-templates/></client>
    </xsl:template>
</xsl:stylesheet>
```

9.4.2   Java Architecture for XML Binding (JAXB)

The Java Architecture for XML Binding (JAXB) puts XML documents at the same conceptual level as Java objects. It enables applications to manipulate XML documents just as they might manipulate Java objects. By using XML data binding, Java programmers can use the same Java constructs with which they are familiar to manipulate XML documents, thus making it easier to write document-handling applications. Developers do not need sophisticated knowledge of XML to handle XML documents because the documents are represented appropriately as Java objects.

JAXB technology includes a schema compiler that generates Java classes based on a schema, typically represented as a DTD. The compiler-generated Java classes provide both access (get) and mutation (set) methods to the XML document data and they enforce the constraints specified in the XML schema. The Java classes also provide methods for marshalling, unmarshalling, and validation of the data represented by the graph of Java objects. Unmarshalling is the process of building an object representation of XML data. Marshalling is the reverse process. Validation is the process of checking whether the objects conform to the specified DTD.

9.4.3   Java API for XML Messaging (JAXM)

The Java API for XML Messaging (JAXM) provides a standard way to send XML messages over the Internet. It is based on the Simple Object Access Protocol (SOAP) technology and can be extended to work with higher level messaging protocols such as ebXML, a standard developed jointly by OASIS (Organization for the Advancement of Structured Information Standards) and UN/CEFACT (United Nations Centre for Trade Facilitation and Electronic Business).

Using JAXM, applications can easily send and receive JAXM messages between each other in a synchronous or asynchronous manner. JAXM provides a framework for exchanging XML business documents, such as purchase orders and invoices, between enterprises. JAXM can also be used to interact with a remote Web service through SOAP messaging.

9.4.4   Java API for XML-based RPC (JAX-RPC)

The Java API for XML-based RPC (JAX-RPC) makes it possible to access Web services using remote procedure calls (RPC). Although Java already provides two APIs for RPCs—Remote Method Invocation (RMI) and CORBA-based Java Interface Definition Language (IDL)—JAX-RPC is geared principally toward Web services and it uses XML as its data format.

Both JAXM and JAX-RPC provide access to Web services. However, JAX-RPC hides the complexity of handling SOAP messages. It also provides a familiar Java RPC programming style. Applications using JAX-RPC can also take advantage of the strong type checking on parameters that the Java programming language offers.

9.4.5 Java API for XML Registries (JAXR)

The Java API for XML Registries (JAXR) provides a standard way to access XML-based business registries over the Internet. A business registry can often be thought of as electronic yellow pages. As more and more businesses conduct transactions using the Internet, it becomes increasingly important to have a central repository where businesses can supply information, such as the format of purchase orders, needed for transactions to take place. Using business registries, companies can interact with each other in a loosely coupled fashion.

Most business registries today are based on ebXML or UDDI. Similar to the Java Naming and Directory Interface (JNDI), JAXR hides the implementation details of registries and provides Java applications with a uniform way to interact with different types of XML-based registries.

Code Example 9.7 shows how to locate registries of businesses whose names contain "EAI." JAXR supports the SQL query mechanism, which is illustrated in this example.

Code Example 9.7   Using JAXR to Locate a Registry

```
RegistryService rs = connection.getRegistryService();
SQLQueryManager sqm = rs.getSQLQueryManager();
BulkResponse result =
    sqm.submitQuery("SELECT id FROM RegistryEntry
                     WHERE name LIKE %EAI%");
```

This code fragment first obtains a reference to the RegistryService. Then it obtains a reference to the SQLQueryManager. Other kinds of query mechanisms, such as the BusinessQueryManager, are also supported. Finally, the code submits an SQL query. The BulkResponse object result will contain a unique identifier for each entry in the RegistryEntry that has "EAI" in its name.

9.5   XML and Connector Architecture

The J2EE Connector architecture and XML are complementary technologies. They can be used together to enable enterprise application integration (EAI) or business-to-business (B2B) interactions. The Connector architecture and XML address two important areas of EAI and B2B: EIS data access and the establishment of a common data format.

The Connector architecture focuses on EIS data access—it provides a standard way to integrate heterogeneous EISs and legacy applications. XML addresses the data format issues—it defines a common data format that many platforms, applications, and tools support. XML APIs, such as JAXP, SAX, DOM, and XSLT, enable applications to easily handle and manipulate data that is in XML format.

9.5.1 XML and Connector Scenario

Our enterprise application example illustrates the use of JAXP and the Connector architecture. Recall the example scenario for ACI's order processing application. As part of the ordering process, ACI's order processing application needs to communicate with the Fulfillment Service provider, an external application, to schedule the shipping of products to customers. In this scenario, the Fulfillment Service provider is implemented by a different company.

Because the fulfillment transaction involves two separate companies, it is important to define a common data format and messaging protocol between the two business entities. XML is a perfect choice for the data format because it is portable and platform independent. It is also a human-readable format, and this allows a certain degree of manual processing if necessary.

In terms of exchanging messages between the two companies, we find it useful to use JAXM. JAXM technology sends and receives SOAP messages using HTTP(S) as transport. SOAP and HTTP(S) are widely adopted standards. In addition, most companies allow HTTP(S) to pass through their corporate firewalls. This makes HTTP(S) an ideal transport protocol for business-to-business transactions.

Although XML technology is suitable for conducting business-to-business transactions, most enterprise data still resides in multiple EISs within the corporation. This is where the Connector technology comes in. The Connector technology, in this case, is used to extract and aggregate enterprise data from multiple enterprise systems. The data is converted into XML format using XML APIs and then sent to the external business entity using XML messaging or similar technologies. The application scenario is illustrated in Figure 9.1.

9.5.2 Example Application Processing

The order processing application, to conduct its interaction with the external shipping fulfillment application, must pass certain customer information to the shipping application. The order application ensures that the customer information exchanged between the two business entities is formatted using XML.

The order application must first extract the required customer information, such as the customer ship-to address, from the customer database. Because the

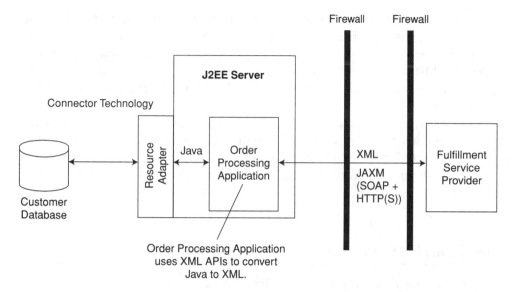

Figure 9.1   Using XML and the Connector Architecture for ACI's Order Processing

customer database is stored on a mainframe system and is separate from the order processing application, the application uses the Connector technology to access the customer EIS. Code Example 9.8 illustrates how the order application uses the Common Client Interface API defined by the Connector architecture to access the EIS within an enterprise bean.

Code Example 9.8   Accessing the Customer EIS

```
// access EIS and get customer address
Context ic = new InitialContext();
ConnectionFactory cf = (ConnectionFactory)
    ic.lookup("java:comp/env/CustomerEIS");
Connection con = cf.getConnection();
Interaction ix = con.createInteraction();
EISInteractionSpec spec = new EISInteractionSpec();
spec.setFunctionName("getCustomerRecord");
RecordFactory rf = cf.getRecordFactory();
IndexedRecord input = rf.createIndexedRecord("customerId");
input.add(new String(custid));
CustomerRecord cust = (CustomerRecord)
    ix.execute(ix, input);
// ...
```

The order application uses a ConnectionFactory instance to establish a connection to the customer EIS. It then instantiates an Interaction object and sets the function name it intends to call, `getCustomerRecord`, in the associated EISInteractionSpec. The application uses the RecordFactory object to create an indexed record, `customerId`, which is an input record. The variable `cust` holds the returned customer data.

CustomerRecord is a custom CCI record implementation supported by the EIS resource adapter. (See Chapter 7, Common Client Interface, for more information about CCI.) CustomerRecord is used to represent customer information, such as the shipping address. It follows the JavaBean pattern of declaring variables as `private` fields and having public get and set methods to access these fields. (See Code Example 9.9.)

Code Example 9.9 CustomerRecord Implementation

```
public class CustomerRecord implements Record {
    private int custid;
    private String address1;
    private String address2;
    private String city;
    // ... more fields
    public int getCustId() {
        return custid;
    }
    public setCustId(int custid) {
        this.custid = custid;
    }
    // ... more get/set methods
}
```

Before the application can send the customer information to the shipping fulfillment provider, we need to convert the CustomerRecord object to an XML document. We do this conversion using the JAXP API by constructing a DOM object from the CustomerRecord object.

Code Example 9.10 shows how to construct a DOM object from the CustomerRecord object:

Code Example 9.10 Constructing a DOM Object from a Java Object

```
CustomerRecord cust = ... // get customer record using Connector
DocumentBuilderFactory factory = DocumentBuilderFactory.newInstance();
```

```
DocumentBuilder builder = factory.newDocumentBuilder();
Document doc = builder.newDocument();
Element elem = doc.createElement("customer");
doc.appendChild(elem);
Element elem1 = doc.createElement("custid");
elem1.appendChild(doc.createTextNode
    (String.valueOf(cust.getCustId())));
elem.appendChild(elem1);
elem1 = doc.createElement("address1");
elem1.appendChild(doc.createTextNode(cust.getAddress1()));
elem.appendChild(elem1);
// ...
```

Recall that a DOM object is a tree structure in which the nodes of the tree represent the XML elements. The example creates a new document object. Then, it creates node elements from the properties of a CustomerRecord object and appends each element to the tree as a child or node. The example first instantiates a new DocumentBuilderFactory, then uses it to create a new DocumentBuilder object. It uses the DocumentBuilder object's `newDocument` method to create the XML document. The example invokes the DocumentBuilder object's `createElement` method for `customer` to create the initial node in the tree. It then adds this variable as the top node to the tree using the document object's `appendChild` method. For each subsequent variable in the CustomerRecord, such as `custid`, `address1`, and so forth, it uses the same `createElement` method to create a new element, which it then appends to the top node with the `appendChild` method. Notice that each variable is converted to a Java String object before it is appended to the DOM object.

The resulting XML document represented by the DOM object would be similar to this:

```
<customer>
   <custid>384659844</custid>
   <address1>445 XYZ Drive</address1>
   ...
</customer>
```

Finally, the order processing application uses JAXM to send the fulfillment request to the external service provider. Code Example 9.11 illustrates how this is done.

Code Example 9.11 Sending a JAXM Message

```
// Obtain connection and create JAXM message
Context ctx = new InitialContext();
ConnectionFactory cf =
    (ConnectionFactory) ctx.lookup("JAXMProvider");
Connection con = cf.getConnection();
MessageFactory mf = con.getMessageFactory();
Message m = mf.createMessage();

// Populate the message with DOM object
Document doc = ... // constructed from a CustomerRecord
SOAPPart soapPart = m.getSOAPPart()
SOAPEnvelope soapEnv = soapPart.getSOAPEnvelope();
DOMSource domSrc = new DOMSource(doc);
soapEnv.setContent(domSrc);

// Send the message
Endpoint endPoint = new Endpoint("http://fulfillment.com/service");
con.send(m, endPoint);
```

In Code Example 9.11, the code first creates a JAXM connection using a JAXM connection factory. It then creates a JAXM message object and populates that object with the DOM object representing the customer information. Finally, the code sends the JAXM message to the external fulfillment server.

9.6 XML Support in Connector Architecture

You'll notice in Code Example 9.11 that the enterprise data represented in Java objects was converted to an XML DOM data structure. This conversion is necessary because most resource adapters today use Java to represent the EIS data types. Using Java types has the benefits of strong typing and seamless integration with other Java-based applications. However, EAI scenarios that use XML as the common data format will require frequent conversions between Java types and XML format.

To avoid these conversions, some resource adapters have begun to support the use of XML to interact with EISs. For example, a resource adapter might represent its input and output records using XML. A resource adapter can support XML in the 1.0 version of the Connector architecture by providing a custom record that represents an XML document. (See Code Example 9.12.)

Code Example 9.12 Using a Custom Record to Represent an XML Document

```
package com.resourceadapter;

import javax.resource.cci.Record;
import org.w3c.dom.Document;

public class XMLRecord implements Record {
    private Document doc;

    public Document getDocument() {
        return doc;
    }
    public setDocument(Document doc) {
        this.doc = doc;
    }
}
```

The resource adapter uses the XMLRecord as the data structure for its input and output records. Let's consider our example application again. Suppose this time we use a resource adapter that can return results as XMLRecords. The customer information returned by the EIS will be in XML format. There is no need to convert between Java objects and XML.

However, it is possible that the XML format returned by the EIS might be different than the format required by the external fulfillment service provider. If so, it is useful to use XSLT technology at this point. The application can use XSLT to transform the XML data it receives from the EIS before using JAXM to send it to the fulfillment provider.

In the 2.0 version of the Connector architecture, the Common Client Interface will likely be enhanced to provide built-in XML support. In addition to supporting the existing record types—such as IndexedRecord, MappedRecord, and Result-Set—the 2.0 version of the Connector architecture plans to add a standard XML record type. With a standard XML record type, it will not be necessary for a CCI-based resource adapter to define its own record structure to represent XML data.

9.7 Conclusion

This chapter presented an overview of XML concepts and described the Java and J2EE XML-related technologies. These technologies, such as JAXP, JAXM, and JAXR, make it easier for developers to use XML in their applications.

The chapter also showed how developers can use the J2EE Connector architecture and XML to integrate enterprise applications and accomplish business-to-business interactions. Using the Connector architecture and XML together helps establish a common data format and simplifies EIS data access. XML defines a common data format supported by many platforms and applications, while the Connector defines a standard for EIS data access among EISs. Resource adapters that adhere to the Connector architecture contracts can support the use of XML for data interactions with EISs.

The next chapter describes how developers build a resource adapter, the system-level software library that applications use to connect to an EIS.

CHAPTER 10

Building a Resource Adapter

A resource adapter is a system-level software library that applications use to connect to an enterprise information system (EIS). EIS vendors, middleware or application server vendors, or even end users of legacy systems provide a resource adapter. This chapter shows the steps involved in building a resource adapter, plus it includes code snippets for a sample resource adapter.

A resource adapter implements the EIS adapter-side of the Connector system contracts. These contracts include connection management, transaction management, and security. A resource adapter also provides a client-level API that applications use to access an EIS. The client level API can be the common client interface (CCI) or an API specific to the resource adapter or the EIS.

A resource adapter can be used within an application server environment, referred to as a managed environment. The application server interacts with the resource adapter using the system contracts while J2EE components use the client API to access the EIS. A resource adapter can also be used in a two-tier or nonmanaged scenario. In a nonmanaged scenario, an application directly interacts with the resource adapter using both the system contracts and the client API to connect to the EIS.

10.1   Implementing a Resource Adapter

A resource adapter consists of the Java classes that implement the system contracts, the client-level API, either the CCI API or an adapter-specific API, and an XML deployment descriptor that describes the capabilities of the resource adapter. The Java classes and the deployment descriptor are packaged together into a Java ARchive (JAR) format with a file extension of `.rar`.

The implementation of a resource adapter can be partitioned into three parts: system contracts, client API, and EIS communication.

- **System contracts**—A resource adapter must implement the three system contracts defined in the Connector specification: connection management, transaction management, and security. These system contracts enable an application server to interact with resource adapters in a standard manner. In general, the system contracts are not exposed to J2EE components, which is the case with managed scenarios. However, in a nonmanaged scenario, an application needs to use parts of the system contracts to connect to an EIS. (Recall that in a managed scenario, the J2EE application server acts as an intermediary and handles most system contract issues, such as connection management, for the application component. However, in a nonmanaged scenario, the application deals directly with the resource adapter to connect to the EIS without the services of the application server.) This chapter focuses on the implementation of the system contracts from the perspective of both managed and nonmanaged environments.

- **Client API**—Applications use the client API to access the EIS. A resource adapter can either implement the Common Client Interface (CCI) or it can implement an API specific to its EIS or itself. For example, a resource adapter can choose to support JDBC as the client API. (Refer to Chapter 7, Common Client Interface, for more information about implementing CCI as the client API.)

- **EIS communication**—A resource adapter has to communicate with the EIS, which it does using an EIS-specific protocol. An adapter either implements this communication support or builds it on top of a low-level communication library provided by the EIS. The J2EE Connector architecture does not specify a protocol or interface between a resource adapter and an EIS. A resource adapter also has to handle marshalling and unmarshalling between EIS and Java data types. This book does not discuss the implementation of the EIS communication module because that is specific to each EIS.

Various implementation options are available to a resource adapter. Because the J2EE Connector architecture is designed to support a diverse set of enterprise information systems, the architecture allows resource adapters to implement different capabilities depending on the underlying EIS support. The XML deployment descriptor included with the resource adapter indicates the supported capabilities. (See "Resource Adapter Deployment Descriptor" later in this chapter for more information about the deployment descriptor.)

In general, a resource adapter has these implementation options:

- Client API

- Transaction support level

- Authentication mechanism

- Reauthentication support

10.1.1   Client API

As noted previously, the client API is the means by which application components access the underlying EIS. The Common Client Interface (CCI), which is specified by the Connector architecture, is the recommended client API. CCI is designed so that it can be implemented and used across heterogeneous EISs.

In general, it is best if a resource adapter provides CCI as its client API instead of inventing a new client API. This enables CCI-based resource adapters to provide support for EAI vendors and application development tools vendors. Of course, if a standard or widely accepted Java API already exists to access the EIS, it is understandable that the resource adapter might want to provide this standard API rather than the CCI.

10.1.2   Transaction Support Level

The J2EE Connector architecture defines three transaction levels that a resource adapter can support: NoTransaction, LocalTransaction, and XATransaction. Transaction support levels are incremental. That is, if a resource adapter supports LocalTransaction level, it must also support NoTransaction. If an adapter supports XATransaction level, it must also support NoTransaction and LocalTransaction.

We recommend that a resource adapter support XATransaction because this capability allows an application to access multiple EISs in the same transaction. If a resource adapter supports LocalTransaction, an application can only access at most one EIS in the same transaction and still maintain proper transaction semantics.

10.1.3   Authentication Mechanism

An application has to authenticate with an EIS before it can connect and access the EIS. The J2EE Connector architecture defines two types of authentication mechanisms: basic password authentication and Kerberos V5.

The basic password mechanism is probably the most commonly used mechanism to sign on with an EIS. This mechanism relies on a PasswordCredential object that contains a username and a password identifying the user or component desiring to sign on to the EIS. An application server passes this PasswordCredential object to the resource adapter for authentication.

Kerberos is a distributed authentication protocol created by the Massachusetts Institute of Technology. It is supported by a GenericCredential object. A

GenericCredential encapsulates generic credential data such as a Kerberos ticket. An application server passes a GenericCredential object to the resource adapter for authentication.

The Connector architecture requires that an application server support the basic password mechanism. It is optional for an application server to support Kerberos and GenericCredential. Therefore, a resource adapter should always support the basic password mechanism to ensure general pluggability into application servers.

10.1.4   Reauthentication Support

Reauthentication refers to the process of changing the security context of existing connections to the EIS. Recall that a connection is a handle that applications use to access the EIS. Typically, a connection is associated with a security context, and the EIS uses the security context to enforce access control. This association normally occurs when an application initially creates a connection.

A resource adapter has the option to support reauthentication of existing connections. Reauthentication allows an application server to switch the security context of an existing connection without creating a new connection. This reauthentication capability enables an application server to support more advanced connection pooling.

10.2   System Contract Interfaces

To properly support the J2EE Connector architecture system contracts, a resource adapter needs to implement several Java interfaces. Table 10.1 lists these system contracts interfaces, grouped together by package, and provides a brief description of each interface's function.

In addition to implementing these interfaces, a resource adapter also needs to provide an implementation of a connection factory and a connection. If a resource adapter supports CCI, its connection factory and connection classes must implement the ConnectionFactory and Connection interfaces defined in the javax.resource.cci package. Otherwise, if the adapter is providing its own client API, the resource adapter's connection factory and connection classes can implement any Java interface.

The next sections discuss these system contracts and the other relevant interfaces.

10.2.1   Implementing Connection Management

A resource adapter has to provide the means to manage connections. To begin with, the adapter must be able to handle the basic steps for creating a connection.

Table 10.1 System Contracts Implemented by Resource Adapters

Interface Name	Description
Package javax.resource.spi	
ConnectionManager	Implemented by a resource adapter to provide connection management support in a nonmanaged environment.
ConnectionRequestInfo	Encapsulates security and client-specific information. A connection factory creates an object that implements this interface, and the resource adapter passes it unmodified to a managed connection factory.
LocalTransaction	Provides methods for local transaction demarcation. Resource adapters at LocalTransaction and XATransaction levels must implement this interface.
ManagedConnection	Represents a physical connection to an EIS.
ManagedConnectionFactory	Represents a factory for managed connections.
ManagedConnectionMetaData	Provides information about the managed connection.
Package javax.transaction.xa	
XAResource	Provides methods for distributed XA transaction demarcation. Provides support for two-phase commit.

To help you understand what is involved in these steps, we present a simplified view of what happens when a J2EE component requests a connection in a J2EE-managed environment. (See Figure 10.1.)

The following interactions happen in this scenario:

1. A J2EE component uses JNDI to look up a connection factory that has been implemented by the resource adapter.

2. The J2EE component calls the `getConnection` method on the connection factory.

3. The connection factory delegates the request to the ConnectionManager. In a managed environment, the ConnectionManager is implemented by the application server.

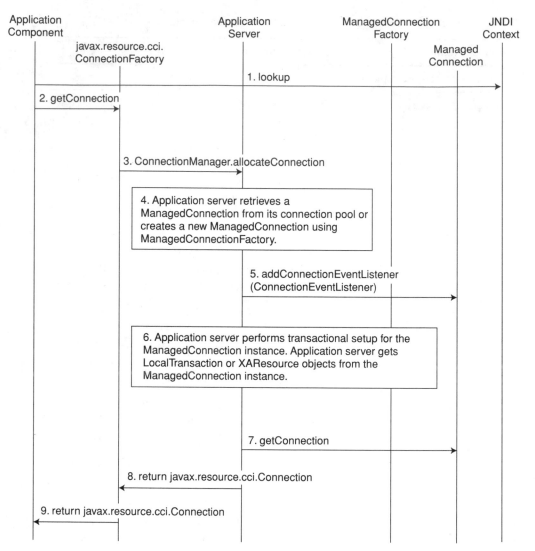

Figure 10.1 Requesting a Connection

4. The ConnectionManager might retrieve an existing connection from the connection pool to satisfy the request. Or, it might call the ManagedConnection-Factory to create a new physical connection, represented by a ManagedConnection object.

5. The application server may register one or more listeners with the Managed-Connection so that it can receive notification on connection events. Closing a connection is an example of a connection event.

6. The application server performs transaction demarcation, if necessary. It obtains LocalTransaction and XAResource objects from the ManagedConnection.

7. The application server requests a connection handle by calling the `getConnection` method on the ManagedConnection.

8. The application returns the connection handle to the connection factory.

9. The connection factory returns the connection handle to the J2EE component.

10.2.2   Connection Factory

J2EE application components use a connection factory to create connections to an EIS. The connection factory may have to implement several interfaces.

A connection factory is usually bound in a JNDI namespace. As a result, it implements two JNDI-related interfaces: java.io.Serializable and javax.resource.Referenceable. In addition, if a resource adapter supports CCI, the connection factory also needs to implement the javax.resource.cci.ConnectionFactory interface. However, if the adapter does not support CCI, it implements some other connection factory interface specified by the resource adapter.

When a resource adapter creates a connection factory, it must associate the connection factory object to a ConnectionManager.

The relevant methods in a connection factory are the `getConnection` methods. Typically, a connection factory interface has two `getConnection` methods, one of which takes no parameters and returns a connection object. For example:

```
...
javax.resource.cci.Connection getConnection()
        throws javax.resource.ResourceException;
...
```

When a J2EE application uses this form of the `getConnection` method, the application server is responsible for passing the client security information to the resource adapter.

The second form of the `getConnection` method takes as parameters client security information, such as username and password, as follows:

```
javax.resource.cci.Connection getConnection
        (javax.resource.cci.ConnectionSpec spec)
        throws javax.resource.ResourceException;
```

This form of the `getConnection` method encapsulates the security information in a ConnectionSpec object.

When a resource adapter receives a request from a `getConnection` method, it is required to call the `allocateConnection` method of the associated Connection-Manager. (Remember that the association between the ConnectionManager and the ConnectionFactory is made when the ConnectionFactory is created.)

In the managed environment, the application server provides the Connection-Manager implementation. Thus, in the managed environment, an application server has the capability of intercepting a connection creation request and hooking in connection pooling or other value-added services. The ConnectionManager implementation is required to either return an appropriate ManagedConnection from the connection pool or request a new ManagedConnection from the ManagedConnectionFactory.

In a nonmanaged environment, however, the resource adapter provides a default ConnectionManager implementation. The ConnectionManager does not provide any pooling or value-added services.

10.2.3   Managed Connection Factory

Applications use a connection factory to create connections, whereas application servers use a managed connection factory to create managed connections. A managed connection represents a physical connection to an EIS.

A resource adapter must provide an implementation of the ManagedConnectionFactory interface. A ManagedConnectionFactory must implement the java.io.Serializable interface, as well as the `equals` and `hashCode` methods. Here we highlight the more significant methods defined in ManagedConnectionFactory:

- **createConnectionFactory**—This method returns an instance of a connection factory that can be used by applications. Associated with the connection factory are the ManagedConnectionFactory and, optionally, a ConnectionManager. (See "ConnectionManager" later in this chapter.)

- **createManagedConnection**—This method creates a new ManagedConnection.

- **matchManagedConnections**—This method returns from the set of ManagedConnection instances a ManagedConnection that matches the security and client information.

In addition to implementing methods defined in the ManagedConnectionFactory interface, a resource adapter must provide get and set methods for the configuration properties. These get and set methods must follow the JavaBean programming pattern. A configuration property contains information for connecting to an EIS, such as, for example, hostname and port number.

For example, the J2EE reference implementation provides a sample CCI XA resource adapter. This CCI XA resource adapter defines a configuration property called `XADataSourceName`. The adapter's ManagedConnectionFactory implementation contains get and set methods for this configuration property, `getXADataSourceName` and `setXADataSourceName`.

10.2.4 ConnectionManager

The ConnectionManager interface provides a hook so that the resource adapter, in the case of a managed environment, can pass a connection request to the application server. In a managed J2EE environment, the application server provides the implementation of the ConnectionManager interface.

However, in a nonmanaged J2EE environment, a resource adapter provides a default implementation of the ConnectionManager interface. In a nonmanaged environment, a resource adapter does not provide connection pooling or other services. As a result, the resource adapter's implementation of the ConnectionManager interface can be very simple—the ConnectionManager only needs to delegate the connection request to the ManagedConnectionFactory. For example, a resource adapter might implement the ConnectionManager `allocateConnection` method as follows:

```
public Object allocateConnection(ManagedConnectionFactory mcf,
                          ConnectionRequestInfo info)
    throws ResourceException {
    ManagedConnection mc =
        mcf.createManagedConnection(null, info);
    return mc.getConnection(null, info);
}
```

10.2.5 ManagedConnection

A ManagedConnection interface represents a physical connection to an EIS. It provides access to XAResource and LocalTransaction implementations for transaction demarcation. It also allows an application server to register for connection event notifications. A J2EE application component does not interact directly with a ManagedConnection. Instead, it interacts with an application-level connection handle returned by a ManagedConnection.

A resource adapter is responsible for properly checking security and identification before issuing a connection handle to an application. When an application server calls the ManagedConnection interface's `getConnection` method, the server passes Subject and ConnectionRequestInfo instances to the method. The Subject and ConnectionRequestInfo objects contain client-specific information and security information. The resource adapter needs to ensure that the `getConnection` method returns a connection handle only when security and client-specific information is consistent with the ManagedConnection.

For example, suppose a ManagedConnection instance is authenticated with user A. It then receives a `getConnection` call that passes in user B as the `subject` parameter. How should the resource adapter handle this disparity? If the resource adapter does not support reauthentication, it should throw a SecurityException. If the adapter supports reauthentication, the adapter should switch the Managed-Connection's security context to user B and return a corresponding connection handle.

It is possible to have multiple connection handles associated with the same ManagedConnection. An application server might call `getConnection` multiple times to enable sharing of a ManagedConnection across multiple connection handles. As a result, it is important that no states are kept in the connection handles. They should be treated as a stateless pipe, or pointer, to the ManagedConnection.

It is also possible to change the association of a connection handle from one ManagedConnection instance to another. The ManagedConnection's `associate-Connection` method allows a connection handle to be associated with a Managed-Connection instance that is different from its original creator. For example, suppose we have two ManagedConnection instances—`mc1` and `mc2`—and a connection handle called `chandle`. The following code snippet illustrates switching a connection handle from one ManagedConnection to another.

```
chandle = mc1.getConnection(subject, info);
// initially chandle is associated with mc1
mc2.associateConnection(chandle);
// chandle is now associated with mc2 and is not associated with mc1
```

At the start of the code snippet, the `getConnection` method executes and the connection handle is associated with the ManagedConnection `mc1`. After the `as-sociateConnection` call, the connection handle is now associated with Managed-Connection `mc2` and it is no longer associated with `mc1`.

Keep in mind that a connection handle can be associated with only one ManagedConnection at any given time. When an application server switches a connection handle's ManagedConnection association, all EIS access through the connection handle must be redirected to the newly associated ManagedConnection instance.

In addition, when an application server calls `associateConnection`, it must make sure that it is passing a compatible connection handle. For example, a connection handle from another resource adapter would be incompatible and thus would not be a valid candidate for switching.

10.2.6   Connection Handle

A J2EE application uses a connection handle to access an EIS. The connection handle is an object returned by the ManagedConnection. The connection handle implements a connection interface that provides methods to interact with an EIS.

If a resource adapter implements CCI, the connection handle must implement the javax.resource.cci.Connection interface. Otherwise, the adapter implements a connection interface that is specific to the resource adapter. For example, one of the sample resource adapters in the J2EE reference implementation implements the java.sql.Connection interface because this sample adapter uses SQL to interact with the EIS rather than CCI.

Regardless of the connection interface that a connection handle implements, it must include a `close` method that allows an application to release the connection. Refer to the three system contract chapters (Chapters 12, 13, and 14) for more details.

10.3   Managing Transactions

Transactions can be managed either at the LocalTransaction level or at the XATransaction level. The resource adapter and its underlying resource manager manage a local transaction. Such a transaction cannot span multiple EISs. A transaction manager that is external to the resource adapter manages XATransactions, also referred to as global transactions. Typically, an external transaction manager resides on the application server.

10.3.1   Using Local Transactions

Recall the three levels of transaction support: NoTransaction, LocalTransaction, and XATransaction. The NoTransaction support level indicates that the resource adapter does not support transactions. When a resource adapter supports either LocalTransaction or XATransaction level, it needs to provide an implementation of the LocalTransaction interface.

The LocalTransaction interface allows an application server to demarcate the local transaction boundaries of a ManagedConnection. Local transactions are managed internally by an EIS. If a resource adapter does not support transactions, the ManagedConnection `getLocalTransaction` method should throw a NotSupportedException.

Refer to Chapter 13, Transaction Management Contract, for more details on the LocalTransaction interface.

10.3.2 Handling XAResource Transactions

When a resource adapter supports XATransaction level, it needs to provide an implementation of the XAResource interface. The XAResource interface is defined in the Java Transaction API (JTA) to support distributed transaction processing. In an XATransaction, an external transaction manager coordinates multiple resource managers to achieve transaction semantics. In the J2EE environment, the application server typically implements the transaction manager. The XAResource interface is the contract between the transaction manager and a resource manager, such as an ERP system.

Keep in mind that when a resource adapter supports XATransaction level, it can participate in global transactions. With global transactions, it is possible that access to the EIS can be together with other resource managers. In this case, updates to the resource managers either all commit or all rollback. This uniform behavior makes it much simpler for an application to maintain data integrity across multiple EISs. As a result, we strongly recommend that a resource adapter support the XATransaction level.

Refer to Chapter 13, Transaction Management Contract, for more details on XATransactions.

10.4 Implementing Security Management

A resource adapter needs to ensure that appropriate security management takes place whenever a new connection is created. The resource adapter authenticates a client when establishing the connection.

When an application requests a resource adapter to create a new connection, the application must pass appropriate security credentials to the resource adapter for authentication. The application has several different options for passing this security information to the adapter. The resource adapter must follow certain prescribed protocols for handling the security credentials, depending on how the security data is passed to it.

Security information that passes between an application and a resource adapter is contained within either a Subject or ConnectionRequestInfo object. The ConnectionRequestInfo interface is a generic interface that a resource adapter can use for representing connection request-specific data.

A Subject object represents a group of related security information for a single entity, such as a user's principal. It includes the entity's identity or identities, because a subject may have multiple identities, as well as its security-related attributes, such as passwords and cryptographic keys, for example. Each identity is represented as a principal within the Subject object. The security-related attributes are referred to as credentials. A Subject object may contain a PasswordCredential or a GenericCredential object. Recall that the PasswordCredential object contains a username and a password identifying the user or component desiring the connection. A GenericCredential encapsulates generic credential data such as a Kerberos ticket.

10.4.1   Container-Managed Sign-on

An application can rely on the application server to pass security credentials to the resource adapter. When the application server passes the security credentials for the application, it is considered to be container-managed sign-on.

When this option is used, the application server passes a Subject instance in two connection-related methods: the ManagedConnectionFactory's `createManagedConnection` and the ManagedConnection's `getConnection` methods. Depending on the particular deployment configuration, the Subject instance contains either a PasswordCredential or a GenericCredential. When a resource adapter receives a non-null Subject instance, it must use the security credentials contained in the Subject instance to authenticate with the EIS. Note that the ConnectionRequestInfo object may contain additional, resource adapter-specific security information, although this is not required.

10.4.2   Application-Managed Sign-on

It's also possible for an application to pass security information, such as username and password, directly when it calls the `getConnection` method of the connection factory. This approach for passing security information is called application-managed sign-on.

When an application uses this approach, the connection factory encapsulates the security information in a ConnectionRequestInfo object. The application server, in turn, passes the unmodified ConnectionRequestInfo object to both the ManagedConnectionFactory's `createManagedConnection` method and the ManagedConnection's `getConnection` method. The application server passes null for the Subject instance. When a resource adapter receives a null Subject, it must use the security information encapsulated in the ConnectionRequestInfo for the connection request.

10.4.3   Using the ConnectionRequestInfo Interface

The ConnectionRequestInfo interface enables a resource adapter to pass its own request-specific data structure across the connection request flow. A resource adapter extends the ConnectionRequestInfo interface to support its own data structures for the connection request.

In addition to security information, ConnectionRequestInfo may also be used to pass client-specific information such as encoding style. However, it is best to minimize the use of ConnectionRequestInfo for passing information other than security information. It is recommended that all information related to an EIS configuration be defined as configuration properties in the ManagedConnection-Factory.

The following code snippet is an example of implementing the ConnectionRequestInfo interface so that it can be used to pass username and password information from the connection factory.

```
public class CciConnectionRequestInfo
          implements ConnectionRequestInfo {
    private String user;
    private String password;
    ...
}
```

10.5 Handling Connection Events

The J2EE Connector architecture defines an event listener mechanism that enables an application server to receive event callbacks from a resource adapter. To use this mechanism, the application server must register one or more connection event listeners with the resource adapter. The application server does this by first implementing the ConnectionEventListener interface. Then it registers a connection event listener with a ManagedConnection object by invoking the ManagedConnection's addConnectionEventListener method.

When might it be useful for a server to register itself as a connection event listener? For example, when an application closes a connection handle, a resource adapter is required to send a connection_closed event to all registered listeners. Sending this event allows an application server to put the connection back into the connection pool, making it available for further use.

Here is a summary of when a resource adapter needs to fire a connection event:

- A connection is closed.

- An error has occurred that makes the corresponding managed connection invalid and unusable.

- A local transaction is started.

- A local transaction is committed.

- A local transaction is rolled back.

Note that a resource adapter should fire an event only when the action is performed by an application via the client-level API. A resource adapter must not fire an event when the action is performed by an application server via the system contracts. For example, if an application server starts a local transaction using the javax.resource.spi.LocalTransaction interface, a resource adapter should not fire a connection event for this action.

10.6 Distributing a Resource Adapter

To distribute a resource adapter to enterprise sites and developers, it's necessary to properly package the adapter. The packaging process includes creating a deployment descriptor file and ensuring that all resource adapter files are correctly inserted into the proper archive module.

10.6.1 Packaging a Resource Adapter

A resource adapter consists of the XML deployment descriptor file and a set of Java interfaces and implementation classes. These files are packaged using the Java ARchive (JAR) format into a Resource ARchive file (RAR). A RAR file is the unit of distribution for a resource adapter. For example, a resource adapter called eisA.rar might include the following files:

```
META-INF/ra.xml
impl.jar
client.jar
```

The ra.xml file represents the resource adapter deployment descriptor. (See "Resource Adapter Deployment Descriptor.") The deployment descriptor file must be stored as /META-INF/ra.xml.

All resource adapter interfaces and classes must be packaged into one or more JAR files. However, the resource adapter developer has a certain amount of leeway in determining how to partition the classes into JAR files. This packaging example, has two JAR files: impl.jar and client.jar. The impl.jar file contains the implementation of the resource adapter, and the client.jar file contains interfaces and classes that are exposed to applications that use the resource adapter.

We recommend that a resource adapter be implemented entirely in the Java programming language, if at all possible. However, it is possible to package platform-dependent libraries in a RAR file. For this to work, a deployer needs to manually extract the appropriate platform-dependent library and configure the application server to use this library.

Keep in mind that, because each RAR file should only contain one resource adapter, you should package multiple resource adapters into separate RAR files.

10.6.2 Resource Adapter Deployment Descriptor

Every resource adapter includes an XML deployment descriptor file. The deployment descriptor describes the capabilities of a resource adapter and provides a deployer with enough information to properly configure the resource adapter in an application server-based environment. An application server also relies on the information in the deployment descriptor so that it knows how to interact properly with the resource adapter.

The deployment descriptor file is meant to be read-only for a deployer or resource adapter user. In other words, a resource adapter provider sets the deployment descriptor, and the deployer should never modify it. For example, it is an error to change the transaction-support element in a resource adapter's deployment descriptor. Such a change may result in incorrect application server and resource adapter interactions.

Here is a summary of the information contained in a resource adapter deployment descriptor:

- General information about the resource adapter

- Interface and implementation classes

- Transaction support level

- Authentication information

- Security permissions

- Configuration properties

The configuration properties define information required to connect to an EIS. The ManagedConnectionFactory implementation further defines the setter and getter methods to the same properties. For example, if the `hostName` and `portNumber` properties are defined in the deployment descriptor, the ManagedConnectionFactory implementation must define get and set methods for these properties: `getHostName`, `setHostName`, `getPortNumber`, and `setPortNumber`.

The properties in the deployment descriptor provide a template that allows the deployer and tools developer to configure connection factories. The deployment descriptor provides the property name and type, and it may also provide an optional default value. Multiple connection factory instances can be configured using the same resource adapter. However, the actual configuration property values are not stored back to the read-only deployment descriptor. Instead, the application server stores them separately in its own copy or representation of the deployment descriptor.

Code Example 10.1 shows an example of a deployment descriptor for the CCI sample local transaction black box resource adapter bundled with J2EE reference implementation.

Code Example 10.1 Deployment Descriptor Example

```xml
<?xml version="1.0" encoding="UTF-8"?>

<!DOCTYPE connector PUBLIC '-//Sun Microsystems, Inc.//DTD Connector
1.0//EN' 'http://java.sun.com/j2ee/dtds/connector_1_0.dtd'>

<connector>
    <display-name>CciBlackBoxLocalTx</display-name>
    <vendor-name>Java Software</vendor-name>
    <spec-version>1.0</spec-version>
    <eis-type>JDBC Database</eis-type>
    <version>1.0</version>
    <resourceadapter>
        <managedconnectionfactory-class>
            com.sun.connector.cciblackbox.
            CciLocalTxManagedConnectionFactory
        </managedconnectionfactory-class>
        <connectionfactory-interface>
            javax.resource.cci.ConnectionFactory
        </connectionfactory-interface>
        <connectionfactory-impl-class>
            com.sun.connector.cciblackbox.CciConnectionFactory
        </connectionfactory-impl-class>
        <connection-interface>javax.resource.cci.Connection
            </connection-interface>
        <connection-impl-class>
            com.sun.connector.cciblackbox.CciConnection
            </connection-impl-class>
        <transaction-support>LocalTransaction</transaction-support>
        <config-property>
            <config-property-name>ConnectionURL
            </config-property-name>
            <config-property-type>java.lang.String
            </config-property-type>
```

```
                <config-property-value>
                    jdbc:cloudscape:rmi:CloudscapeDB;create=true
                </config-property-value>
            </config-property>
            <authentication-mechanism>
                <authentication-mechanism-type>BasicPassword
                </authentication-mechanism-type>
                <credential-interface>
                    javax.resource.security.PasswordCredential
                </credential-interface>
            </authentication-mechanism>
            <reauthentication-support>false</reauthentication-support>
        </resourceadapter>
    </connector>
```

10.7 Using an Adapter in the Runtime Environment

When a resource adapter is used within a J2EE application server, the adapter is executed under a default Java security permission set. The security permission set restricts a resource adapter's ability to access system resources. By default, a resource adapter is allowed to access the file systems, read system properties, and connect to remote hosts. If a resource adapter requires additional security permissions, it must document the permissions in the deployment descriptor. When a deployer configures the resource adapter, he or she must explicitly grant the extra security permissions requested. The method to grant permissions is specific to an application server. In the J2EE reference implementation, for example, the deployer must manually edit a security policy file.

Keep in mind that some J2EE components, such as enterprise beans, are normally granted fewer permissions than a resource adapter would be granted. For example, an enterprise bean is not allowed to access the underlying file systems. To ensure that a resource adapter can still access system resources when it is called from a J2EE component such as an enterprise bean, the resource adapter must enclose all its system access invocations in doPrivileged blocks, as follows:

```
AccessController.doPrivileged(new PrivilegedAction() {
    public Object run() {
        // perform system access operations here
    }
});
```

10.8 Conclusion

This chapter described how a developer might implement a resource adapter, providing code snippets to illustrate the process. It showed how to provide a client API and appropriate connection, transaction, and security support, according to the EIS adapter-side of the Connector architecture's system contracts. In addition, the chapter described how to set up a deployment descriptor for a resource adapter, and how to package and distribute the adapter so that it can be used in a runtime environment.

The next three chapters discuss the three Connector system contracts—connection management, transaction management, and security—in greater detail.

CHAPTER 11

Resource Adapter Packaging and Deployment

IN Chapter 10, Building a Resource Adapter, we described how to build a resource adapter. After you have developed and built a resource adapter, you must package and deploy it on a J2EE application server to make it available to J2EE applications. This chapter describes how to package and deploy a resource adapter.

First, we begin with some background on packaging and deployment, and then we focus on how the deployment process occurs within an application server environment.

Deployment is the process whereby software modules are installed into an operational environment. In the J2EE operational environment, all J2EE applications are composed of one or more J2EE modules. A J2EE module represents the basic unit of composition for a J2EE application. That is, a module consists of one or more J2EE application components and one module-level deployment descriptor. J2EE application components are enterprise beans, servlets, and JSPs. The deployment descriptor is an XML file that describes how the module should be deployed. The deployment descriptor describes specific configuration requirements that are resolved at deployment by the *deployer*. A deployer is an expert in the target operational environment who installs, and possibly customizes, software modules into the operational environment.

Within the context of the J2EE platform, a resource adapter corresponds to a J2EE module. In most regards, a resource adapter module is just like other J2EE modules, such as enterprise bean modules, application client modules, and Web client modules. Like other modules, the resource adapter must be deployed into an application server. To that end, the J2EE Connector architecture supports the modular and portable deployment of a resource adapter into a J2EE application server. However, whereas most other J2EE modules contain multiple application components in addition to the deployment descriptor, a resource adapter module contains exactly one component: a resource adapter.

Figure 11.1 shows how the composition of a resource adapter module compares with the composition of other J2EE modules. The icon labeled "DD" in the diagram represents the deployment descriptor file. One J2EE application is illustrated in the figure. It is composed of four J2EE modules: an EJB module, a Web

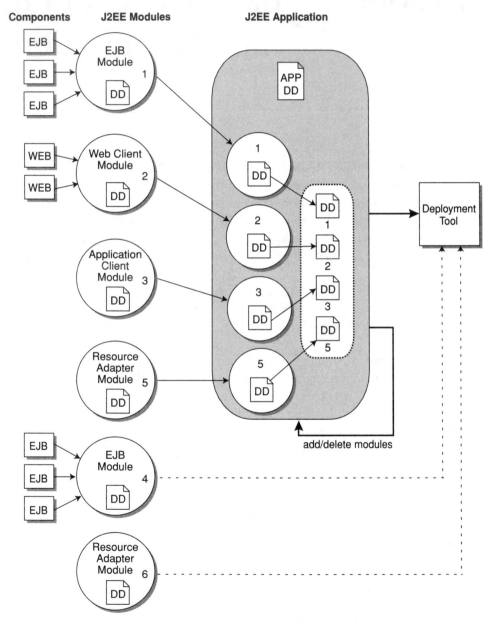

Figure 11.1 Deploying a Resource Adapter Module

client module, an application client module, and a resource adapter module. The J2EE application is a unit of deployment. In addition, the figure also shows a stand-alone EJB module and resource adapter module. A J2EE module can also be directly deployed into a J2EE application server.

11.1   Deployment Approaches

Similar to the other J2EE modules, a resource adapter module must be deployed and configured before it can be made available for other J2EE components and applications to use. There are two approaches or options for deploying a resource adapter:

- **Standalone deployment**—The resource adapter is deployed as a standalone module.

- **Bundled deployment**—The resource adapter is first assembled into a J2EE application and then it is deployed as part of that J2EE application.

The next sections discuss these two resource adapter deployment approaches.

11.1.1   Standalone Deployment

A resource adapter module can be deployed as a standalone unit into an application server. When deployed in this manner, the J2EE platform ensures that the resource adapter is available to all J2EE applications running on the application server. The principal benefit of using this deployment option is to allow multiple J2EE applications to share a single resource adapter.

You use this deployment option if the majority of the J2EE applications in your operational environment use the same type and version of a resource adapter. That way, you need only deploy the resource adapter once, rather than having to deploy the adapter separately for each application.

Keep in mind, though, that this option has some disadvantages for the individual deploying the application at the operational site. The deployer must resolve the external resource adapter dependencies—such as a resource factory reference that manages a connection—for the J2EE application. The deployer also must be sure to deploy the correct version of the resource adapter.

In Figure 11.1, the resource adapter module 6 (which appears at the bottom of the figure) is deployed as a standalone unit.

11.1.2   Bundled Deployment

All J2EE modules can be assembled together with other J2EE modules into one J2EE application. Because a resource adapter is one type of J2EE module, it can be assembled or bundled with other J2EE modules into an application. For example, a three-tier J2EE application may contain a resource adapter module for EIS connectivity, an EJB module for business logic, and a Web client module for Web presentation. Referring again to Figure 11.1, resource adapter module 5 is bundled together with EJB module 1, Web client module 2, and application client module 3 into one J2EE application.

When you bundle a resource adapter module within an application and then deploy that application, the J2EE platform makes that resource adapter available only to the modules and components within the same application. The bundled resource adapter is not visible to other applications deployed in the same application server.

The bundled deployment option enables you to ship the J2EE application together with the resource adapter. By doing so, the deployer (at the operational site) need not resolve any external resource adapter dependencies. This also ensures that the deployer does not mistakenly install an incorrect version of a resource adapter, a scenario best avoided.

11.2   Packaging a Resource Adapter

Packaging a resource adapter entails defining the deployment descriptor for the adapter and including all elements of the resource adapter. Generally a packaged resource adapter includes these elements:

- The Java classes and interfaces that implement the functionality of the resource adapter

- Any utility Java classes the resource adapter uses

- The resource adapter's platform-dependent native libraries

- Help files and documentation

- The deployment descriptor containing descriptive meta information that ties together all the elements of the resource adapter

A resource adapter is packaged into a Resource Adapter Archive (RAR) file using the Java Archive (JAR) format. A resource adapter archive file is identified by the file extension .rar. For example, you might package the resource adapter myEIS into the archive file myEIS.rar.

A resource adapter RAR file must contain a correctly formatted deployment descriptor. The implementation—the Java classes and interfaces—of a resource adapter is typically packaged in one or more JAR files, and these JAR files are in the resource adapter module. (Note that JAR files use the .jar extension.) The deployer must ensure that all the JAR files are loaded in the operational environment.

It's possible that the resource adapter module may contain platform-specific native libraries. If so, the deployer must also ensure that these native libraries are installed in the operational environment.

For example, you might have the following files in a resource adapter module:

```
/META-INF/ra.xml
/howto.html
/images/icon.jpg
    /ra.jar
    /cci.jar
    /win.dll
/solaris.so
```

In this example, the file `ra.xml` is the deployment descriptor, The files `ra.jar` and `cci.jar` contain the Java interfaces and implementation classes for the resource adapter. Last, `win.dll` and `solaris.so` represent native libraries that the adapter uses.

As we've noted, each resource adapter module includes a deployment descriptor. A deployment descriptor is an XML file containing deployment-specific information about the resource adapter. The deployment descriptor defines the contract between a resource adapter provider and a deployer. The file contains declarative information about the resource adapter and is intended for the deployer's use. The information in the descriptor enables the deployer to deploy the resource adapter in a target operational environment.

Before deploying a resource adapter, the deployer should examine the resource adapter deployment descriptor to understand the resource adapter's capabilities and requirements. In particular, the deployer needs to pay attention to the following elements of the deployment descriptor, all of which pertain to the resource adapter: version information, transactional support, configuration properties, authentication mechanisms, and security permissions.

- **Version information**—The deployer must ensure that he or she is deploying the correct version of the resource adapter for a particular application.

- **Transactional support**—The deployment descriptor includes a transaction support level that determines the transactional capability of a resource adapter. There are three levels of transactional support:

  - NoTransaction—At this level, the resource adapter does not support any transaction semantics.

  - LocalTransaction—When this level of support is specified, the resource adapter supports only local transactions internal to a particular EIS resource manager.

- **XATransaction**—When this level is specified, the resource adapter supports both local and XA transactions. With XA transaction support, the resource adapter can participate in a JTA (or global) transaction involving multiple EISs.

The deployer must ensure that the resource adapter meets the transactional needs of the J2EE applications intending to use the resource adapter. That is, the deployer ensures that the resource adapter's transaction support level is sufficient to support the transactional requirements of the J2EE applications. For example, if a J2EE application needs to access two EISs in the same transaction, the transaction support level of both resource adapters should be XATransaction.

(See Chapter 4, Working with Transactions, and Chapter 13, Transaction Management Contract, for more information on handling transactions.)

- **Configuration properties**—The deployment descriptor specifies the properties for the configuration of multiple connection factories. The deployer needs to configure at least one connection factory for each resource adapter. The deployer may have to configure more than one connection factory for each resource adapter. The J2EE applications use these connection factories to create connections to the underlying EIS.

Each connection factory has a corresponding managed connection factory that the application server uses. Each managed connection factory requires configuration information, such as server and connection port information, typically specified as name-value pairs. The configuration properties in the deployment descriptor define a template for the name-value pairs that must be specified for each managed connection factory. For example, a resource adapter may define the following configuration properties:

- **ServerName**—Name of the server for the EIS instance

- **PortNumber**—Port number for establishing a connection to an EIS instance

The deployer must specify the proper configuration properties for each managed connection factory. But why would an operational site want to have more than one managed connection factory for a single resource adapter? Different managed connection factories allow the same resource adapter to be used to connect to different EIS instances of the same type. Each managed connection factory must be configured with different property values, reflecting the particular EIS instance for which it provides a connection.

(See Chapter 3, Managing Connections, and Chapter 12, Connection Management Contract, for more information.)

- **Authentication mechanisms**—The resource adapter deployment descriptor specifies the authentication mechanisms that the resource adapter supports. A resource adapter may support one or both of the following authentication mechanisms:

- **BasicPassword**—This is a user password-based authentication mechanism that is specific to an EIS.

- **Kerbv5**—This refers to Kerberos version 5-based authentication mechanism.

Depending on the authentication mechanism supported by the resource adapter, the deployer ensures that the proper security mechanism is set up in the operational environment.

- **Security permissions**—Every resource adapter is granted the same default set of Java security permissions. A resource adapter may request additional security permissions (such as thread creation) beyond this default permission set. The deployment descriptor lists these additional or changed security permissions. If the resource adapter requests additional security permissions, or wants to change the security permissions, the deployer needs to evaluate the security implications of the changed or additional permissions and decide whether or not to grant the extra permissions in the operational environment.

11.3 Deployment and Configuration

Deployment entails two actions: installation and configuration. The deployer installs a resource adapter module on an application server and then configures it into the target operational environment.

Generally most application servers provide some tools to simplify the deployment process. However, the tools cannot handle all the deployment steps, and the deployer may need to perform some deployment tasks manually.

After a resource adapter is deployed successfully, the deployer should configure the application server based on the configuration information contained in the resource adapter deployment descriptor. For example, the deployer may need to configure the security authentication mechanism and grant extra security permissions requested by the resource adapter.

The deployer performs certain tasks to configure a resource adapter. The deployer

- Configures one or more property sets per ManagedConnectionFactory instance to create connections to different underlying EIS instances. Values for the fields in a property set are specified in the deployment descriptor. Note that each property set provides a specific configuration for creating a connection to a specific EIS instance.

- Configures the application server mechanisms for transaction management based on the resource adapters' level of transaction support

- Configures security in the target operational environment based on the resource adapter's security requirements, the adapter's authentication mechanism, and its credentials interface. The deployment descriptor specifies the security requirements. The deployer needs to consider the security mechanisms supported by the application server.

11.4   Connection Factory Creation

For a J2EE application component to use a deployed resource adapter, the application component needs to be able to look up a connection factory and create a connection using the connection factory. This requires the deployer to perform an additional step after deploying a resource adapter. The deployer must create one or more connection factories for the resource adapter and then must bind these connection factories to the JNDI namespace.

A J2EE application uses the JNDI to locate and look up a connection factory for a resource adapter. The application then uses the connection factory to create a connection to the resource adapter's underlying EIS.

A deployer uses the tools provided by the application server to create connection factories. Keep in mind that each connection factory has an associated managed connection factory. The resource adapter deployment descriptor defines the set of configuration properties that need to be defined for each managed connection factory. The deployer configures each configuration property for the managed connection factory based on the property's name, type, and description as specified in the deployment descriptor.

11.5   Using Packaging and Deployment Tools

Generally you package and deploy a resource adapter using the tools that are part of your particular application server. Although each application server's tool is different, functionally they all accomplish similar tasks. We use the J2EE Software Development Kit (SDK) Version 1.3 deployment tool, called deploytool, to illustrate some of these packaging and deployment tasks. Using the J2EE SDK, we will deploy a sample resource adapter that has been provided with the SDK.

Note that you can download the J2EE SDK from `http://java.sun.com/j2ee/download.html`.

Two sample resource adapters come with the J2EE SDK. The CciBlackBoxLocalTx supports local transactions, and the CciBlackBoxXA supports global transactions. We use deploytool to deploy these adapters onto the server called localhost.

As we've already noted, resource adapters may contain configuration properties. Properties are name-value pairs containing information specific to the resource adapter and its underlying EIS. Configuration properties are defined in the deployment descriptor of each resource adapter's RAR file.

Deployment tools let you view and set up the configuration properties for a resource adapter. For example, you can view and edit the properties that provide general information about a resource adapter—these properties provide such information as the adapter name, version description, vendor name, licensing requirements, type of EIS supported, and supported specification version. You can also edit a resource adapter's default configuration properties, security properties, and RAR file.

Figure 11.2 shows some of the properties for a resource adapter, including its managed connection factory, its ConnectionFactory interface and implementation, and its Connection interface and implementation.

Figure 11.3 shows example screens that you might see for the configuration properties, security, and RAR file.

Generally a deployment tool shows the available resource adapters and the adapters that have been deployed on a particular server. The top screen in Figure 11.4 shows that the J2EE deploytool has two available resource adapter files, CciBlackBoxLocalTx and CciBlackBoxXA, and that currently only the cciblackbox-xa.rar adapter has been deployed to the localhost server. The lower screen

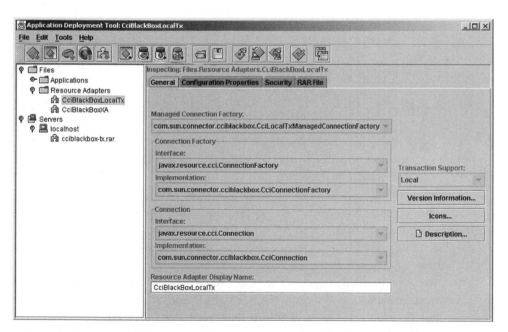

Figure 11.2 deploytool Configuration Properties

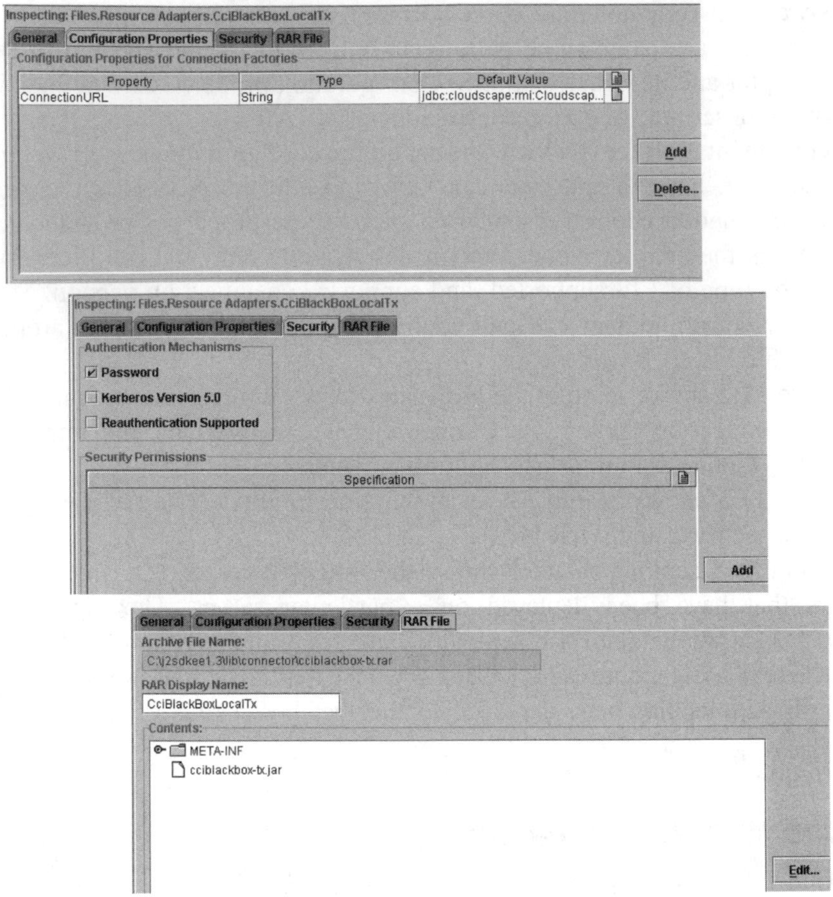

Figure 11.3 Configuration, Security, and RAR Properties

shows a typical dialog box for deploying a resource adapter file to a specific server. You indicate the resource adapter that you want to deploy and the name of the target server on which it should be deployed.

After you have deployed a resource adapter, you must set up at least one connection factory for that adapter. Your application uses a resource adapter's connection factory to establish a connection to an adapter's underlying EIS instance. When you create a connection factory for an adapter, you specify a JNDI name to identify the connection factory.

You use your application server's deployment tool to view, create, and edit these connection factories. For example, we use the J2EE deployment tool to look at the connection factories already set up for our two resource adapters. The cci-blackbox-tx resource adapter has a connection factory whose JNDI name is eis/

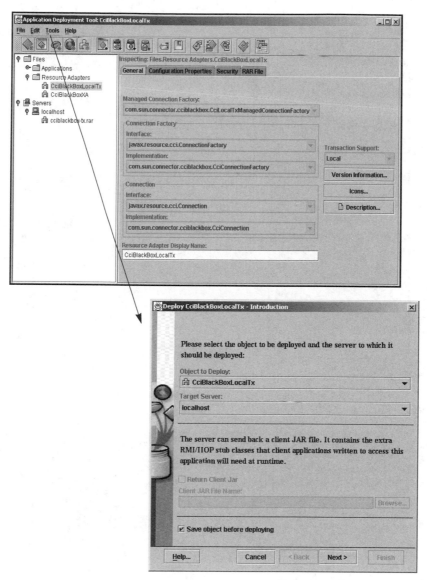

Figure 11.4 Deploying a Resource Adapter

newFactory, and the cciblackbox-xa resource adapter's connection factory is identified as eis/myfactory. (See Figure 11.5.)

Deployment tools also provide a means to create a new connection factory for a resource adapter. Figure 11.6 shows a sample screen to create a new connection factory with a JNDI name of eis/testFactory for the cciblackbox-tx resource adapter.

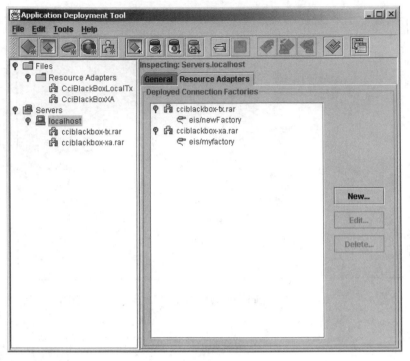

Figure 11.5 Viewing a Resource Adapter's Connection Factory

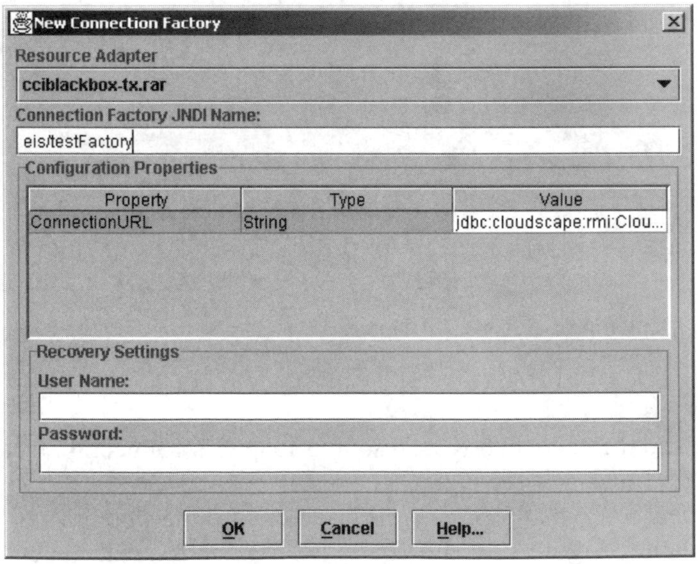

Figure 11.6 Creating a New Connection Factory

The tools also provide a means to undeploy a particular resource adapter from a specific server. When you *undeploy* an adapter, you remove its association with the specified server.

11.6 Conclusion

This chapter summarized the packaging and deploying of a resource adapter. It explained the elements that make up a resource adapter module and showed what a deployer must do to configure a resource adapter.

Most deployers use special deployment tools provided by their own application server to accomplish these packaging and deployment tasks. We used the J2EE SDK and its deployment tool to illustrate the typical functionality provided by these tools.

Chapter 12 discusses some of the features that are expected to be included in future releases of the Connector architecture.

Connection Management Contract

THIS is an advanced chapter that discusses the Connector architecture's connection management contract. The connection management contract supports connection pooling and management. This chapter provides an "under the hood" view of the contract. It examines the interfaces and classes that are specified in the Connector architecture specification.

Keep in mind that these system-level details are intended for application server and resource adapter providers. However, application developers may find it useful to understand what is happening behind the scenes, especially if they are interested in gaining insight into the subtleties of the connection management concepts and mechanisms.

12.1 Connection Management Contract

An application component uses a connection factory to access a connection instance, which the component then uses to connect to the underlying EIS. A resource adapter acts as a factory of connections.

Connection pooling manages connections that are expensive to create and destroy. Connection pooling of expensive connections leads to better scalability and performance in an operational environment.

The goal of the Connector architecture is to enable efficient, scalable, and extensible connection pooling mechanisms, not to specify a mechanism or implementation for connection pooling. The goal is accomplished by defining a standard architected contract for connection management with the providers of connections—that is, resource adapters. An application server uses the connection management contract to implement a connection pooling mechanism in its own implementation-specific way.

The connection management contract provides the following features:

- A consistent application programming model for connection acquisition for both managed and nonmanaged (two-tier) applications.

- A generic mechanism by which an application server can provide different quality of services (QoS)—transactions, security, advanced pooling, error tracing/logging—for its configured set of resource adapters.

- Support for connection pooling.

12.2 Contract Overview

The application server uses the deployment descriptor mechanism to configure the resource adapter in the operational environment.

The resource adapter provides connection and connection factory interfaces. A connection factory acts as a factory for EIS connections. For example, the javax.sql.DataSource and java.sql.Connection interfaces are JDBC-based interfaces for connectivity to a relational database. The CCI defines javax.resource.cci.ConnectionFactory and javax.resource.cci.Connection as interfaces for a connection factory and a connection, respectively.

The application component does a lookup of a connection factory in the JNDI namespace. It uses the connection factory to get a connection to the underlying EIS. The connection factory instance delegates the connection creation request to the ConnectionManager instance.

The ConnectionManager enables the application server to provide different quality of services in the managed application scenario. These quality of services include transaction management, security, error logging and tracing, and connection pool management. The application server provides these services in its own implementation-specific way. The Connector architecture does not specify how the application server implements these services.

The ConnectionManager instance, on receiving a connection creation request from the connection factory, does a lookup in the connection pool provided by the application server. If no connection in the pool can satisfy the connection request, the application server uses the ManagedConnectionFactory interface (implemented by the resource adapter) to create a new physical connection to the underlying EIS. If the application server finds a matching connection in the pool, it uses the matching ManagedConnection instance to satisfy the connection request.

If a new ManagedConnection instance is created, the application server adds the new ManagedConnection instance to the connection pool.

The application server registers a ConnectionEventListener with the ManagedConnection instance. This listener enables the application server to get event notifications related to the state of the ManagedConnection instance. The application server uses these notifications to manage connection pooling, manage transactions, clean up connections, and handle any error conditions.

The application server uses the ManagedConnection instance to get a connection instance that acts as an application-level handle to the underlying physical connection. An instance of type javax.resource.cci.Connection is an example of such a connection handle. An application component uses the connection handle to access EIS resources.

The resource adapter implements the XAResource interface to provide support for transaction management. The resource adapter also implements the LocalTransaction interface so that the application server can manage transactions internal to a resource manager. Chapter 13, "Transaction Management Contract," describes this transaction management contract between the application server (and its transaction manager) and the resource adapter (and its underlying resource manager).

Figure 12.1 depicts the connection management interfaces—ConnectionManager, ConnectionFactory, Connection, ManagedConnectionFactory, ManagedConnection, and ConnectionEventListener. In this diagram, the solid lines represent architected contracts, and the dotted lines represent implementation-specific interactions.

The definitions of these interfaces and classes are shown in "Connection Management Classes and Interfaces" later in this chapter.

12.3   Scenarios

The scenarios presented in this section in the form of sequence diagrams illustrate the scope of the connection management contract. They show how the resource adapter and application server work together to manage connection requests, either by creating new connections or matching existing connections to these requests. Each scenario illustrates the methods of the connection management interfaces. (For complete information on these connection management interfaces, you should refer to the *J2EE Connector Architecture Specification, v. 1.0.*)

In this section, the CCI interfaces—javax.resource.cci.ConnectionFactory and javax.resource.cci.Connection—represent connection factory and connection interfaces, respectively.

Figure 12.2, the object diagram for the connection management contract, clearly shows the flow of control between the various objects on the application server and resource adapter.

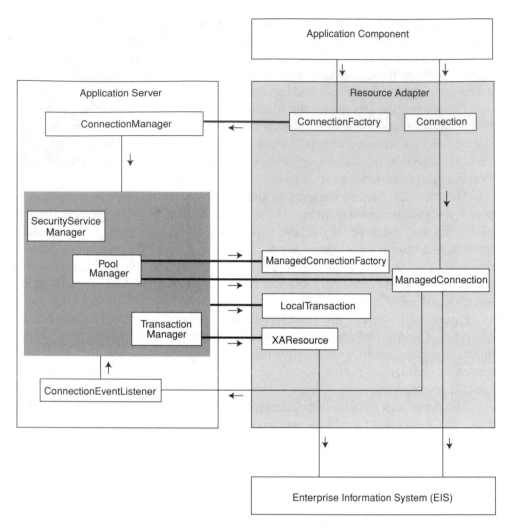

Figure 12.1 Architecture Diagram: Managed Application Scenario

12.3.1   Creating New Connections

Figure 12.3 shows the object interaction diagram for creating a new connection. This diagram provides detailed information about each step of the connection management contract.

The following object interactions happen in this scenario:

1. An application component calls the getConnection method on a Connection-Factory instance to obtain a connection to an EIS instance. This Connection-Factory instance is obtained from a JNDI lookup.

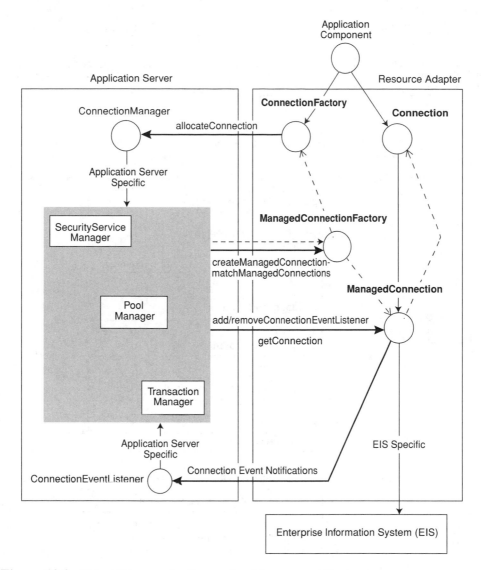

Figure 12.2 Object Diagram for Connection Management Contract

2. The ConnectionFactory instance, which at its instantiation was associated with a ConnectionManager instance provided by the application server, delegates the request to its associated ConnectionManager instance by calling the ConnectionManager's `allocateConnection` method. That is, the resource adapter essentially passes the connection request to the application server. The application server then manages the interaction between the ConnectionManager and the connection pool manager, and does so in an application server-specific manner.

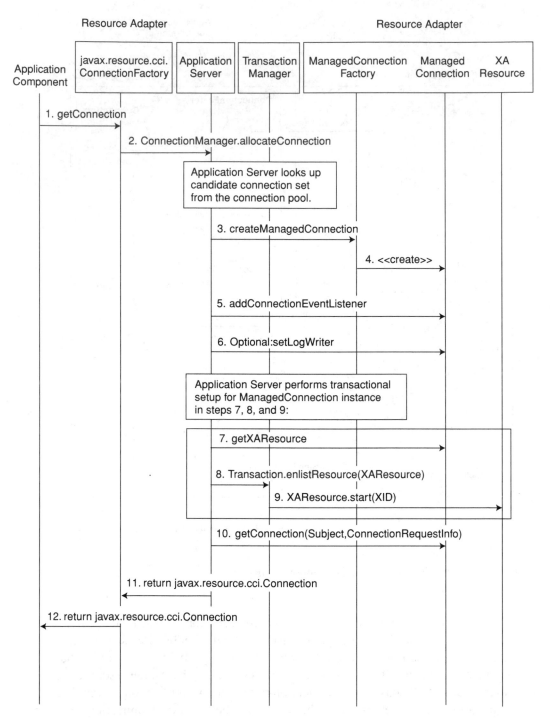

Figure 12.3 Creating a New Connection

3. The application server, using its own connection lookup criteria, checks the connection pool for ManagedConnection instances that can handle the current connection request. If the server finds a suitable ManagedConnection instance, it uses that ManagedConnection instance to create a connection handle. Then it merely returns the connection handle to the resource adapter. However, if the server finds no suitable match, it needs to create a new physical connection to the EIS, which it does by creating a new ManagedConnection instance. To do this, the server calls the ManagedConnectionFactory's `createManagedConnection` method. Note that both the ManagedConnection and ManagedConnectionFactory interfaces are implemented by a resource adapter.

4. The ManagedConnectionFactory instance creates a new physical connection, represented as a ManagedConnection instance, and returns this instance to the application server. The ManagedConnectionFactory instance creates a new physical connection to the underlying EIS to handle the createManagedConnection method. This new physical connection is represented by a ManagedConnection instance. The ManagedConnectionFactory uses the security information (passed as a Subject instance), ConnectionRequestInfo, and its default set of configured properties (port number, server name) to create a new ManagedConnection instance. (Refer to the security contract for more details on the createManagedConnection method.)

5. The application server calls the `addConnectionEventListener` method and registers a ConnectionEventListener with the new ManagedConnection instance so that the server can receive event notifications for this connection. These event notifications enable the application server to manage connection pooling. The application server also does the required transactional setup for the ManagedConnection. (See Chapter 4 for more information on transaction management.)

6. The application server may call the `setLogWriter` method to manage error logging and tracking.

   The application server performs a transactional setup for the ManagedConnection instance. (Steps 7 through 9 pertain to this transactional setup.)

7. The application server calls the `getXAResource` method on the ManagedConnection instance.

8. The application server enlists the transaction with the transaction manager, by calling the `Transaction.enlistResource` method.

9. The transaction manager starts the transaction by invoking the `XAResource.start` method on the XAResource instance.

10. The application server calls the ManagedConnection instance's `getConnection` method to obtain an application-level connection handle. It is this connection handle that the application server returns to the resource adapter.

11. The application server returns the connection handle to the resource adapter's ConnectionFactory instance.

12. The resource adapter returns the application-level connection handle (either the newly created one or the one that the server retrieved using the connection pool) to the application that initiated the connection request.

12.3.2   Matching Existing Connections

In many cases, the application server finds a set of ManagedConnection instances in its connection pool that it considers potential matches for the connection request from an application component. In this situation, the application server calls on the resource adapter to ascertain the correct matching connection for the connection request.

The application server uses the methods of the ManagedConnectionFactory to find a matching existing connection, or to create a new connection if a match cannot be found. An application server uses the ManagedConnectionFactory's `matchManagedConnection` method to enable the resource adapter to perform connection matching from a candidate set of connections. The application server finds what it believes to be a candidate set of connection instances from its connection pool, based on its application server-specific criteria, and it then passes this set of connections to the `matchManagedConnection` method. The `matchManagedConnection` method, in turn, tries to find a matching connection from this candidate set of connections—in terms of security and connection state requirements—using criteria internal to the resource adapter.

Figure 12.4 shows the object interaction diagram for the connection matching scenario. (Note that the initial steps are the same as in the previous scenario.) The object interactions are:

1. The application component calls the `getConnection` method to request a connection.

2. The ConnectionFactory delegates the connection request to the ConnectionManager instance by invoking the `allocationConnection` method.

3. Using its own internal implementation, the application server identifies the candidate set of ManagedConnection instances for this connection request from its connection pool. Then the application server calls the ManagedConnectionFactory method `matchManagedConnections` to pass the resource adapter the candidate connection set, security information, and any information related to the

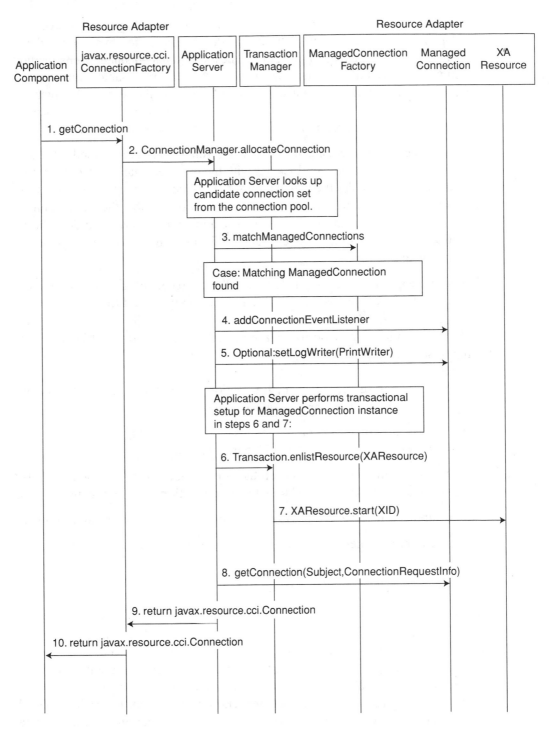

Figure 12.4 Matching ManagedConnections

connection request. This `matchManagedConnections` enables the resource adapter, using its own internal criteria, to do the connection matching in the ManagedConnectionFactory instance. The `matchManagedConnections` method returns a ManagedConnection instance that the resource adapter considers an acceptable match for the connection request. Because the resource adapter knows best about the internal specifics of the ManagedConnection instances, it helps the application server achieve optimal connection matching.

4. The application server calls the `addConnectionEventListener` method and registers a ConnectionEventListener with the matched ManagedConnection instance. This enables the application server to receive event notifications for connection-related events. These event notifications enable the application server to manage connection pooling. The application server also does the required transactional setup. (See Chapter 4 for more information on transaction management.)

5. The application server optionally may call the `setLogWriter` method on the ManagedConnection instance to manage error logging and tracing.

The application server performs a transactional setup for the ManagedConnection instance (steps 6 and 7).

6. The application server enlists the transaction with the transaction manager by calling the `Transaction.enlistResource` method.

7. The transaction manager starts the transaction by invoking the `XAResource.start` method on the XAResource instance.

8. The application server now can call the `getConnection` method on the ManagedConnection instance to obtain a new application-level connection handle.

9. The application server returns the connection handle to the resource adapter.

10. The resource adapter, in turn, passes the connection handle to the application.

12.3.3   Handling Connection Events

J2EE Connector architecture provides an event callback mechanism that enables an application server to receive event notifications from a ManagedConnection instance. An application server uses the connection event mechanism to manage connection pooling. It uses these event notifications to clean up any invalid or terminated connections, and also to manage local transactions.

An application server registers a ConnectionEventListener for each ManagedConnection instance in its connection pool. The ConnectionEventListener receives both close and error events (ConnectionEvents) for the connection.

A ConnectionEvent provides information about the source of a connection-related event. It contains such information as the type of the connection event, the ManagedConnection instance that generated the connection event, a connection handle associated with this ManagedConnection instance, and possibly an exception indicating the connection-related error.

To understand connection management, we discuss the steps that happen when an application component initiates a close of a connection. Figure 12.5 shows the object interaction diagram for handling connection event notifications.

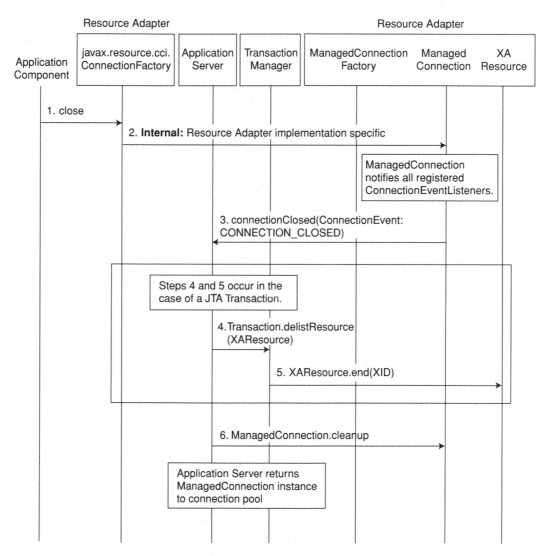

Figure 12.5 Connection Event Notification

The steps are as follows:

1. The application component releases an allocated connection handle using the `close` method on the Connection instance.

2. The Connection instance, in turn, delegates the method to its associated ManagedConnection instance in the resource adapter. Note that each resource adapter uses its own mechanism to establish this association.

3. The ManagedConnection instance starts the actual close operation. First, the ManagedConnection instance notifies all registered listeners of the close request by invoking the ConnectionEventListener method `connectionClosed` with the event type set to `CONNECTION_CLOSED`.

   The application server, when it receives notification of the close event, performs transaction management related cleanup of the ManagedConnection instance. (See Chapter 4 for transaction management information.)

   The application server performs a transactional setup for the ManagedConnection instance (steps 4 and 5).

4. The application server delists the transaction with the transaction manager, by calling the `Transaction.delistResource` method.

5. The transaction manager ends the transaction by invoking the `XAResource.end` method on the XAResource instance.

6. The application server calls the `cleanup` method on the ManagedConnection instance that raised the close event. This method prepares the instance to be reused for subsequent connection requests. When the `cleanup` method completes, the server puts the ManagedConnection instance in the pool of available connections.

12.3.4   Nonmanaged Environment

The connection management contract enables a resource adapter to be used in a two-tier application directly from an application client. For applications running in a two-tier nonmanaged environment, an application client can use a resource adapter to connect to an underlying EIS.

In a nonmanaged environment, either an application developer or the resource adapter provides the ConnectionManager implementation class. The ConnectionManager class provided by the resource adapter is the default. Other third-party vendors may provide additional quality of services components.

When an application requests a connection from the ConnectionFactory instance, the ConnectionManager instance interposes on the connection request and delegates it to the ManagedConnectionFactory instance. The ManagedConnectionFactory instance creates the physical connection to the EIS, and this connection is represented by a ManagedConnection instance. The ConnectionManager obtains an application-level handle to the physical connection represented by the ManagedConnection instance. The ConnectionManager returns the application-level handle to the ConnectionFactory, which, in turn, passes the handle to the application. To be consistent with the application programming model in the managed environment, an application should use the JNDI namespace to look up a ConnectionFactory instance.

Figure 12.6 illustrates the connection management contract in the nonmanaged environment. Here we show the object interactions for the creation of a connection in a nonmanaged environment. Figure 12.7 shows the object interaction diagram for this scenario.

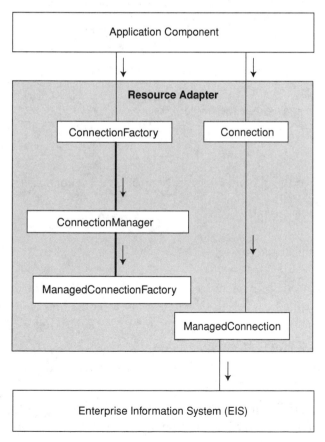

Figure 12.6 Nonmanaged Environment

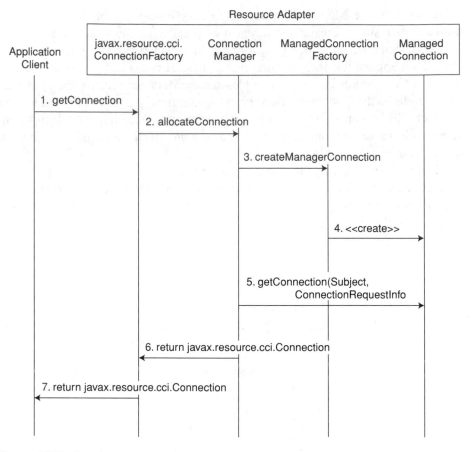

Figure 12.7 Creating a Connection in a Nonmanaged Environment

Here are the steps:

1. An application component looks up a ConnectionFactory instance from the JNDI namespace. It invokes the getConnection method on the Connection-Factory instance to request a connection to an underlying EIS.

2. The ConnectionFactory instance uses the allocateConnection method to pass the request to the default ConnectionManager instance provided by the resource adapter.

3. The ConnectionManager instance calls the createManagedConnection method on the ManagedConnectionFactory instance to create a new physical connection to the EIS.

4. The ManagedConnectionFactory instance creates a new ManagedConnection instance to represent the physical connection. It initializes the ManagedConnection instance state.

5. The ConnectionManager instance calls `getConnection` on the ManagedConnection instance to obtain an application-level connection handle. It is important to emphasize that `getConnection` does not create a new physical connection to the EIS; instead, it produces an application-level connection handle that an application uses to access the underlying physical connection represented by the ManagedConnection instance.

6. The ConnectionManager returns the application-level handle to the ConnectionFactory instance.

7. The ConnectionFactory instance returns the application-level handle to the application initiating the request.

12.4   Connection Management Classes and Interfaces

Now that we've presented the scenarios describing the connection management contract and examined the object interactions, let's focus on the specific classes and interfaces.

There are two principal packages of interest: `javax.resource.spi` and `javax.resource.cci`. The javax.resource.cci package defines the two connection interfaces, ConnectionFactory and Connection, to which an application component relates. The javax.resource.spi package defines the system contracts between the application server and the resource adapter.

12.4.1   ConnectionFactory and Connection Interfaces

Application components use two key connection interfaces: connection factory and connection. A connection factory provides an interface for establishing a connection to an EIS instance. A connection provides connectivity to an underlying EIS.

The Connector architecture supports a consistent application programming model across clients that use both the Common Client Interface (CCI) and an EIS-specific API. To achieve this consistent programming model, the Connector architecture specifies an interface template to be used as a design pattern for both the connection factory and the connection interfaces. The CCI interfaces (defined in the javax.resource.cci package) ConnectionFactory and javax.resource.cci.Connection are based on this design pattern.

A resource adapter provides implementations for both the ConnectionFactory and the Connection interfaces.

Code Example 12.1 shows the ConnectionFactory interface.

Code Example 12.1 ConnectionFactory Interface

```
package javax.resource.cci;
public interface ConnectionFactory
        extends java.io.Serializable, javax.resource.Referenceable {
    public Connection getConnection()
            throws ResourceException;
    public Connection getConnection(
        javax.resource.cci.ConnectionSpec properties)
            throws ResourceException;
    ...
}
```

The javax.resource.cci.ConnectionFactory interface defines multiple variants of the getConnection method. An application invokes this method when requesting a connection to an underlying EIS instance. Different resource adapters may add more getConnection methods if they require additional flexibility in connection requests beyond those offered by the default interface specification.

Code Example 12.2 shows the definition of the Connection interface.

Code Example 12.2 Connection Interface

```
package javax.resource.cci;
public interface Connection {
    public void close() throws ResourceException;
    ...
}
```

The javax.resource.cci.Connection interface defines a close method. An application invokes the close method to indicate that it no longer requires the connection to the EIS. This allows the resource adapter or application server to release the connection and free system resources, if necessary.

12.4.2 Connection Management Contract

The interfaces most relevant for resource adapters and application servers are contained in the javax.resource.spi package. See Appendix A.

The javax.resource.spi.ConnectionManager provides a hook for a resource adapter to pass a connection request to an application server. An application server provides different quality of services as part of its handling of the connection request. (See Figure 12.8.)

The ConnectionManager interface defines the allocateConnection method. A resource adapter's connection factory instance invokes the allocateConnection method so that it can delegate a connection request to the ConnectionManager instance.

It is the application server that provides the implementation of the ConnectionManager interface. This is a generic implementation that is not tied to a specific resource adapter or connection factory interface. Through this ConnectionManager interface, the server provides its additional services, including security, connection pool management, transaction management, and error logging. After the application server has used its "hooked-in" services, it delegates the connection request to a ManagedConnectionFactory instance implemented by a resource adapter.

Code Example 12.3 shows the ConnectionManager interface.

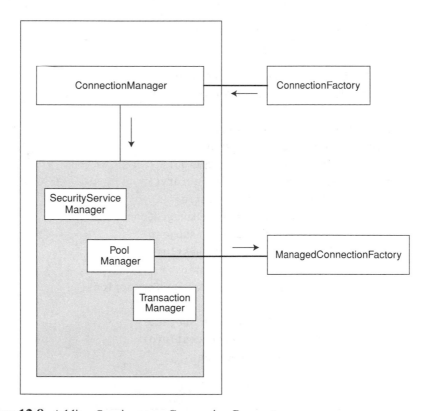

Figure 12.8 Adding Services to a Connection Request

Code Example 12.3 ConnectionManager Interface

```
package javax.resource.spi;
public interface ConnectionManager extends java.io.Serializable {
    public Object allocateConnection(
        ManagedConnectionFactory mcf,
        ConnectionRequestInfo cxRequestInfo)
            throws ResourceException;
    }
    ...
}
```

The ManagedConnectionFactory interface is a factory of both ManagedConnection instances and connection factory instances. It defines a number of methods of interest, as shown in Code Example 12.4.

Code Example 12.4 ManagedConnectionFactory Interface

```
package javax.resource.spi;
public interface ManagedConnectionFactory
        extends java.io.Serializable {

    public Object createConnectionFactory(
        ConnectionManager connectionManager)
            throws ResourceException;
    public Object createConnectionFactory()
            throws ResourceException;
    public ManagedConnection createManagedConnection(
        javax.security.auth.Subject subject,
        ConnectionRequestInfo cxRequestInfo)
            throws ResourceException;
    public ManagedConnection matchManagedConnections(
        java.util.Set connectionSet,
        javax.security.auth.Subject subject,
        ConnectionRequestInfo cxRequestInfo)
            throws ResourceException;
    ...
}
```

The createConnectionFactory method creates a connection factory instance that can be used in either managed or nonmanaged scenarios. The createManagedConnection method creates a new physical connection (represented by a ManagedConnection instance) to an underlying EIS instance. The matchManagedConnections method enables the application server to use a resource adapter-specific criterion for matching a ManagedConnection instance in order to service a connection request. The application server finds a candidate set of ManagedConnection instances from its connection pool based on application server-specific criteria and passes this candidate set to the matchManagedConnections method.

An instance of the ManagedConnection interface represents a physical connection to the underlying EIS. Code Example 12.5 shows the methods of this interface that pertain to the connection management contract.

Code Example 12.5 ManagedConnection Interface

```
package javax.resource.spi;
public interface ManagedConnection {
    public Object getConnection(
            javax.security.auth.Subject subject,
            ConnectionRequestInfo cxRequestInfo)
                throws ResourceException;
    public void destroy() throws ResourceException;
    public void cleanup() throws ResourceException;
    // Methods for Connection and transaction event notifications
    public void addConnectionEventListener(
            ConnectionEventListener listener);
    public void removeConnectionEventListener(
            ConnectionEventListener listener);
    public ManagedConnectionMetaData getMetaData()
            throws ResourceException;
    ...
}
```

Creating a ManagedConnection instance for a physical connection results in the allocation of EIS and resource adapter resources, such as memory and network socket resources. Because these resources are often costly and scarce, in a managed environment the application server typically pools ManagedConnection instances to conserve resources.

Keep in mind that the Connector architecture does not specify how the application server should implement connection pooling, although it does recommend that the server should structure its connection pooling to be efficient with resources.

The ManagedConnection interface method `getConnection` creates a new application-level connection handle, which is tied to the physical connection represented by the ManagedConnection instance.

The ManagedConnection interface also includes the `addConnection-EventListener` method, which allows a connection event listener to register its interest with a ManagedConnection instance. Its `removeConnectionEventListener` method removes a previously registered connection event listener (represented by a ConnectionEventListener instance) from a ManagedConnection instance. Last, the interface's `getMetaData` method obtains metadata information for a ManagedConnection instance and its connected EIS instance. It returns this data as a ManagedConnectionMetaData instance.

The ManagedConnectionMetaData interface provides identifying information about a ManagedConnection and the connected EIS instance if a valid physical connection exists to the EIS instance.

The application server implements the javax.resource.spi.ConnectionEventListener interface. It uses the `ManagedConnection.addConnectionEventListener` method to register a connection listener with a ManagedConnection instance.

```
package javax.resource.spi;
public interface ConnectionEventListener {
    public void connectionClosed(ConnectionEvent event);
    public void connectionErrorOccurred(ConnectionEvent event);

    // Local Transaction Management related events
    public void localTransactionStarted(ConnectionEvent event);
    public void localTransactionCommitted(ConnectionEvent event);
    public void localTransactionRolledback(ConnectionEvent event);
}
```

A javax.resource.spi.ConnectionEvent class provides information about the source of a connection-related event. A ConnectionEvent instance contains the following information:

- Type of connection event

- ManagedConnection instance that has generated the connection event. A ManagedConnection instance is returned from the `ConnectionEvent.getSource` method.

- Connection handle associated with the ManagedConnection instance

- Optionally, an exception indicating a connection-related error

12.4.3 Support for Error Handling

The connection management contract provides support for error logging and tracing for both the managed and nonmanaged environments. This enables the application server to detect resource adapter errors and to use error information for debugging purposes.

The ManagedConnectionFactory interface defines two methods for error logging. The `setLogWriter` method registers a character output stream, or log writer, with a ManagedConnectionFactory instance. All error logging and tracing messages for the instance are output to this log writer. The `getLogWriter` method returns the current log writer for the ManagedConnectionFactory instance.

The application server manages the association of a log writer with a ManagedConnectionFactory instance. When the ManagedConnectionFactory instance is first created, no log writer is associated with the instance and logging is disabled. Invoking `setLogWriter` on the instance enables error logging and tracing for the instance. Note that the error information is at the system level, and it is used primarily by the application server administrator. Most application developers would not be directly interested in this error information.

12.5 Conclusion

At this point, you have seen the classes and interfaces that play key roles in the connection management contract. This chapter also described scenarios and object interactions related to the connection management contract.

A J2EE application server uses the connection management contract to support connection pooling and to hook in its quality of services. Connection pooling leads to better scalability and performance in a managed multi-tier environment.

Chapter 13 describes the transaction management contract.

Transaction Management Contract

THIS chapter describes the transaction management contract supported by the J2EE Connector architecture. The transaction management contract is defined between an application server and an EIS resource adapter. This chapter focuses on the system-level aspects of transaction management.

A resource manager can support two types of transactions:

- A transaction that is controlled and coordinated by a transaction manager external to the resource manager. The Connector architecture refers to such a transaction as a JTA, XA, or global transaction.

- A transaction that is managed internal to a resource manager. The coordination of such transactions involves no external transaction managers. The Connector architecture refers to such a transaction as a local transaction.

The transaction management contract extends the connection management contract to provide support for the management of both local and XA transactions.

An application component deployed on an application server uses the transactional services provided by that application server, and, in doing so, the component performs transactional access to one or more resource managers. The application server manages these transactions using the services of its transaction manager. A transaction manager coordinates transactions across multiple resource managers. It also provides additional low-level services that enable the transactional context to be propagated across systems. The services provided by a transaction manager are not visible directly to an application component.

Both local and global transactions can be demarcated by either the container or by the application component. When performed by the container, transaction demarcation is referred to as *container-managed transaction demarcation*. When performed by the application component, it is called *component-managed transaction demarcation.* (Refer to Chapter 5, Managing Security which describes transaction management from the application programming model perspective.)

13.1   Transaction Management Contract

Figure 13.1 depicts the three key interfaces of the transaction management contract:

- javax.resource.spi.ManagedConnection
- javax.transaction.xa.XAResource
- javax.resource.spi.LocalTransaction.

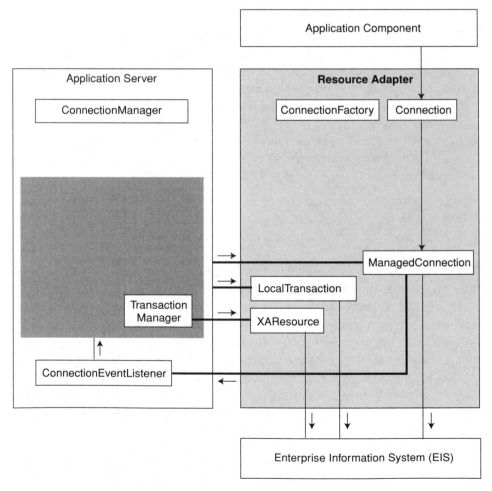

Figure 13.1   Transaction Management Contract

The diagram shows only the interfaces and flows that are relevant to transaction management. It does not depict the flows that pertain to connection management. In the diagram, the bold lines represent the architected contracts in the Connector architecture.

A ManagedConnection represents a physical connection to the underlying EIS. The ManagedConnection interface defines two methods that pertain to the transaction management contract. These two methods, `getXAResource` and `getLocalTransaction`, provide an application server with access to the two transaction management interfaces:

- javax.transaction.xa.XAResource

- javax.resource.spi.LocalTransaction

See Code Example 13.1.

Code Example 13.1 ManagedConnection Interface

```
package javax.resource.spi;
public interface ManagedConnection {
    public XAResource getXAResource() throws ResourceException;
    public LocalTransaction getLocalTransaction()
            throws ResourceException;
    ...
}
```

Depending on the transaction support level of a resource adapter, these methods throw appropriate exceptions. For example, if the transaction support level for a resource adapter is NoTransaction, invoking the `getXAResource` method throws a ResourceException.

The application server invokes the `getLocalTransaction` method on a ManagedConnection instance to create a new LocalTransaction instance. Similarly, the application server invokes the `getXAResource` method on a ManagedConnection instance to create a new XAResource instance. The application server's transaction manager uses the XAResource instance to associate and disassociate a transaction with the underlying EIS resource manager instance, and also to perform a two-phase commit. Notice that the transaction manager itself does not directly use a ManagedConnection instance.

Figure 13.2 depicts the object diagram for transaction management. The bold arrows in the diagram represent the architected contracts, and the dotted line arrows represent object instantiations.

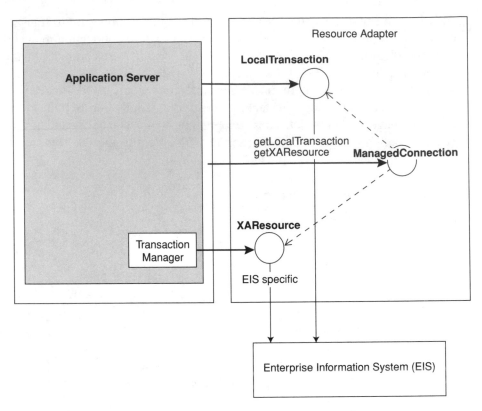

Figure 13.2 Object Diagram for the Transaction Management Contract

The application server invokes two methods on the ManagedConnection instance in the resource adapter: getLocalTransaction and getXAResource. This is an architected interface. The ManagedConnection instance performs two transaction-specific operations. It creates a new LocalTransaction instance and a new XAResource instance.

Although not shown on the diagram, the interfaces between the EIS and ManagedConnection, XAResource, and LocalTransaction are specific to the underlying EIS. For example, a resource adapter implementation can use a low-level EIS-specific API to interface with the underlying EIS.

13.2   Local Transaction Management

Transactions managed internal to a resource manager are local transactions. If a single resource manager instance participates in a transaction, regardless of whether that transaction is component managed or container managed, the application server has two choices for managing the transaction:

- The application server can use the transaction manager to manage this transaction. The transaction manager uses a one-phase commit optimization to coordinate the transaction for this single resource manager instance.

- The application server can let the resource manager coordinate this transaction internally without involving an external transaction manager.

Keep in mind that, had the application component used the XA interface to manage transactions on the resource manager, there would have been additional performance overhead. This performance overhead occurs even when accessing a single resource manager because the XA interface involves the external transaction manager.

To avoid the overhead of using an XA transaction in a single resource manager scenario, the application server can optimize this scenario by using a local transaction instead of an XA transaction.

Figure 13.3 shows a local transaction managed internal to an EIS instance.

13.2.1   Example Local Transaction

Code Example 13.2 shows the code for the business method `getQuantityAvailable` in the InventoryManagerEJB. The method uses a local transaction, and container-managed transaction demarcation to interact with the inventory management application. The underlying EJB container takes responsibility for managing the local transaction using the transaction management contract. When the transaction completes, the mainframe system's transactional resource manager ensures that all read and write access to the inventory management application is either entirely committed or rolled back.

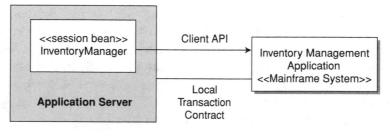

Figure 13.3 Local Transaction Management

Code Example 13.2 Local Transaction on a Single EIS Resource Manager

```
public class InventoryManagerEJB implements SessionBean {
    private javax.resource.cci.ConnectionFactory cf;
    // ...

    public int getQuantityAvailable(String productId)
            throws InventoryException {
        try {
            Connection cx = getConnection();
            // Operations on the underlying EIS resource manager
            // ...
            cx.close();
            return command.getProductQuantity();
        }
        catch (Exception e) {
            throw new InventoryException();
        }
    }
    // ...
}
```

13.2.2   Local Transaction Management Contract Interfaces

The local transaction management contract has two parts: a LocalTransaction interface and event notification. The application server manages local transactions using the javax.resource.spi.LocalTransaction interface, which makes the application server's management of transactions transparent to an application component.

The local transaction management contract also specifies the local transaction-related event notifications. A resource adapter notifies the application server of events related to the local transaction's begin, commit, and rollback methods.

The javax.resource.spi.LocalTransaction interface defines the contract between an application server and resource adapter for local transaction management. A resource adapter implements the LocalTransaction interface so that it can provide support for local transactions performed on the underlying EIS resource manager. The LocalTransaction interface defines three methods: begin, commit, and rollback. An application server uses the methods of the LocalTransaction interface to manage local transactions for a resource manager.

Code Example 13.3 shows the definition of the LocalTransaction interface.

Code Example 13.3 LocalTransaction Interface

```
package javax.resource.spi;
public interface LocalTransaction {
    public void begin() throws ResourceException;
    public void commit() throws ResourceException;
    public void rollback() throws ResourceException;
}
```

An application server invokes the LocalTransaction `begin` method to explicitly start a local transaction. When the work of the transaction completes, the application server commits the transactional changes made to the EIS by calling the `commit` method. Or, the application server can undo whatever changes were made by calling the `rollback` method. The `rollback` method rolls back the EIS to the state it was in prior to the start of the transaction. Both the `commit` and `rollback` methods end the current transaction.

An application server implements the javax.resource.spi.ConnectionEventListener interface so that it can register itself as a listener with the appropriate Managed-Connection instance. An application server registers a ConnectionEventListener instance to a ManagedConnection instance by invoking the ManagedConnection instance's `addConnectionEventListener` method. Code Example 13.4 shows the local transaction-related methods of the ConnectionEventListener interface.

Code Example 13.4 ConnectionEventListener Interface

```
package javax.resource.spi;
public interface ConnectionEventListener {
    // Local Transaction Management related events
    public void localTransactionStarted(ConnectionEvent event);
    public void localTransactionCommitted(ConnectionEvent event);
    public void localTransactionRolledback(ConnectionEvent event);
    ...
}
```

The ConnectionEventListener interface specifies three methods that pertain to local transaction management: `localTransactionStarted`, `localTransactionCommitted`, and `localTransactionRolledback`. When a local transaction starts, a ManagedConnection instance calls the `localTransactionStarted` method to notify its registered listeners that the transaction has started. Similarly, a ManagedConnection instance calls the `localTransactionCommitted` method to notify its listeners that the transaction has committed, and it calls `localTransactionRolledback` to notify its registered listeners that the transaction has been rolled back.

13.3   XAResource Transaction Management

The XAResource transaction management contract is based on the X/Open transaction model. The javax.transaction.xa.XAResource interface is a Java mapping of the industry standard XA interface based on the X/Open CAE specification. In the J2EE environment, the Java Transaction API (JTA) represents the Java mapping of the XA specification.

The application server uses a transaction manager to support a transaction management infrastructure that enables an application component to perform transactional access across multiple EIS resource managers. The transaction manager manages transactions across multiple resource managers and supports the propagation of the transaction context across distributed systems.

The transaction manager supports a JTA XAResource-based transaction management contract with a resource adapter and its underlying resource manager. An EIS supports JTA transactions by implementing the XAResource interface through its resource adapter. The transaction manager uses the XAResource interface to manage transactions across the multiple underlying resource managers.

The XAResource transaction management contract supports a two-phase commit protocol that ensures that a transaction across multiple resource managers either entirely commits or entirely rolls back. If even one resource manager is not prepared for commit, the transaction manager rolls back the transaction across all participating resource managers.

For example, an application might perform transactional work that makes updates to a mainframe transaction processing (TP) system and to an ERP system. The application client invokes one EJB component, X, which invokes the transaction programs on the TP system. EJB component X calls EJB component Y, which accesses the ERP system. Figure 13.4 illustrates this scenario.

In this scenario, the application server uses the services of a transaction manager. The transaction manager supports a transaction management infrastructure that enables the application component to perform transactional access across the two EIS resource managers, the TP system and the ERP system.

What is happening between the transaction manager and the ERP and TP systems? The transaction manager and resource adapters support a transaction management contract that is based on the JTA XAResource interface. To participate in a JTA (or global) transaction managed and coordinated by this transaction manager, the EIS supports the XAResource interface. In our example, the ERP system sup-

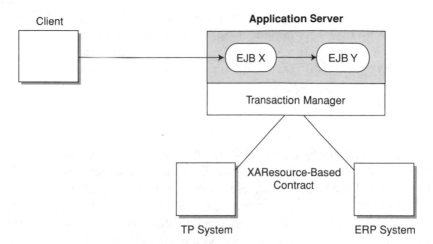

Figure 13.4 Transactions Across Multiple Resource Managers

ports JTA transactions by implementing the XAResource interface in its resource adapter. Likewise, the resource adapter for the TP system implements the XAResource interface. The transaction manager can then use the methods of the XAResource interface to manage transactions across both underlying resource managers.

The EJB components in Figure 13.4 access the ERP and TP systems using their respective client-access API. Behind the scenes, the application server enlists the connections to the two systems obtained from their respective resource adapters as part of the JTA transaction. When the transaction completes, the transaction manager performs a two-phase commit across both resource managers. As previously noted, this ensures that all read and write access to both the ERP and TP system resources is either entirely committed or entirely rolled back.

13.3.1 XAResource Interface

The XAResource interface is a Java JTA mapping of the standard XA interface. The XA interface is based on the X/Open CAE specification. It defines methods pertaining to managing a two-phase commit XA transaction. See Code Example 13.5.

Code Example 13.5 XAResource Interface

```
package javax.transaction.xa;
public interface XAResource {
    public void commit(Xid xid, boolean onePhase) throws XAException;
    public void end(Xid xid, int flags) throws XAException;
    public void forget(Xid xid) throws XAException;
```

```
        public int prepare(Xid xid) throws XAException;
        public Xid[] recover(int flag) throws XAException;
        public void rollback(Xid xid) throws XAException;
        public void start(Xid xid, int flags) throws XAException;

    }
```

A resource adapter for an EIS resource manager implements the XAResource interface. By implementing this interface, the resource adapter gains the ability to participate in JTA transactions that are controlled by an external transaction manager. The external transaction manager uses the XAResource interface to communicate transaction-related information through the resource adapter to the EIS resource manager. For example, the transaction manager uses the XAResource interface to communicate such information as transaction association, completion, and recovery to the resource manager.

A resource adapter typically implements the XAResource interface using a low-level library available for the underlying EIS resource manager. This library either supports a native implementation of the XA interface or provides a proprietary vendor-specific interface for transaction management.

In addition, a resource adapter is responsible for maintaining a one-to-one relationship between the ManagedConnection and XAResource instances. This means that, for each time a ManagedConnection.getXAResource method is called, the resource adapter must return the same XAResource instance.

A transaction manager can use any XAResource instance, assuming that the XAResource instance refers to the proper resource manager instance, to initiate transaction completion. The XAResource instance used during the transaction completion process need not be the one initially enlisted with the transaction manager for this transaction.

A resource adapter supports a one-phase commit optimization protocol by implementing the XAResource commit method when the boolean flag onePhase is set to true.

13.3.2 Java Transaction API (JTA)

The Java Transaction API (JTA) is a specification of standard interfaces between a transaction manager and the other parties that are involved in a distributed transaction processing system. These other parties include application programs, resource managers, and an application server. One of the real benefits of standard JTA interfaces is that JTA allows applications to access the application server's transaction management services in a way that is independent of any specific implementation.

A JTA transaction is a transaction managed and coordinated by the J2EE platform, and such a transaction can span multiple components and EISs. If a component is managing its own transaction demarcation, the component begins a JTA transaction using the javax.transaction.UserTransaction interface.

A principal benefit of a JTA transaction is that it enables combining multiple components and EIS accesses into a single transaction with little programming effort. To illustrate, suppose component A begins a JTA transaction and then invokes a method on component B. Because this is a JTA transaction, the platform will transparently propagate the transaction context from component A to component B. Likewise, if component B updates a table in a relational database, the update is automatically under the same transaction scope without the need to do extra programming. Last, applications using enterprise beans with container-managed transaction demarcation do not need to programmatically begin or commit transactions; the EJB container automatically handles this.

The Java Transaction Service (JTS) API is a Java binding of the CORBA Object Transaction Service (OTS) 1.1 specification. JTS specifies the implementation of a transaction manager that supports JTA and propagates transactions between distributed servers. A JTS transaction manager provides the services and management functions to support transaction demarcation, manage transactional resources, synchronize transactions, and propagate transaction context. A vendor uses the JTS API to implement a transaction processing infrastructure for enterprise middleware. An application server vendor can use this JTS implementation as the underlying transaction manager.

The JTA TransactionManager interface enables the application server to control the transaction boundaries for its application components. For example, an EJB container uses the TransactionManager interface and the calling thread's transaction context to demarcate transaction boundaries when it manages the transactional state for its EJB components.

The JTA Transaction interface enables the application server to enlist and delist transactional connections with the transaction manager. This is important because the transaction manager must be able to coordinate the transactional work performed by all enlisted resource managers within a transaction.

13.3.3 Two-Phase Commit Protocol

In this section, we describe the steps taken by the transaction manager to commit a transaction across multiple resource manager instances. These steps are executed after the transaction manager calls the XAResource.end method for each enlisted resource manager instance. (See Figure 13.5.)

1. The transaction manager invokes the prepare method on the XAResource instances associated with each resource manager participating in a JTA or global transaction. The prepare method notifies each resource manager instance to prepare for the transaction commit. A resource manager can veto the transaction commit operation.

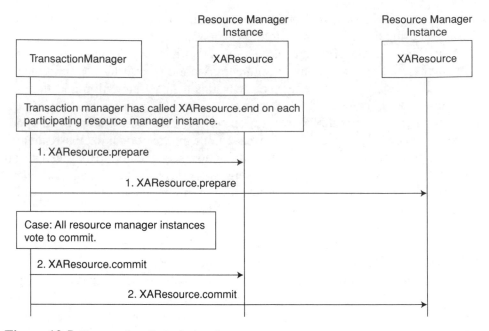

Figure 13.5 Transaction Completion Steps

2. If all resource managers participating in the transaction agree to commit, the transaction manager invokes the `commit` method on each XAResource instance to commit the transaction. If even one resource manager does not vote for the commit, the transaction manager rolls back the transaction by calling the `rollback` method on all participating XAResource instances.

13.4   Requirements for Transaction Management Contract

A resource adapter can be classified based on its level of transaction support, as follows:

- **Level NoTransaction**—The resource adapter supports neither resource manager local nor JTA transactions. It does not implement the XAResource or LocalTransaction interfaces.

- **Level LocalTransaction**—The resource adapter supports resource manager local transactions by implementing the LocalTransaction interface.

- **Level XATransaction**—The resource adapter supports both resource manager local and JTA transactions by implementing the LocalTransaction and XAResource interfaces, respectively.

Depending on its transactional capabilities and the requirements of its underlying EIS, a resource adapter can choose to support any of the preceding transaction levels.

Note that a resource adapter is not required to support the JTA XAResource-based transaction contract. If it does support this contract, the resource adapter must adhere to certain implementation requirements specified by the Connector architecture. Although these requirements apply to the resource adapter and the resource manager together, they may be split between them in any way that the resource manager and adapter deem appropriate. (Refer to the J2EE Connector architecture specification for more details on these requirements.

An application server is required to support resource adapters with all three levels of transaction support—NoTransaction, LocalTransaction, and XATransaction.

In addition, a J2EE-compliant application server provides support for several transaction scenarios. In brief, a J2EE application server supports

- **Transactions that span multiple components and transactional resources**—This includes such resources as JDBC connections, JMS sessions, and resource adapter connections at the XATransaction level.

- **Transactions that comprise servlets or JSPs that access multiple enterprise beans**—Each such component (servlet, JSP, or enterprise bean) may acquire one or more connections to access transactional resources.

- **Transactions that involve resource adapters at the XATransaction level**—This means that multiple application components can access each such resource adapter from within a single transaction.

- **Transactions in which access to a nontransactional resource is combined with access to one or more transactional resources within a single transaction**—For example, in a container-managed transaction, an enterprise bean accesses JDBC and JMS resources and also accesses a nontransactional EIS using the EIS's resource adapter.

The application server supports only these scenarios and no additional transaction scenarios. Although it is possible that a particular J2EE application server might optionally support another scenario, a J2EE application should not rely on this support.

13.5   Connection Sharing

Connection sharing, which refers to sharing connections within the same transaction scope, typically results in a more efficient use of resources and better performance. A container may attempt to share connections within the same transaction scope when multiple connections acquired by a J2EE application use the same re-source manager.

Connections to resource managers that are acquired by J2EE applications are considered potentially shared or shareable. A J2EE application component that intends to use a connection in an unshareable way needs to leave a deployment hint to that effect to prevent the container from sharing the connection. Otherwise, the container assumes a connection to be shareable if no deployment hint is provided. Examples of an application's unshareable usage of a connection include changing the connection's security attributes, isolation levels, character settings, or localization configuration. J2EE application components may use the optional deployment descriptor element `res-sharing-scope` to indicate whether a connection to a resource manager is shareable or unshareable. (Refer to the EJB specification for a description of this deployment descriptor element.)

Containers do not share connections that are marked unshareable. If a connection is marked shareable, it is transparent to the application whether the connection is actually shared or not, provided that the application is properly using the connection in a shareable manner.

Connection sharing may be useful with local transactions. We present a scenario that illustrates using the connection sharing mechanism to enable a local transaction to span multiple components.

In Figure 13.6, the stateful session beans A and B use container-managed transaction demarcation with the transaction attribute set to Required. Both EJBs A and B access a single EIS resource manager as part of their business logic. Both EJBs use the same local transaction-capable resource adapter.

A local transaction is associated with a single physical connection. Both EJB components in this scenario share the same physical connection under the local transaction scope.

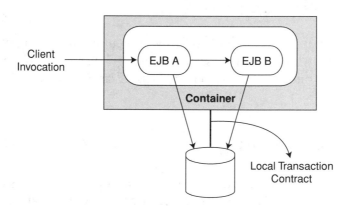

Figure 13.6 Connection Sharing

In this scenario, the container takes responsibility for managing connection sharing. To share a physical connection in the local transaction scope, the container assumes the connection to be shareable unless it has been marked `unshareable` in the deployment descriptor element `res-sharing-scope`. The container uses connection sharing in a manner that is transparent to the application components.

13.6   Transaction Scenarios

To illustrate the transaction management contract, we describe two typical transaction scenarios and illustrate these scenarios with object interaction diagrams. The first scenario covers transaction setup, and the second scenario focuses on transaction cleanup.

13.6.1   Transaction Setup

The first scenario illustrates how transactions are set up for a ManagedConnection. The scenario begins with the client invoking a method on an enterprise bean. The method is invoked as part of a transaction, because either the client was already participating in a transaction or the EJB container started a transaction before the invocation of the bean method. (See Figure 13.7.)

Notice that the enterprise bean instance calls the `getConnection` method on the ConnectionFactory instance. The connection management contract specifies how the resource adapter delegates the connection request to the application server. This is step 2 in the diagram. (See Chapter 3, Managing Connections, for more information on delegating connection requests.)

The following steps take place in this scenario:

1. The application component calls the `getConnection` method on the ConnectionFactory instance.

2. The resource adapter delegates the connection request to the application server using the ConnectionManager `allocationConnection` method.

3. At this point, the application server controls the connection request. The server either obtains an existing ManagedConnection instance from the connection pool or it creates a new ManagedConnection instance. The server then registers itself as a ConnectionEventListener with the ManagedConnection instance so that it can receive connection and transaction-related event notifications.

4. The application server may decide that the transaction manager should manage the current transaction as a JTA transaction. If so, steps 4 through 6 occur (shown in the gray area in Figure 13.7). In step 4, the server proceeds to perform transactional setup on the ManagedConnection instance. It begins by

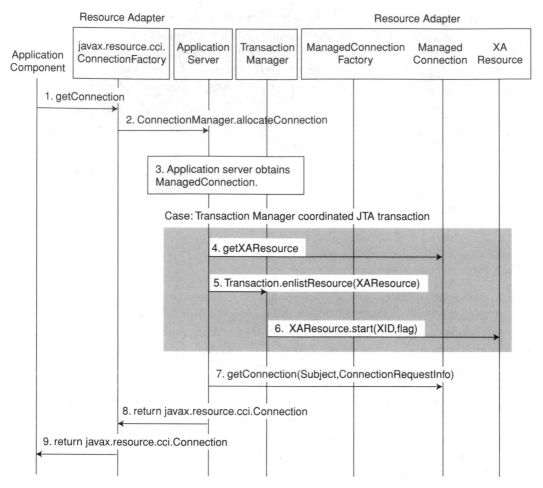

Figure 13.7 Transaction Setup for ManagedConnection Instances

invoking the ManagedConnection getXAResource method to obtain the XAResource instance associated with the ManagedConnection instance.

5. The application server uses the Transaction.enlistResource method to enlist the XAResource instance with the transaction manager for the current transaction context. (The enlistResource method is a JTA method.)

6. The transaction manager invokes the XAResource start method to associate the current transaction with the underlying resource manager instance. This enables the transaction manager to inform the participating resource manager that all units of work performed by the application on the underlying ManagedConnection instance should now be associated with this transaction.

7. The application server calls the `getConnection` method on the ManagedConnection to obtain a new application-level connection handle. The underlying physical connection is represented by a ManagedConnection instance.

8. The application server returns the connection handle to the resource adapter.

9. The resource adapter passes the connection handle to the application component that initiated the connection request.

13.6.2   Transaction Cleanup

Transactional cleanup occurs when an application component initiates a request to close a connection. Figure 13.8 illustrates the object interactions that occur during a connection close initiated by an application and the subsequent transaction cleanup.

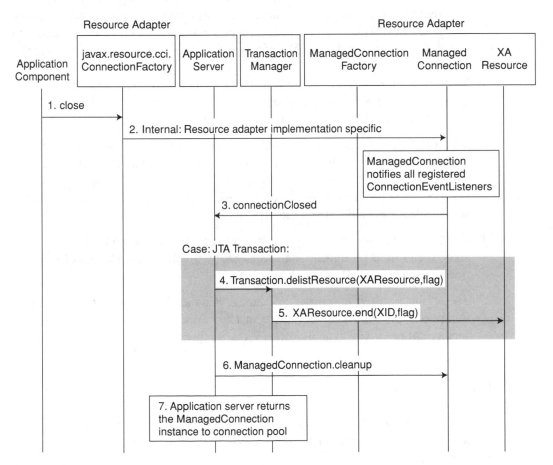

Figure 13.8   Transaction Cleanup

The following steps take place in this scenario.

1. The application component starts the process by calling the `close` method on the Connection instance to release an application-level connection handle.

2. The Connection instance, using a resource adapter-specific implementation, delegates the connection close operation to its associated ManagedConnection instance.

3. The ManagedConnection instance notifies all its registered listeners that it has received a connection close request from the application component. It does this by using the ConnectionEventListener interface's `connectionClosed` method and passing a ConnectionEvent instance with event type set to `CONNECTION_CLOSED`.

Steps 4 and 5 occur if the ManagedConnection is participating in a transaction manager-enlisted JTA transaction. These two steps perform the necessary transaction disassociation. When the application server receives the connection close notification, it performs transactional cleanup for the ManagedConnection instance.

4. The application server uses the `Transaction.delistResource` method to first disassociate the XAResource instance that corresponds to the ManagedConnection instance from the transaction manager.

5. The transaction manager then invokes the `XAResource.end` method to inform the resource manager that further operations on the ManagedConnection instance are no longer associated with the transaction. Note that the transaction is represented by the `Xid` parameter passed to the method. This method disassociates the transaction from the underlying resource manager instance.

6. The application server initiates the cleanup of the physical connection instance after the JTA transaction completes by invoking the ManagedConnection `cleanup` method.

7. The application server returns the ManagedConnection instance to the connection pool. This ManagedConnection instance is now available to the server to service future connection allocation requests from any application component.

13.7   Conclusion

This chapter showed how the transaction management contract extends the connection management contract to add support for local and global JTA (or XA) transactions.

An external transaction manager manages an XA transaction that spans multiple resource managers. The transaction management contract supports JTA transactions using the XAResource interface, which is part of JTA and is based on the X/Open XA specification. The XAResource interface supports the two-phase commit protocol.

A local transaction can only span a single resource manager, which manages such local transactions internally. The transaction management contract supports local transactions using the LocalTransaction interface.

The Connector architecture allows a resource adapter to be at different transaction levels so that an adapter can be developed for EISs that have different transactional capabilities. That is, a resource adapter may be nontransactional, or it may support only local transactions. The highest level of transaction support is when a resource adapter supports both local and XA transactions. The J2EE application server is required to support resource adapters at all transaction levels.

CHAPTER 14

Security Management
Contract

THE Connector architecture provides a security management contract to support secure integration with EISs. The security management contract extends the J2EE security model to include support for secure connectivity to EISs.

The security management contract is defined to be independent of any particular security technology or mechanism. It allows the use of different security mechanisms to protect an EIS against security threats such as unauthorized access and loss or inaccuracy of information. The contract supports *authentication* of users, ensuring that they are who they say they are. It also enforces *authorization* and access control privileges for authenticated users.

The security contract also provides support for security mechanisms that, in turn, support secure communication links between an application server and an EIS. It accomplishes this by supporting protocols that provide authentication, integrity, and confidentiality services. The contract also supports secure communication protocols such as secure socket layer (SSL).

This chapter focuses on the interfaces and classes supported by the security management contract. These interfaces and classes enable the EIS or J2EE application server to use different security mechanisms and technologies for EIS sign-on. Refer to Chapter 5, Managing Security, for more information on security concepts and EIS sign-on.

14.1   Interfaces and Classes

The security contract extends the connection management contract to support EIS sign-on. The security contract uses the following interfaces and classes:

- **javax.security.auth.Subject class**—Represents an end user or component requesting a connection and on whose behalf EIS sign-on is performed.

- **java.security.ResourcePrincipal interface**—Represents a resource principal.

- **javax.resource.spi.security.GenericCredential interface**—Represents a security credential independent of any particular mechanism.

- **javax.resource.spi.security.PasswordCredential class**—Represents a security credential that holds a user name and a password.

Before we delve into the details of these classes and interfaces, let's look at the class hierarchy, shown in Figure 14.1.

14.1.1   Subject Class

The Subject class, which is defined by the JAAS specification (see the Preface for the reference for this specification), contains security information for a single entity, such as an end user. This information includes the entity's security-related identities and attributes, such as passwords and cryptographic keys. A principal represents an identity within a Subject class—the principal actually binds a name to a Subject—and a subject instance can contain multiple identities.

A subject may also own security-related attributes, and these attributes are referred to as credentials. Credentials may be shared or kept private. Credentials that

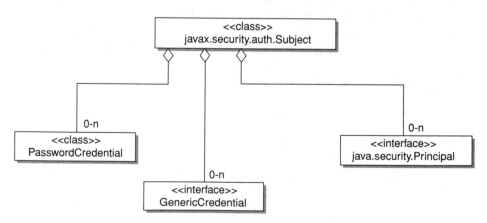

Figure 14.1 Security Interface Hierarchy

are sensitive require special protection, such as private cryptographic keys, and these credentials are stored within a private credential set. Credentials that are intended to be shared, such as public key certificates or Kerberos server tickets, are stored within a public credential set. Different access permissions may be associated with different credential sets.

The Subject class defines a `getPrincipals` method that retrieves all principals associated with a Subject instance. All credentials within a subject's public or private credential set may be retrieved with either the `getPublicCredentials` method or the `getPrivateCredentials` method.

14.1.2 Principal Interface

The java.security.Principal interface represents a resource principal. An EIS connection is established under the security context of a resource principal. The interface is defined as shown in Code Example 14.1. (Note that this class is part of the Java 2 Standard Edition platform.)

Code Example 14.1 Principal Interface

```
package java.security;
public interface Principal {
    public boolean equals(Object another);
    public String getName();
    public String toString();
    public int hashCode();
}
```

The `getName` method is of most interest because it returns the name of the resource principal. The application server uses the Principal interface, or an interface derived from this interface, to pass a resource principal to a resource adapter. This is defined as part of the security management contract. It passes the resource principal as part of a subject.

14.1.3 PasswordCredential

The PasswordCredential class holds the user's name and password. An application server uses the PasswordCredential class to pass the user name and password to the resource adapter via the security contract. Code Example 14.2 shows the definition of this class.

Code Example 14.2 PasswordCredential Class

```
package javax.resource.spi.security;
public final class PasswordCredential
        implements java.io.Serializable {
    public PasswordCredential(String userName, char[] password)
        { ... }
    public String getUserName() { ... }
    public char[] getPassword() { ... }

    public ManagedConnectionFactory getManagedConnectionFactory()
        { ... }
    public void setManagedConnectionFactory(
        ManagedConnectionFactory mcf) { ... }

    public boolean equals(Object other) { ... }
    public int hashCode() { ... }
}
```

The `getUserName` method retrieves the name of the resource principal. (Recall that the Principal interface represents a resource principal.) The `getManagedConnectionFactory` method returns the ManagedConnectionFactory instance for which the application server has set a user name and password.

14.1.4   GenericCredential Interface

The GenericCredential interface defines a security mechanism-independent representation of the security credentials of a resource principal.

The interface provides a Java wrapper to the mechanism-specific security credentials. For example, the GenericCredential interface can be used to wrap Kerberos credentials. It is important that there be a wrapper interface such as this because the security system contract is defined to be security mechanism-independent and thus it does not define any standard representation of security credentials. Each security mechanism-specific representation of security credentials can differ, and GenericCredential provides a uniform wrapper interface for such credentials

A J2EE application server passes a GenericCredential instance as part of a subject, according to the security management contract. (This is discussed later in this chapter.) A resource adapter uses the GenericCredential interface to extract information about a security credential. With this information, the resource adapter can manage an EIS sign-on for a resource principal.

The GenericCredential interface defines several methods that obtain information about a security credential. (See Code Example 14.3.)

Code Example 14.3 GenericCredential Interface

```
package javax.resource.spi.security;
public interface GenericCredential {
    public String getName();
    public String getMechType();
    public byte[] getCredentialData()
        throws javax.resource.spi.SecurityException;
    public boolean equals(Object another);
    public int hashCode();
}
```

The getName method retrieves the name of a GenericCredential instance's associated resource principal, whereas the getMechType method returns the instance's security mechanism type. The getCredentialData method obtains the credential representation, which it returns as an array of bytes. The architecture does not define a standard format for the returned credential data.

14.1.5   ManagedConnectionFactory Interface

Code Example 14.4 shows the methods on the ManagedConnectionFactory interface that are relevant to the security contract:

Code Example 14.4 ManagedConnectionFactory

```
package javax.resource.spi;
public interface ManagedConnectionFactory
    extends java.io.Serializable {

    public ManagedConnection createManagedConnection(
        javax.security.auth.Subject subject,
        ConnectionRequestInfo cxRequestInfo)
            throws ResourceException;
    ...
}
```

During the JNDI lookup, or during the deployment of a resource adapter, the application server configures the ManagedConnectionFactory instance with a set of configuration properties. These properties include default security information and EIS instance-specific information, such as hostname and port number, required for initiating a sign-on to the underlying EIS during the creation of a new physical connection.

The default security configuration on a ManagedConnectionFactory instance can be overridden by security information provided either by a component, with component-managed sign-on, or by the container, with container-managed sign-on.

The application server uses the `createManagedConnection` method when it requests a resource adapter to create a new physical connection to the underlying EIS.

14.2   Security Management Contract

Figure 14.2 shows what happens from a security point of view between the resource adapter and the application server when an application component calls the `getConnection` method to request an EIS connection.

14.2.1   Resource Adapter to Application Server Contract

Recall that when an application component requests a connection to an EIS, the resource adapter receives the request and passes it to the application server. It does this by having its ConnectionFactory instance invoke the `allocateConnection` method on the application server's ConnectionManager. The application server can now add its security services, among other services. Code Example 14.5 shows the definition of the `allocateConnection` method on the ConnectionManager.

Code Example 14.5 ConnectionManager Interface

```
package javax.resource.spi;
public interface ConnectionManager
    extends java.io.Serializable {

    public Object allocateConnection(
        ManagedConnectionFactory mcf,
        ConnectionRequestInfo cxRequestInfo)
            throws ResourceException;
}
```

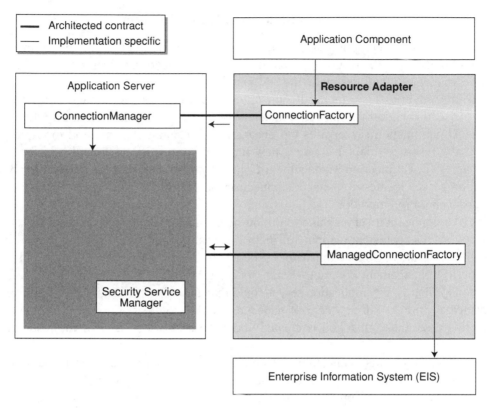

Figure 14.2 Security Management Contract

The resource adapter calls the `allocateConnection` method in one of two ways:

1. **Calling the `allocateConnection` method with the container-managed sign-on option**—It uses this option when the application server manages EIS sign-on. The application component passed no security information in the `getConnection` method. Instead, the application server uses its configured security policies and mechanisms, such as principal mapping, to provide the required security information.

2. **Calling the `allocateConnection` method with the component-managed sign-on option**—When this option is used, the application component provides explicit security information through the ConnectionSpec parameters in its call to the `getConnection` method. The resource adapter, in turn, passes this security information to the application server in the `ConnectionRequest-Info` parameter of the `allocationConnection` method.

14.2.2   Application Server to Resource Adapter Contract

Regardless of which option the resource manager uses when invoking the ConnectionManager's `allocateConnection` method, the application server's security service manager integrates with the ManagedConnectionFactory provided by the resource adapter. The ManagedConnectionFactory defines one method of interest to the security contract, `createManagedConnection`. (See Code Example 14.4.)

An application server uses the `createManagedConnection` method to request that the resource adapter create a new physical connection to the EIS. Refer to Chapter 12, Connection Management Contract, for more details on how an application server locates a ManagedConnectionFactory and invokes the `createManagedConnection` method.

An application server has the option of providing some specific security services, such as principal mapping, principal delegation, and single sign-on, before it calls the ManagedConnectionFactory provided by the resource adapter as part of the security management contract. (Refer to Chapter 5, Managing Security, for more details.) That is, the application server could map the caller principal to the resource principal prior to calling `createManagedConnection` to create the new connection. In this case, the connection is created under the security context of the resource principal.

When sign-on is managed by the container (the resource manager invoked the ConnectionManager's `allocateConnection` method with the container-managed sign-on option), the application server creates a new Subject instance using its own security information configuration before invoking the `createManagedConnection` method.

An application server has the following three options when invoking the `createManagedConnection` method. The resource adapter has specific responses to each option.

1. The application server can invoke the `createManagedConnection` method by passing in a non-null Subject instance that holds a single resource principal, represented by the java.security.Principal interface, and the principal's password-based credentials, represented by the PasswordCredential class. (Recall that the PasswordCredential class holds the user name and password.)

   Response: The resource adapter invokes the `Subject.getPrivateCredentials` method to verify that the Subject instance contains a PasswordCredential instance. If there is a PasswordCredential instance, the resource adapter extracts the user name and password. Using the user name and password, the resource adapter authenticates the resource principal that corresponds to this user name to the EIS when creating the connection.

2. The application server can invoke the `createManagedConnection` method by passing in a non-null Subject instance that holds a single resource principal,

represented by the java.security.Principal interface, and its security credentials. Here the GenericCredential interface represents the security credentials. A typical example is a Subject instance with Kerberos credentials.

Response: The resource adapter uses the resource principal and its credentials (from the Subject instance) for the EIS sign-on process. The resource adapter must explicitly check that the Subject instance carries a GenericCredential instance, which it does using the Subject's `getPrivateCredentials` and `getPublicCredentials` methods. Once it determines that it carries a GenericCredential, the resource adapter extracts the credentials and principal information using the GenericCredential interface's get methods. The resource adapter then uses the resource principal and its extracted credentials for EIS sign-on.

3. The application server can invoke the `createManagedConnection` method by passing a null Subject instance. Invoking the method in this manner serves as a request to the resource adapter to manage the EIS sign-on in its implementation-specific manner, and it is the option the application server uses for component-managed sign-on. The ConnectionRequestInfo instance holds the security information, and the application server does not provide any additional security information or a Subject instance.

Response: The resource adapter has two options for handling this scenario:

a. It can extract security information passed through the ConnectionRequestInfo instance. The resource adapter must also authenticate the resource principal, which it does by combining the ManagedConnectionFactory instance's configured security information with the ConnectionRequestInfo security information. In case of conflict, the ConnectionRequestInfo information overrides the ManagedConnectionFactory information.

b. When the ConnectionRequestInfo instance holds no security configuration, the resource adapter uses the default security configuration on the ManagedConnectionFactory instance to do its authentication.

14.3 Conclusion

This chapter covered the security-related interfaces that are available to a resource adapter. It explained how a resource adapter uses these interfaces to implement the security management contract.

CHAPTER 15

Future Directions

Up to this point, this book has focused on version 1.0 of the J2EE Connector architecture. This chapter provides a preview of the features that we anticipate will be available in future versions of the Connector architecture, and especially version 2.0 of the architecture. We will also briefly look at the future relationship between the J2EE platform and EAI.

15.1 Connector Architecture 2.0

The main goal of the Connector architecture version 2.0 is to further enable pluggability to the J2EE platform. The Connector architecture is being developed and expanded to allow vendors to easily extend the functionality or connectivity of the J2EE platform on their application servers. In the Connector architecture version 1.0, we concentrated on traditional enterprise information systems, such as enterprise resource planning systems and mainframe transaction processing monitors. In version 2.0, we will look to support a broader range of EISs, including messaging, business-to-business, and telecommunication systems and applications.

The following main features of the Connector architecture version 2.0 are proposed:

- Asynchronous resource adapter support

- Java Message Service provider pluggability

- XML support in the Common Client Interface

- Metadata support in the Common Client Interface

Because the Connector specification is developed under the Java Community Process, the exact feature set will ultimately be determined by the Connector expert group. What we present here is a set of proposed features as described in the Connector 2.0 JSR.

15.1.1   Asynchronous Resource Adapter Support

The Connector architecture version 1.0 supports an interaction model that is principally synchronous request and reply. With this type of interaction model, a J2EE application calls an EIS function and then waits to receive the EIS reply before proceeding further.

The Connector architecture version 2.0 extends the interaction model to support both asynchronous inbound and outbound interactions. In the asynchronous outbound direction, a J2EE application can call an EIS function and immediately continue processing without waiting for the reply from the EIS. In the asynchronous inbound direction, an external EIS can initiate a request into a J2EE application. Figure 15.1 illustrates this.

The advantage of an asynchronous resource adapter is that it enables support for more complex integration scenarios. This can be particularly significant if a J2EE application needs to perform a time-consuming EIS task. For example, by using such an asynchronous resource adapter, a J2EE application can asynchronously request the task and continue processing without blocking. When the EIS completes the task, it can send a notification asynchronously to the application.

To support an asynchronous resource adapter, the Connector architecture version 2.0 will need to extend the existing system contracts. This includes extending the connection management, transaction, and security contracts. In addition, the Connector architecture will be defining new system contracts, including contracts for thread management and a dispatch interface.

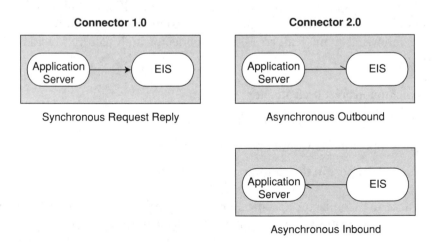

Figure 15.1 Asynchronous Request to J2EE Application

15.1.2 Java Message Service Provider Pluggability

All J2EE 1.3-compatible application servers are required to provide support for the Java Message Service (JMS) API and for message-driven beans. However, at the same time, the J2EE platform does not specify a standard architecture for the integration of a JMS provider and a J2EE application server. To support this requirement, a J2EE vendor has to integrate its application server with a JMS provider in an implementation-specific manner.

There are problems when a vendor must rely on its own implementation-specific approach for integrating its application server with a JMS provider. Principally, such implementation-specific approaches require that the vendor perform a different and distinct integration effort for each JMS provider and application server combination. If a vendor wants its application server to support several JMS providers, or if the vendor has more than one application server product, considerable effort may be necessary to provide a complete integration solution. In addition, these implementation-specific approaches make it difficult for end users to plug in their preferred JMS provider to their application server.

The Connector architecture version 2.0 will address this issue by standardizing the contracts between a JMS provider and a J2EE application server. Once a vendor builds a Connector 2.0 resource adapter for a particular JMS provider, that JMS provider can then be integrated into any Connector 2.0-compatible application server without additional integration effort.

This JMS provider pluggability feature will also leverage the contracts that the Connector 2.0 architecture defines for the asynchronous resource adapter support. (See the preceding section, "Asynchronous Resource Adapter Support.") This leverage is possible because a JMS provider can be thought of as an external EIS that needs to be integrated with an application server in an asynchronous manner.

15.1.3 XML Support in Common Client Interface

XML is playing an increasingly important role in the area of enterprise application integration. XML is useful for standardizing data format, particularly for data that must be shared among various entities. For example, some users would like to export data stored in an EIS in XML format. Other users would also like to interact with an EIS by exchanging XML documents. Currently these scenarios can be supported using the Connector architecture version 1.0. Such support is achieved by using an EIS-specific API provided by a resource adapter.

However, the Connector architecture version 2.0 intends to augment this support. With Connector 2.0, the Common Client Interface will be enhanced to provide first-class XML support. To prevent reinventing the wheel, Connector 2.0 will leverage and align with the existing XML-related APIs, including Java API for XML Parsing and Java API for XML binding.

15.1.4   Common Client Interface Metadata Support

Because of the complexity of most EISs, developers rely on tools to help them construct applications that access an EIS. For example, a tool might generate Java-Beans or enterprise beans to simplify EIS data access in applications.

Generally most tools leverage the CCI to access the target EIS. The CCI enables a tool to use a uniform way to access the EIS. However, just having a uniform approach does not solve the entire problem. A tool needs to obtain meta information about the target EIS to be able to generate the appropriate data access objects. The Connector architecture version 1.0 has no standard APIs as part of the CCI to retrieve EIS metadata. Instead, a tool has to obtain this information in some EIS-specific manner. As a result of this limitation, most tools work only with a pre-defined set of resource adapters or EISs.

The Connector architecture version 2.0 extends the CCI to provide an API for retrieving meta information. The API can be used to obtain such information as a list of EIS function names, as well as the corresponding input and output record types. This functionality will greatly simplify the integration between tools and EISs. It should make it possible for users to use a development tool with arbitrary third-party resource adapters. In other words, this feature enables design-time pluggability between development tools and resource adapters.

15.2   J2EE and EAI

With the addition of such technologies as APIs capable of processing XML, Java Message Service, and the Connector architecture, the J2EE 1.3 platform is becoming the standard integration platform for the enterprise.

In the past, application servers and EAI middleware software were largely viewed as technologies designed to solve different problems, but today that is changing. The boundary between application servers and EAI middleware software is becoming more and more blurred. We see more application server vendors adding integration support to their products. They are bundling various Connector-compliant resource adapters into their products along with providing workflow and business processing features. EAI vendors, on the other hand, are moving away from proprietary programming models and instead they are adding J2EE support, including support for the Connector architecture.

Web services are often viewed as the next-generation technology for enterprise application integration. With the development of the latest XML technologies, including JAXM, JAX-RPC, JAXB, and JAXR, the next version of the J2EE platform promises to be the ideal platform for developing and deploying Web services and for supporting the next wave of enterprise and business-to-business integration.

15.3   Conclusion

This chapter provided a brief look at the new features of the next version of the Connector architecture specification. Version 2.0 of the architecture will make it easier for tools to integrate with resource adapters and EISs. It will increase the availability of asynchronous communication modes and also simplify integrating JMS with the J2EE platform and J2EE application servers. There will also be enhanced support for XML and metadata. With integrated support of Connector architecture, JMS and XML technologies, the J2EE platform is well positioned to be the best EAI platform.

CHAPTER 16

The SAP Connector

Stephan Heik and Stefan Schneider[1]

THE J2EE connector for the SAP System (referred to in this chapter as the SAP Connector) is a plug-in that supports standardized access from a J2EE server to a mySAP.com system (referred to in this chapter as a SAP system). It supports the J2EE Connector architecture specification version 1.0 described in previous chapters of this book and is considered an accessible back-end service.

SAP AG's mySAP.com product is one of the most comprehensive products to operate entire enterprises that has been released in the last decade. Its success is based on the integration of all relevant business workflows in one customizable, homogenous environment.

SAP R/3 systems, which is the former name of the mySAP.com product, began by leveraging SAP's expertise gained with SAP R/2 in the financial, material management, sales, and distribution domains. It extended the SAP R/2 functionality quickly to all business processes of an enterprise.

Today's SAP systems are able to simultaneously process transactions for several thousand online users, a common situation in most Fortune 500 companies today.

mySAP.com's virtual ABAP machine enables enterprises to run the same business application on all major operating systems and relational database systems available in the market.

---

1. Stephan Heik has been a Java development architect at SAP since 1998. There he took part in the development of a RAD framework for implicit persistency. In 2000, he joined In-Q-My Technologies, a 100% subsidiary of SAP, which develops its own J2EE application server. He has worked on different Java technologies and has focused on JSP/Servlet and EJB. Stephan holds a Master's degree in mathematics from the University of Osnabrueck.

Stefan Schneider is a Staff Engineer at Sun Microsystems GmbH, where he's been working with Sun's software partners on client-server technologies since 1994. Before he was development manager at GOPAS Software developing object-relational mapping database products for three years. Stefan holds a PhD from the University of Karlsruhe, where he worked on object-oriented database technologies for computer-aided design applications.

Connecting external applications to mySAP.com systems is not trivial because a single SAP transaction triggers other corporate activities on the fly. The results of online transactions typically become available to all other users instantaneously.

The SAP Connector uses existing and published connectivity components for R/3, and these components are used in other contexts as well. The following sections provide an overview of the different connectivity layers beneath the SAP Connector. They should give you a better understanding of where and when to use which components.

16.1   Architecture of SAP Systems

The mySAP.com system, as of R/3 version 4.6D, may consist of large federations of SAP R/3 systems using specialized components to route and process presentation layer and business application layer transactions. The architecture presented within this context is limited to a single SAP R/3 system because this is the level of interest to a SAP Java connector.

The R/3 three-tier client/server architecture consists of a presentation layer, an application layer, and a database layer. Figure 16.1 illustrates the SAP architecture.

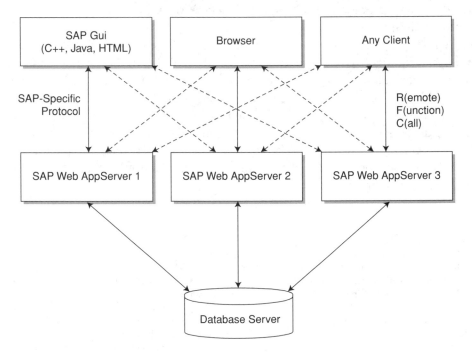

Figure 16.1 SAP Architecture

The database layer is of minor interest in the context of this document because the relational database is accessed exclusively through the R/3 application layer. The database layer consists of relational database products, and all major database products are currently supported. Although the database may be of minor interest in the J2EE context, it is however the storage medium for all data. Typically, several thousand tables are needed to store all information important to an enterprise. Keep in mind that the size of live SAP databases often reaches the terabyte level.

SAP's application layer consists of an application server using a virtual machine that is able to execute SAP's proprietary programming language, called ABAP. The virtual ABAP machine hides all the details of the underlying operating system. The programming language ABAP is tightly integrated into the following:

- ABAP development workbench

- Version and configuration management system

- A database-neutral SQL interface

- A platform-independent screen description language DYNPRO

- A data dictionary tracking all objects and function calls

SAP's presentation layer uses proprietary communication protocols such as DYNPRO and RFC (remote function call). The most important presentation layer products are as follows:

- **The traditional SAP GUI for Windows or Java platforms**—This user interface targets power users with heavy data input.

- **The Internet Transaction Server (ITS)**—The ITS renders GUI transactions and propagates them to browser-based end users.

- **The RFC library**—This library is the programmatic way to access back-end R/3 systems.

J2EE-based applications using the Connector architecture and the SAP resource adapter will access SAP systems just like any other application through the RFC library as low-level access technology.

16.1.1 SAP's Remote Function Call

Prior to release 4.6D, the typical ways to integrate external systems consisted of exchanging idoc documents or using SAP's RFCs. For example, the appropriate way to access a SAP system to execute a SAP transaction contained in a function module such as an interactive user was to use the SAP RFC call interface.

The SAP RFC is implemented as a library with a C call API. The library is available for all platforms supported by SAP. It is cumbersome to directly access this library from Java applications because older versions of the RFC library do not meet the Java Virtual Machine requirements, especially as to multithreading and multithreading safety. In addition, the exception handling and error processing of RFC calls were designed for a C programming environment, and this adds to the complexity of using the library in a Java application.

For application developers, the value of the RFC is based on the fact that SAP supports a well-defined set of calls and these calls are not going to change from version to version. These calls are referred to as Business Application Function Calls, or BAPI for short. Using the set of BAPIs ensures that a published and supported subset of the available RFC-enabled function calls are being used to access a SAP system.

16.1.2   The Java Connector (JCO)

SAP provides a freely available solution to the previously mentioned problems. This solution is called Java Connector (abbreviated as JCO or JayCo). JCO is a Java language wrapper to the RFC library that allows any Java application access to SAP systems. A Java application does not have to be a J2EE application to use JCO. The current JCO library is not a 100% pure Java application due to the nature of the incorporated RFC library. SAP's legacy platform-dependent implementation of the back-end communication (RFC), as of revision 4.6D, will be enhanced by a Simple Object Access Protocol (SOAP) based protocol layer starting with release 6.10.

16.2   Architecture of the SAP Connector

JCO is important to the SAP Connector because it is being used as a lower level transport mechanism. The benefit of the SAP Connector, as opposed to the JCO or any other Java library, is its seamless integration with the following features of a J2EE server:

- Portability across J2EE servers supporting the Java Connector architecture
- Support for connection pooling and connection sharing
- Use of transactions in a J2EE-typical way, either via explicit UserTransactions (using the JTA-specification) or via container-managed transactions, which can be defined for enterprise beans
- Support for security mapping of users in a J2EE server to users in the SAP system, either via user/password or certificates

Figure 16.2 shows the architecture of the SAP Connector, referred to in the diagram as the SAP resource adapter.

16.2.1   Connection Management of the SAP Connector

The SAP Connector supports connection pooling and connection sharing. Note that the J2EE server provides this feature automatically for every J2EE Connector. Application developers can influence the connection management by specifying the particular connection that can be reused and under which circumstances it should be reused.

J2EE Connectors may support the reauthentication of connections. This implies that a connection that has been opened for one user can later be reused for another user. The underlying SAP system does not support this feature because it assumes that the user does not change connections from within an open connection.

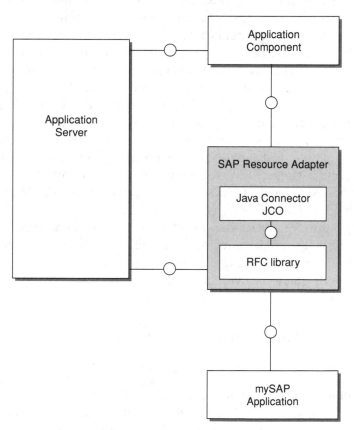

Figure 16.2 Architecture of the SAP Connector

16.2.2   Transaction Management of the SAP Connector

In general, J2EE Connectors are able to support the following transactions:

1. **Local transactions**—These are simple begin-commit/rollback transactions that are completely independent from other systems and transactions.

2. **XAResource-based transactions**—These transactions allow a two-phase commit over different systems or transactions.

3. **No transactions at all**

The ability of SAP connectors to support the preceding features is limited by the functionality of the underlying remote function call (RFC) layer. Therefore, it is necessary to look closer at the transactional aspects of the underlying RFC layer to understand the behavior of the SAP J2EE connector.

The SAP Connector supports local transactions because adequate support for these kinds of transactions exists on the back-end SAP system. However, the SAP Connector does not support XAResource-based transactions. Such support is not possible because SAP R/3 doesn't support two-phase commit.

Regarding underlying functionality, the SAP system executes an automatic database-commit at the end of every remote function call. This automatic commit does not allow database transactions to cover multiple function calls.

A workaround for this limited functionality is the SAP asynchronous update technology, which is being implemented in many RFCs. This technology gathers all database statements and executes them on the database after a specific commit function (or rollback function) is called. The remote function calls in question do not execute database statements directly. The execution of the database statements is triggered by a separate RFC that commits or aborts the submitted database statements. (The separate RFC can be either a BAPI_COMMIT or BAPI_ROLLBACK.)

Although this feature is used to implement transactions spanning multiple RFCs, it is currently cumbersome to use because there is no comfortable way to determine whether or not a RFC uses the "update technology" option. Future versions of the SAP Connector will tackle this issue in order to provide an environment that is easier for software developers to use.

16.2.3   Security Management of the SAP Connector

The SAP Connector applies the following security strategy:

1. **Usage of a subject**—A subject is an object that represents a user in the J2EE server. The subject may contain passwords and certificates for the user in question. The subject may contain different passwords and certificates for every connected system. The subject actually describes the mapping between

users in the J2EE server and users in connected systems. This mapping can be maintained by the administrator of a J2EE server, and it is used automatically when a connection to another system is established.

The SAP Connector currently supports the UserName/Password information of a subject. Certificates are not supported yet, but it is anticipated that such support will follow soon.

2. **Usage of ConnectionSpec**—If either no subject is defined or the defined subject has no specific parameters for the SAP Connector, the ConnectionSpec is used. The ConnectionSpec is an object that is always given as a parameter when getting a connection. It can be of any class because it is used only via reflection. If the ConnectionSpec supports the `getUserName` and `getPassword` methods, those user/password pairs are used to log on to the SAP system. Certificates are not supported here. Although those two methods are optional, the ConnectionSpec supports other methods that are not optional, namely, `getClientNumber` and `getLanguage`.

3. **Usage of the default UserName/Password**—If the ConnectionSpec does not contain the UserName/Password pair, the default UserName/Password pair is used. The administrator of the J2EE server must maintain this information for every SAP Connector.

16.2.4   The Common Client Interface of the SAP Connector

The Common Client Interface (CCI) is a generic application interface (API) allowing any external system to exchange data. The SAP Connector uses this API in the following manner:

1. **InteractionSpec interface**—The SAP Connector gathers all relevant information, such as the function name, through the input record. The InteractionSpec interface is therefore not required as a parameter. (The parameter can be set to null.)

2. **Record interface**—This interface is used to specify all parameters of a specific function call. The parameters are basically the input and output parameters. The SAP connector supports MappedRecord but not IndexedRecord types. The function name of the RFC must be specified to create an instance of a MappedRecord, for example, `RecordFactory.createMappedRecord("BAPI_BANK_CREATE")`. A MappedRecord has three mandatory entries: "import," "export," and "tables." The type for these keys must be ResultSet (see next list item).

The output record has to be identical to the input record.

If `outputRecord = Interaction.execute(null, inputRecord)` is called, outputRecord refers to the same object to which inputRecord refers.

An exception is raised if `interaction.execute(null, inputRecord, output-Record)` is called and outputRecord does not refer to the same object to which inputRecord refers. The reason for this design decision is execution performance. This approach avoids unnecessary copies of the tables that are always used as input and output parameters for calls to the SAP system.

3. **ResultSet interface**—A ResultSet is an interface that permits the parsing and manipulation of tables. The SAP Connector uses this interface for tables as well as for any other input and output data.

Parameter ResultSets are the result sets returned as values of MappedRecord data types, for example, `ResultSet=mappedRecord.get("import")`). A parameter ResultSet data structure contains exactly one row. Applying row manipulating methods such as `resultSet.next` does not work and instead raises an exception. The column names are the parameter names to the function as they are defined in the SAP system. The value of each parameter must match the data type of the corresponding data type of the SAP function call. (See the SAP Java Connector documentation to understand the complete type mapping between BAPIs and result sets.)

Structure ResultSets are returned by the parameter ResultSet in the `getObject` method, for example, `ResultSet.getObject(structureName)`. The handling of structure ResultSets is identical to that of parameter ResultSets. They consist of a single row, and the columns are the parameters of the structure in question.

Table ResultSets are returned by the parameter ResultSet in the `getObject` method, for example, `ResultSet.getObject(tableName)`. As opposed to the other ResultSets, these can have multiple rows. Their usage is identical to that of a structure ResultSet.

Note that the input parameters do not need to be specified completely. Scalar parameters that are optional to the SAP function call can be left out.

16.3   Example

The following example should help you to understand how everything comes together. The example includes the SAP Connector and is freely available through `http://www.inqmy.com`. The complete example also provides a simple JSP-based front end that allows calls to the bean in the example.

The class BankBean, which is described in this section, provides code examples that show how to perform the following tasks:

- Configure the SAP Connector through the `connect` method.
- Obtain a list of banks (BAPI BAPI_BANK_GETLIST).

EXAMPLE   **269**

- Transform the result set into an array.

- Create a new instance of a bank (BAPI BAPI_BANK_CREATE).

16.3.1   Package and Class Declaration

Code Example 16.1 illustrates the package and class declarations.

Code Example 16.1   Package and Class Declarations

```
package com.inqmy.test.sapadapter;

import java.util.*;
import java.io.PrintStream;
import java.rmi.RemoteException;
import javax.ejb.*;
import javax.naming.*;
import javax.resource.cci.*;
import java.sql.ResultSetMetaData;
import java.sql.SQLException;

public class BankBean implements SessionBean {
    SessionContext m_sessionContext;
    public void ejbActivate() {}
     public void ejbCreate() throws
        RemoteException, CreateException {}
    public void ejbPassivate() {}
    public void ejbRemove() {}
    public void setSessionContext(SessionContext sessionContext)
    {
        m_sessionContext = sessionContext;
  }
 }
```

16.3.2   Member Variables

Code Example 16.2 shows the member variables used to configure the class. They cover the information about the SAP system to which the client connects and the bank country of interest.

The connect method allows for the configuration of the instance and sets all private variables.

Code Example 16.2   Member Variables

```
private static String m_resourceAdapter;
private static String m_sapClient;
private static String m_sapLanguage;
private static String m_bankCountry;

public void connect(String resourceAdapter, String sapClient,
            String sapLanguage, String bankCountry) {
  m_resourceAdapter = resourceAdapter;
  m_sapClient = sapClient;
  m_sapLanguage = sapLanguage;
  m_bankCountry = bankCountry;
}
```

16.3.3   Getting the Bank List

The method in Code Example 16.3 extracts banks up to the maximum number given as a parameter. The method relies on the bank country and the connection information specified in the previously called connect method.

Code Example 16.3   Getting the Bank List

```
public Object[][] callBapiBankGetList(int maxRows){
Connection connection = null;
try { // lookup J2EE Connector
    InitialContext initialcontext = new InitialContext();
    ConnectionFactory connectionfactory = (ConnectionFactory)
        initialcontext.lookup
        ("java:comp/env/EISConnections/" + m_resourceAdapter);

    // connect with default-info
    SAPConnectionSpec connectionSpec =
        new SAPConnectionSpec(m_sapClient, m_sapLanguage);
    connection = connectionfactory.getConnection(connectionSpec);
```

EXAMPLE **271**

```
        // get InteractionObject and create input-record
        Interaction interaction = connection.createInteraction();
        MappedRecord parameters =
            connectionfactory.getRecordFactory().createMappedRecord
            ("BAPI_BANK_GETLIST");
        ResultSet importResultSet = (ResultSet)
            parameters.get("import");
        ResultSet exportResultSet = (ResultSet)
            parameters.get("export");
        ResultSet tablesResultSet = (ResultSet)
            parameters.get("tables");

        // set input-parameters
        importResultSet.updateInt("MAX_ROWS", maxRows);
        importResultSet.updateString("BANK_CTRY", m_bankCountry);

        // call function
        interaction.execute(null, parameters);

        // extract results
        ResultSet bankList = (ResultSet)
            tablesResultSet.getObject("BANK_LIST");

        // transform into Object[][]
        Object result[][] = transformResultSetToArray(bankList);
        return result;
    }
    catch (Exception e) {
        e.printStackTrace();  // helpful for debugging
        throw new EJBException(e.getMessage());
    }
    // ...
    }
```

16.3.4   Creating a New Bank

The callBapiBankCreate method creates a new bank in the SAP system. It accepts the required parameters as String types and converts them into the appropriate types. See Code Example 16.4.

Code Example 16.4   Creating a Bank

```
public void callBapiBankCreate(String bankKey,
        String bankName, String bankCity) {
    Connection connection = null;
    try
        { // lookup J2EE Connector
        InitialContext initialcontext = new InitialContext();
        ConnectionFactory connectionfactory = (ConnectionFactory)
            initialcontext.lookup("java:comp/env/EISConnections/"
            + m_resourceAdapter);
        RecordFactory recordfactory =
            connectionfactory.getRecordFactory();

        // connect with default-info
        SAPConnectionSpec connectionSpec =
                new SAPConnectionSpec(m_sapClient, m_sapLanguage);
        connection =
            connectionfactory.getConnection(connectionSpec);

        // get InteractionObject and create input-record
        Interaction interaction = connection.createInteraction();
        MappedRecord parameters =
            connectionfactory.getRecordFactory().createMappedRecord
            ("BAPI_BANK_CREATE");
        ResultSet importResultSet = (ResultSet) parameters.get
            ("import");
        ResultSet exportResultSet = (ResultSet) parameters.get
            ("export");
        ResultSet tablesResultSet = (ResultSet) parameters.get
            ("tables");

        // set input-parameters
        importResultSet.updateString("BANK_CTRY", m_bankCountry);
        importResultSet.updateString("BANK_KEY", bankKey);
        ResultSet bankAddressResultSet =
            (ResultSet) importResultSet.getObject("BANK_ADDRESS");
        bankAddressResultSet.updateString("BANK_NAME", bankName);
        bankAddressResultSet.updateString("CITY", bankCity);

        // call function
        interaction.execute(null, parameters);
```

EXAMPLE   **273**

```
        // check results
        ResultSet returnResultSet =
            (ResultSet) exportResultSet.getObject("RETURN");
        String resultMessage = returnResultSet.getString("MESSAGE");
        if (resultMessage != null && resultMessage.trim().length()
                != 0)
            throw new Exception("Error-Message from SAP-system: "
            + resultMessage);
    }
    catch (Exception e) {
        e.printStackTrace();   // helpful for debugging
        throw new EJBException(e.getMessage());
    }
    finally { try { connection.close(); } catch (Exception e) { } }
}


private Object[][] transformResultSetToArray(ResultSet rs)
        throws SQLException {
    ResultSetMetaData rsm = rs.getMetaData();

    // convert into array
    Vector allLines = new Vector();
    Object line[] = new String[rsm.getColumnCount()];
    for (int pos = 0; pos < line.length; pos ++)
        line[pos] = rsm.getColumnName(pos + 1);
    allLines.add(line);
    // position on first line
    while (rs.next()) {
        line = new Object[rsm.getColumnCount()];
        for (int pos = 0; pos < line.length; pos++)
            line[pos] = rs.getObject(pos + 1);
        allLines.add(line);
    }
    Object allLinesArray[][] = new
        Object[allLines.size()][rsm.getColumnCount()];
    allLines.copyInto(allLinesArray);
    return allLinesArray;
  }
}
```

CHAPTER 17

Developing Applications with JCA-based Tools

Michael Beisiegel, Piotr Przybylski, and Gary Bist[1]

Tools make the difference when you want to apply architecture to application development. Tools turn architecture into products. In this section, you will see the practical aspects of the J2EE™ Connector Architecture (JCA) by using JCA-based tools from IBM® to build, test, deploy, and run a J2EE enterprise bean ap-

1. Michael Beisiegel is a Senior Technical Staff Member working for the architecture team of IBM's Application and Integration Middleware (AIM) Division in Somers, NY. He is responsible for IBM's connector/adapter runtime and tools architecture. He is IBM's expert on the J2EE Connector Architecture effort. He joined IBM in 1989 and began working for the 390 software development organization at the IBM Lab in Boeblingen, Germany. Later, he took an assignment (1998-2000) to lead the development effort of the VisualAge for Java Enterprise Access Builder (EAB) and the Common Connector Framework (CCF) at the IBM Toronto Lab in Canada. He received his M.S. (1989) in Electrical Engineering from the University of Kaiserslautern, Germany.

Piotr Przybylski is an Advisory Staff Member at the IBM Toronto Laboratory working on Connector architecture and tools. Piotr Przybylski joined IBM in 1996, working on tools and libraries to access enterprise applications from Java. He has contributed to several releases of the VisualAge for Java Enterprise Access Builder (EAB) and Common Connector Framework (CCF). He received his B.S. in Computer Science from Concordia University in Montreal in 1994 and his M.S. in Computer Science from the University of Waterloo in 1996.

Gary Bist is a technical writer at the IBM Toronto Lab. He has developed product documentation for the EAB feature in VisualAge for Java for the past 3 years. He also has been an educator, developing courses in VisualAge for Java and DB2, IBM's relational database. He holds an M.A. in English from the University of Western Ontario.

Michael and Piotr are developers from IBM who designed and developed many of the JCA tools shown. Gary is a technical writer who has documented many of the same tools.

We would like to thank Mike Andrea, Sandy Minocha, Kevin Sutter, and Leigh Davidson for their help with this article.

© Copyright International Business Machines Corporation 2001. All rights reserved.

IBM, CICS, IMS, MQSeries, VisualAge, and WebSphere are trademarks of International Business Machines Corporation in the United States, or other countries, or both.

Java and all Java-based trademarks and logos are trademarks or registered trademarks of Sun Microsystems, Inc., in the United States or other countries.

J.D. Edwards and OneWorld are registered trademarks of J. D. Edwards & Company.

Oracle is a registered trademark of Oracle Corporation.

PeopleSoft is a registered trademark of PeopleSoft, Inc.

SAP is a registered trademark of SAP AG.

Windows is a registered trademark of Microsoft Corporation in the United States, or other countries, or both.

plication. Let's begin with a brief overview of the Enterprise Access Builder (EAB) feature in IBM's VisualAge® for Java™, Enterprise Edition, Version 4.0. EAB contains the JCA-based tools that we will use to build our application.

17.1   Enterprise Access Builder (EAB) 101

To an application developer, a connector is a set of related classes that lets an application access business logic and data in an Enterprise Information System (EIS). A simple analogy is to think of these connector classes collectively as a pipeline that allows you to flow request and response data between your application and the EIS.

In Figure 17.1, the connector classes are between the application classes and the server with the EIS, in this case a CICS™ transaction server. In VisualAge for Java, the connector classes are subset into the EAB classes, which interact with your application, and the specific connector classes, in this case, the CICS connector classes. When we say EAB classes, we mean the classes generated by using the EAB tools and EAB runtime libraries. Note that an application never directly accesses specific connector classes.

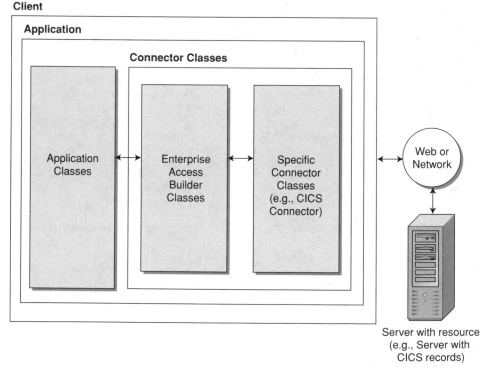

Figure 17.1 Application, Connector, and EIS Relationship

This separation means that once you are familiar with the EAB tools, you can develop an application in an identical way for any connector supported by VisualAge for Java because your application only interacts with the EAB classes. The application that we will develop accesses CICS transactions. But using the same EAB tools, we could write an application to access IM™ transactions, MQSeries™ messaging queues, PeopleSoft® ERP data, Oracle® applications and so on. (The connectors that come with VisualAge for Java are listed at the end of this section.) Using EAB, then, is a standard way to develop any connector-related application.

17.2   JCA Application Development Process

What is the JCA application development process? How does EAB fit into it? Although there are no absolute rules for developing a JCA-based application, Figure 17.2 shows a process that many developers using EAB have found effective when creating an application. It begins by developing the application in VisualAge for Java. By developing, we mean using the EAB tools to generate code that can

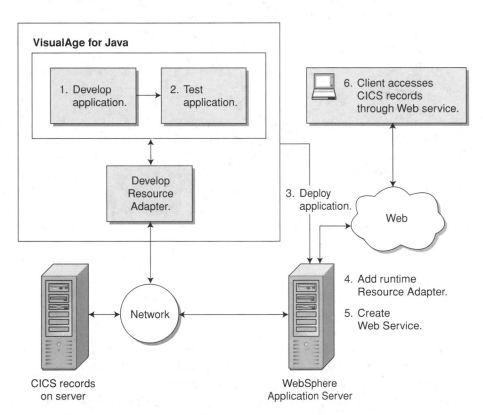

Figure 17.2 JCA Application Development Process

access an EIS through the JCA connector and be called by your application. Once the code is generated, another tool in VisualAge for Java is used to test it. The WebSphere® Test Environment emulates the server, in this case, the WebSphere Application Server.

Testing a JCA-based application before you deploy it is a very good idea. Testing lets you address any problems in your application while still in the development environment. Remember that deployment of an application and setup of that application on a server take time. You do not want to find errors in your application after you have invested time in deployment because then you must return to the development environment, fix the problems, and redeploy until you get it right. Those who have painfully experienced redeployment will find the WebSphere Test Environment a valuable tool.

After testing, comes deployment of the application. At this point, you are switching from a development environment to a production environment. How you use your deployed application varies, of course, according to your needs. Any application, however, would need to install the runtime resource adapter at the application server. The runtime resource adapter is packaged in a Resource Adapter ARchive (RAR) file. It contains a deployment descriptor, help files, and the interface, implementation and helper classes of the resource adapter. If you were to develop a Web service from an enterprise bean, as seen in our diagram, the final step would be to access it over the Web.

17.2.1 Overview of the Application

Let's walk through how we will build our application. We will follow the standard JCA application development process mentioned previously to develop our application. We will use VisualAge for Java, Enterprise Edition, Version 4.0; WebSphere Application Server, Advanced Edition, Version 4.0; the development version of the CICS ECI connector included in VisualAge for Java; and the CICS ECI connector RAR file included with the CICS Transaction Gateway, Version 4.0. We will develop and run our application on Windows 2000 Professional. Our application will call a CICS transaction that requires as input a customer number and that will return the name of the customer that matches the customer number. Obviously, it is a simple application, but it will demonstrate the heart of the JCA architecture, which is to interact with EIS systems as if the data on the EIS systems is available in the local application.

We will use the EAB session bean tool to create our enterprise bean. The tool first defines the connection information; that is, the type of connection and configuration. In the next stage, it imports a COBOL file, which defines the input and output data structure for the CICS transaction accessed.

Then records representing COBOL structures are generated in the application; that is, input and output records. The tool handles code generation, data type conversion, "endianness" issues, and optimization. The code generated will, at run-time, handle the marshalling and unmarshalling of the different data representation formats used by the application and EIS system. Afterwards, we will use a related editing tool, which can be automatically invoked after record generation, to further specify connection information necessary for the Java Naming and Directory Interface (JNDI) at runtime. With this information, a factory object at runtime can generate a connection when needed by the application.

To test our application within VisualAge for Java, that is, before deployment, we will use the WebSphere Test Environment. As its name implies, it emulates an application server within a development environment. Once we know our application works, we will switch to the production environment. We will add the CICS ECI RAR file to the application server. Then we will deploy the application to the application server using another tool. Finally, we will run our application again from the application server.

We will show you all of the above as we step you through our tools. Note that VisualAge for Java comes with similar step-by-step samples that let you try out these JCA-based tools in a safe environment.

17.2.2 Using the EAB Session Bean Tool

Launch the EAB session bean tool from within VisualAge for Java's EJB Development Environment. This environment is an IDE for developing enterprise beans. In the EJB Development Environment, create an EJB group, in order to contain an enterprise bean, and then launch the tool. An initial page gives you the option of migrating a session bean; that is, if you had an existing session bean created in the preceding IBM Common Connector Framework (CCF) architecture, you could migrate it to the JCA architecture at this point. On the first page, shown in Figure 17.3, enter the basic information such as the project, package, and name of the session bean. Also, enter the connection information.

The connection information is the critical information at this point. In particular, the choice of a managed connection factory and the type of managed connection factory affects the subsequent properties that appear in the tool. The property sheet for connection information, which opens when you click Edit, is shown in Figure 17.4. You can fill in all the connection properties immediately or wait until after the code is generated and use the session bean editor tool. All of the properties are documented in the online help, if you happen to get lost. The key connection properties are the JNDI-related information (res_ref, res_type, and res_auth) and the type of managed connection factory, and its properties specifying the address of the CICS gateway and the CICS server name.

Eventually you reach the method page. A method for an EAB session bean comprises interaction properties and an input and an output record. Starting with the input record, the session bean tool lets you import an existing COBOL structure

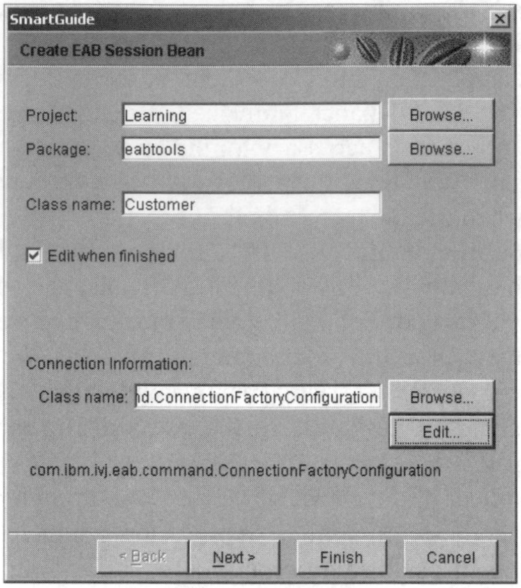

Figure 17.3 Initial Information for EAB Session Bean

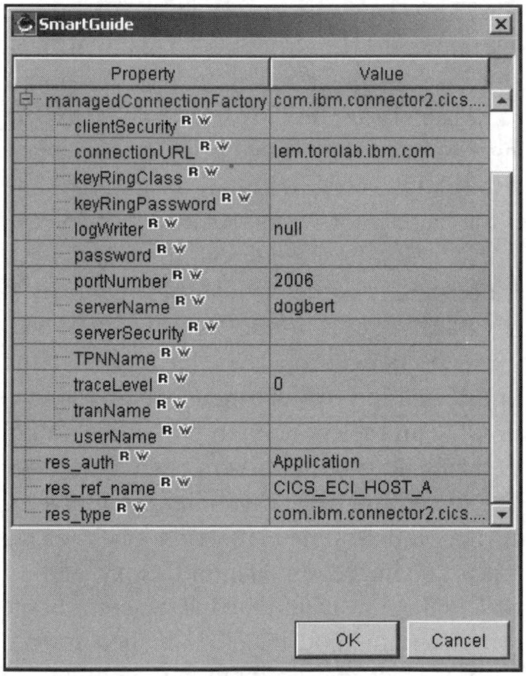

Figure 17.4 Connection Properties

to create your input record bean. If you import a COBOL file, it leads to the page shown in Figure 17.5. In the foreground is the COBOL file.

In the following page, select an option called Generate as javax.resource.cci.Record interface. This option means that your input and output record beans will comply with JCA. The other options shown on that page can impact the performance of your session bean. The performance implications of these options are discussed in "Connectors in J2EE" (see the References at the end of this chapter). In most cases, the default options offer the best performance. You are also given the opportunity to change critical machine-to-machine properties such as code page and endianness.

Completing similar fields generates an output record. The completed input and output record beans, as specified in the method page, are shown in Figure 17.6. The invocation of the `getCustomerInfo` method would result in the customer number being passed from the application to the input record and then to the EIS. Then customer information would be returned from the EIS in the output record and then to the application. The function called has to be expressed in terms understood by the EIS. In the connector architecture, you do this using an InteractionSpec class. In our application, we specified an ECIInteractionSpec class. Figure 17.6 shows how to specify the class.

At this point, you generate the session bean. If you had selected to edit the session bean when finished in the first page (see Figure 17.3), you would automatically launch the EAB Session Bean editor after generation.

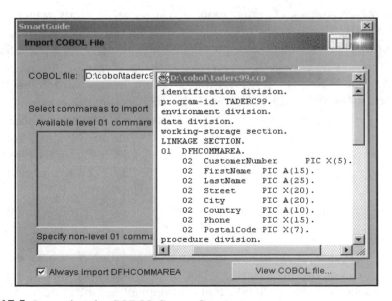

Figure 17.5 Importing the COBOL Source Structure

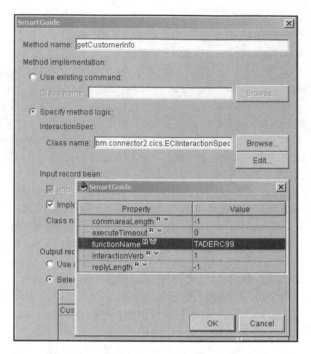

Figure 17.6 Method Page with Interaction to EIS Properties

17.2.3   Using the Session Bean Editor

Application developers greet visual tools with suspicion. Exactly what is going on underneath? IBM has tried to strike a balance between those who want a fully automatic code generator and those who want more control over the generated code. Editors are provided so that developers can make modifications to the code after generation. The EAB Session Bean editor, for example, lets you edit the generated session bean. The information is grouped into connection information and methods (input and output records). Review the values you entered when building the session bean, make any changes you wish, and save the session bean. Figure 17.7 shows the session bean editor. Now it is time to test, while still in the development stage, that your enterprise bean can, in fact, get the data expected from the EIS.

17.2.4   Testing the Application in the WebSphere Test Environment

Once you have built your application with the EAB tools, you need to test it while still in the development environment. As indicated earlier, it's better to verify in the development environment that you can get your data from the EIS than to deploy your application into the production environment and then find out it does not work. IBM created the WebSphere Test Environment for this very reason. As its

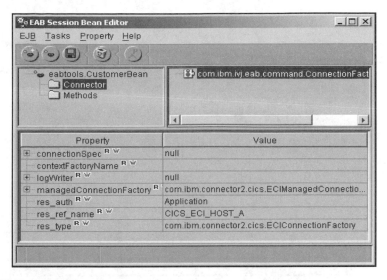

Figure 17.7 EAB Session Bean Editor with Connection Properties

name implies, it emulates the application server within the VisualAge for Java IDE. Testing does not need to be elaborate, but it should verify that you can get the expected values from the EIS. Also, a test should check for error conditions, such as incorrect input, or failure at the server end, such as failure of a gateway.

Begin in the EJB Development Environment where your previous tool will have created your enterprise bean. Figure 17.8 shows the customer enterprise bean we created in the enterprise beans pane. Note that the method, `getCustomerInfo`, is in the Members pane. Begin to test your enterprise bean by adding that method to the EJB remote interface. Then generate your deployed code, which creates code similar to the code you would actually create if you really had deployed an application to an application server. Then, while still in the EJB Development Environment, generate an access bean for your enterprise bean. The access bean is a simplified client interface to an enterprise bean.

Once everything is ready in the EJB Development Environment, launch the WebSphere Test Environment. This runtime environment emulates the actual application server from within the VisualAge for Java IDE. Figure 17.9 shows the console window for the test environment. Your enterprise bean needs the persistent name server to be up and running, as is shown. The persistent name server is necessary to support applications using JNDI. The WebSphere Test Environment has its own database, and so it can emulate persistence. Add your enterprise bean to the server configuration, just as you would add an enterprise bean to a regular application server. Optionally, you may wish to set an option that lets you step through code a line at a time. This debugging feature can be extremely helpful when you do experience a failure and need to pinpoint precisely the line that caused it.

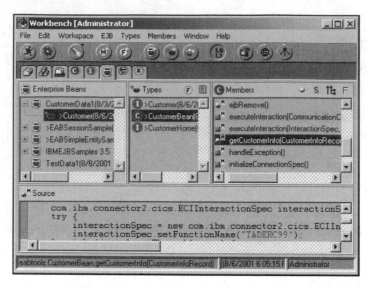

Figure 17.8 Testing the Enterprise Bean in the EJB Development Environment

Finally, write some additional simple client code, which creates an input record. In our case, we passed a customer number to the enterprise session bean running in the WebSphere Test Environment. Then, capture the returning output from the CICS server and print the result to the console. A fragment of code for the client bean we created is shown in Code Example 17.1. The point of the test is to show that your application can access the CICS Transaction Server and return correct values, in this case, the customer's first name.

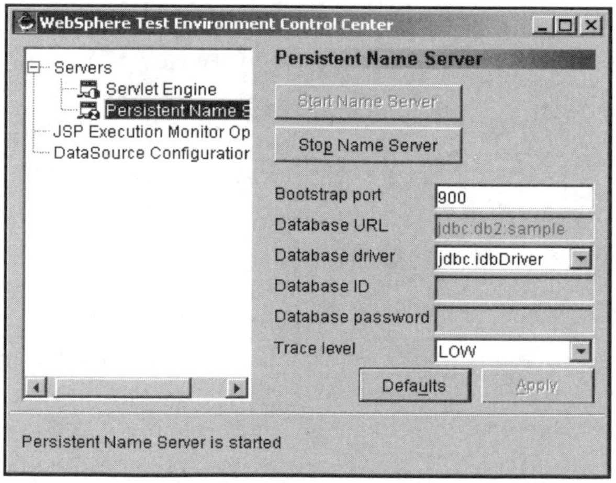

Figure 17.9 WebSphere Test Environment with the Persistent Name Server Running

Code Example 17.1 Sample Client Code

```
Context initial = new InitialContext();

Object objref = initial.lookup("MyCustomerBean");
CustomerBeanHome home =
            (CustomerBeanHome)PortableRemoteObject.narrow(objref,
         CustomerBeanHome.class);
CustomerBean customer = home.create();

// Create an input record
CustomerInfoRecord input = new CustomerInfoRecord();
// Pass customer number as input
input.setCustomerNumber("12345");
// Get output record
CustomerInfoRecord output = customer.getCustomerInfo(input);
// Print the first name of the customer
System.err.println(output.getFirstName());
```

17.2.5   Moving Your Application to the WebSphere Application Server

Once you have developed and tested your application, it is time to move from the development environment to the production environment and put the application onto an application server. Deployment is a two-stage process: first, deploying the RAR file and setting up optimal runtime values at the application server, and second, deploying the application itself.

When deploying the application, you need to export a Java archive file (JAR file) containing the application and the libraries the application accesses. Exporting a JAR file is handled through the EJB Development Environment tools. The JAR file can contain either an individual EAB session bean or a group of session beans. Include in the JAR file all the libraries used by the exported beans that are not provided by the WebSphere Application Server. For example, you will need to include in the archive the generated records representing the COBOL copybooks but not the CICS ECI connector classes.

17.2.6   Deploying the RAR File

A runtime JCA resource adapter is shipped in a Resource Adapter Archive (RAR) file. You need to make that resource adapter accessible to the WebSphere instance running the application. Deployment of the RAR file into WebSphere is done using the WebSphere Administrative Console. From the console menu, select an option to add a J2C resource adapter. Then browse the file system and locate the RAR file. Once the file contents are read, the administrative console displays the properties of the resource adapter as defined by its deployment descriptor. The XML deployment descriptor provides information about the service that the resource adapter is providing, with details such as the properties descriptions and their default values. Figure 17.10 shows the list of resource adapter properties as described in its XML deployment descriptor.

You can also view additional information besides the configurable properties. For example, you can look at version numbers. These numbers tell you the specification level of the connector architecture and the version of the EIS necessary for communication. Other information tells you the authentication mechanism supported. More instructions concerning the libraries used by the connector are found in the HowTo.html file contained in the RAR file.

The next step is to create the instance of the JCA connection factory and configure its properties. The connection factory, as its name implies, provides connections to the EIS. From the menu, select Create J2C Connection Factory, and the administrative console tool creates an editable properties set associated with the particular connection factory instance. Specify all the information needed by the resource adapter to connect to the particular instance of the EIS. For the CICS ECI connector, specify at least the ServerName and ConnectionURL properties that determined the CICS server to connect to and the address of the CICS transaction

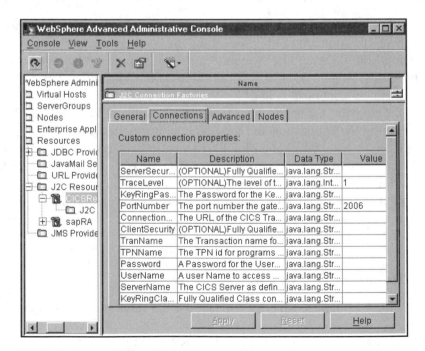

Figure 17.10 Resource Adapter Properties

gateway, respectively. These values determine the server and gateway that will be accessed through all the connections created by this instance of the connection factory. The resource adapter documentation provides the details of these two properties and all the other properties.

Next, you can specify the JNDI lookup name, instead of the provided default name, under which the new connection factory instance will be available to the components, as shown in Figure 17.11. The components use the JNDI lookup name to retrieve the instance of the connection factory. The instance is used, in turn, to create a connection to the EIS.

17.2.7 Specifying the Connection Pooling Properties

The last step in the deployment of the connection factory instance is to specify the management properties to be used when pooling the physical connections to the EIS. Connection pooling can significantly improve performance, so these values deserve some attention. Typically, a system administrator sets up the values of the properties based on the system requirements, load, and availability as shown in Figure 17.12. The properties that can be specified include

- **Reap Time**—The interval, in seconds, between runs of the garbage collector. Garbage collection can be disabled by setting Reap Time or Unused Timeout to the default value of 0. The garbage collector discards all connections that have been unused for the time specified by Unused Timeout.

- **Unused Timeout**—The interval, in milliseconds, after which the unused connection is discarded. Setting this value to the default value of 0 disables the garbage collector.

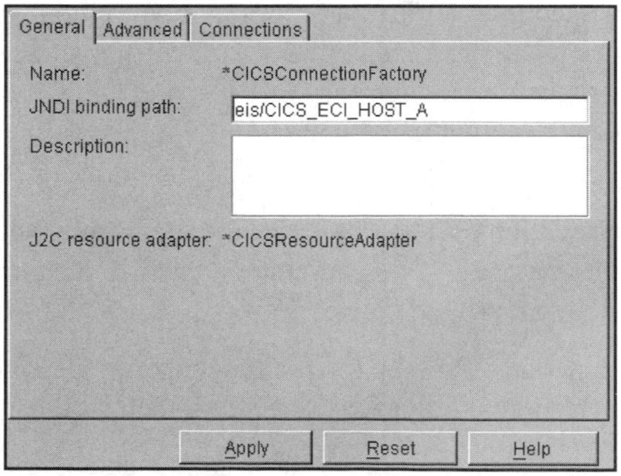

Figure 17.11 Specifying the JNDI Lookup Name of the Connection Factory

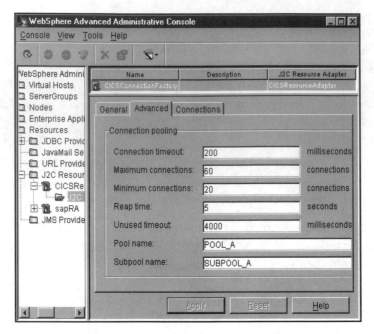

Figure 17.12 Connection Pooling Values

- **Connection Timeout**—The interval, in milliseconds, after which a ResourceAllocationException is thrown if the maximum number of connections has been reached. If Connection Timeout is set to the default value of 0, the pool manager waits indefinitely until a connection can be allocated; that is, until the number of connections falls below the maximum number of connections or a connection becomes available for reuse.

- **Maximum Connections**—The maximum number of connections that can be created by a particular managed connection factory instance. Once this number is reached, no new connections are created and the requester waits or a ResourceAllocationException is thrown. If Maximum Connections is set to the default of 0, the number of connections can grow indefinitely.

- **Minimum Connections**—The minimum number of managed connections that should be maintained. If this number is reached, the garbage collector will not discard any managed connections.

- **Pool Name**—The name used by the pool manager to group managed connections created by different managed connection factories.

- **Subpool Name**—The name used by the pool manager to further subgroup pools of managed connections within a particular pool.

17.2.8 Assembling and Deploying the Application onto the WebSphere Application Server

The first step in assembling and deploying the application is to create the Enterprise Application Archive (EAR file) from the JAR file exported from the development environment. At this time, you can also add Web components such as JSPs or HTML files to your EAR file. Using the WebSphere Application Assembly Tool, provide the name for a new EAR file and the location of the JAR file with the application code. Look at the deployment descriptor for your application. You can also modify the deployment descriptor at this point, too. Figure 17.13 shows the resource references section of the deployment descriptor that describes the resource adapter used by an application.

The EAR file created by the Application Assembly Tool can now be deployed into the WebSphere Application Server. Using the Administrative Client tool, the Install Enterprise Application wizard guides you through the steps necessary to deploy your application. Select the WebSphere server, provide your application name, and, finally, add the location of your EAR file. Next, the wizard will take you through several panels, allowing you to specify deployment options for the application. One option, mapping of the resource references to resources, is particularly helpful.

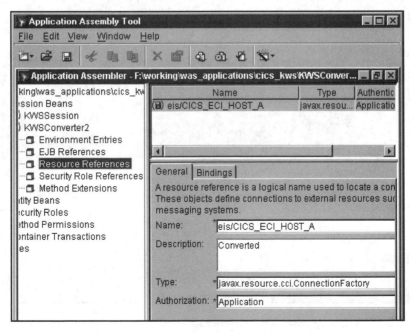

Figure 17.13 Resource Reference Section of the Deployment Descriptor

When you create your application, you specify a resource reference name
(`res_ref_name`, see Figure 17.4). It is a name used by the application to look up the
instance of the connection factory in the JNDI context at runtime. When the application is deployed, the value of the `res_ref_name` retrieved from the deployment
descriptor overrides the value you specified during creation of your application.
This allows the deployer, by modifying the deployment descriptor, to set the lookup
name to the value specific to the server on which the application is deployed. In
WebSphere, this can be achieved even easier. The deployment tool lets you map the
`res_ref_name` specified in your application to the resource name on the server
without requiring you to modify the deployment descriptor. Figure 17.14 shows the
page that lets you perform the mapping operation between the resource reference of
the application and the resource defined on the particular server.

17.2.9   Using the Deployed Application

You are finished at this point. After deployment, there are several ways to use a session bean that accesses a CICS server. You can access the session bean directly
from a client program. You can also provide access to it from a servlet or use it with
other enterprise bean components as a part of a more complex business application.

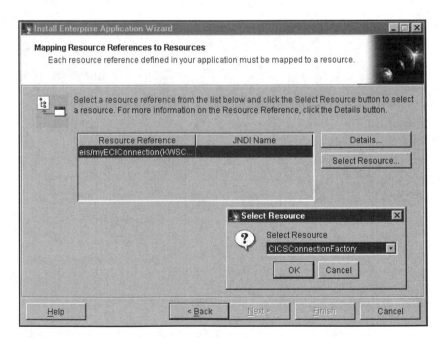

Figure 17.14 Mapping Resource References

17.2.10   Accessing Session Beans as Web Services

Setting up a session bean as a Web service is a new way of providing easy access to EIS systems. In this section, we will show you how a session bean could be made available as a Web service.

The WebSphere Application Server support for the Simple Object Access Protocol (SOAP) lets you expose a session bean as a Web service. Here's how to take advantage of that support with JCA-based applications today. Begin by creating a SOAP deployment descriptor specifying the particular session bean you would like to expose as Web service. The information to include in the deployment descriptor includes the service URN, the list of exposed methods, and the session bean home interface name as well as other information. Code Example 17.2 shows the SOAP deployment descriptor for the session bean we created previously.

Code Example 17.2 SOAP Deployment Descriptor

```
<isd:service xmlns:isd="http://xml.apache.org/xml-soap/deployment"
             id="urn: customerinfo-service ">
<isd:providertype="com.ibm.soap.providers.WASStatelessEJBProvider"
             scope="Application" methods="getCustomerInfo">
  <isd:java class="eabtools/Customer" />
  <isd:option key="FullHomeInterfaceName"
             value="eabtools.CustomerHome" />
  <isd:option key="ContextProviderURL"
             value="iiop://localhost:900" />
  <isd:option key="FullContextFactoryName"
  value="com.ibm.ejs.ns.jndi.CNInitialContextFactory" />
  </isd:provider>
  <isd:faultListener>org.apache.soap.server.DOMFaultListener
    </isd:faultListener>
  <isd:mappings>
    <isd:map xmlns:x=" urn: customerinfo-service " qname="x:customer"
             encodingStyle="http://schemas.xmlsoap.org/soap/encoding/"
             javaType="eabtools.CustomerRecord"
             java2XMLClassName=
               "org.apache.soap.encoding.soapenc.BeanSerializer"
             xml2JavaClassName=
               "org.apache.soap.encoding.soapenc.BeanSerializer"/>
                </isd:mappings>
</isd:service>
```

Finally, use the WebSphere tool, the SOAPEAREnabler, to add the EAR file containing the session bean to the WebSphere SOAP configuration. After WebSphere SOAP is configured with your deployment descriptor and you deploy the EAR file, the session bean connecting to the EIS can be accessed as a Web service.

To describe this service, you will need to use other IBM tools to create the corresponding Web Services Description Language (WSDL) file. The WSDL file shown in Code Example 17.3 describes the service offered by the server.

Code Example 17.3 WSDL File

```
<?xml version="1.0" encoding="UTF-8"?>
<definitions name="exportejb_Service-interface"
  targetNamespace="http://www.exportejbservice.com/exportejb-
interface"
  xmlns="http://schemas.xmlsoap.org/wsdl/"
  xmlns:soap="http://schemas.xmlsoap.org/wsdl/soap/"
  xmlns:tns="http://www.exportejbservice.com/exportejb"
  xmlns:xsd="http://www.w3.org/1999/XMLSchema">

<message name="IngetCustomerInfoRequest">
  <part name="meth1_inType1" type="xsd:eabtools.CustomerRecord"/>
</message>

<message name="OutgetCustomerInfoResponse">
  <part name="meth1_outType" type="xsd:eabtools.CustomerRecord"/>
</message>

<portType name="exportejb_Service">
  <operation name="getCustomerInfo">
    <input message="IngetCustomerInfoRequest"/>
    <output message="OutgetCustomerInfoResponse"/>
  </operation>
</portType>

<binding name="exportejb_ServiceBinding" type="exportejb_Service">
  <soap:binding style=
      "rpc" transport="http://schemas.xmlsoap.org/soap/http"/>
  <operation name="getCustomerInfo">
    <soap:operation soapAction="urn:customerinfo-service"/>
```

```
<input>
  <soap:body
      encodingStyle="http://schemas.xmlsoap.org/soap/encoding/"
      namespace="urn:customerinfo-service"
      use="encoded"/>
</input>
<output>
  <soap:body
      encodingStyle="http://schemas.xmlsoap.org/soap/encoding/"
      namespace="urn:customerinfo-service"
  use="encoded"/>
</output>
</operation>
</binding>

<types>
  <xsd:schema
      targetNamespace="http://www.exportejbservice.com/exportejb"
xmlns="http://www.w3.org/1999/XMLSchema/">
      </xsd:schema>
</types>

</definitions>
```

Once you have the WSDL representation of your service, you can make the service available. Availability is achieved by sharing the WSDL file with the intended users of the service. Depending on your service type, you can either directly send the WSDL file to specific users or, if your service is to be used publicly, you can publish its description through a public registry. For example, you could publish publicly using the Universal Description, Discovery and Integration (UDDI) standard registry.

17.3   Future Directions

The J2EE Connector Architecture makes the J2EE platform the preferred platform for enterprise application integration. In particular, this architecture does an excellent job in making connectors a pluggable system component. It also provides a common client programming model for access to EIS resources. A common client programming model simplifies life for both programmers and tool vendors.

It is important to understand that when the connector architecture discusses EISs, the discussion is not limited to legacy enterprise systems. We will see the JCA architecture evolve into a service connector architecture for inter- and intra-enterprise service invocation. Besides extending the runtime architecture itself (inbound connectivity, XML support, provider pluggability, and so forth), it is important that the next version of the JCA architecture provide pluggability into tool environments (that is, metadata, import and generation support).

IBM will continue to play a leading role in the evolution and support of the J2EE Connector Architecture.

17.4   Conclusion

We have shown you how to get up and running with the JCA architecture today, using tools that are currently available. Although you could hand-code your own application to access EIS systems, the cost in development and maintenance time is enormous. For example, you would have to code your own Quality of Service (QoS) and you would need to access proprietary EIS interfaces. These tools simplify the process by generating most of the code you will need to access many EIS systems and the code generated is nonproprietary. At runtime, the code will handle the marshalling and unmarshalling needed to pass data from your application to the EIS system while maintaining data integrity in all environments.

We have also shown you tools to help in the deployment of your application along with the RAR file to the application server, as you move your application from the development to the production environment. And we have shown how JCA-based applications are suited to the move to XML-based ways of exchanging data. With a few changes to some files, an application becomes a Web service, available publicly or privately for clients requesting this kind of service. Last, we have indicated how IBM will lead and support future JCA architecture directions.

Our section ends with a list of the current connectors that come with Visual-Age for Java and some references you will find helpful. If you wish to follow IBM's commitment to the JCA architecture and to Java in general, you should bookmark IBM's WebSphere Developer Domain (`www.ibm.com/websphere/developer`). Technical articles on tools and products that will support the JCA architecture are posted at this popular Web site.

17.4.1   Connectors in VisualAge for Java, Enterprise Edition, Version 4.0

Connector support is an ongoing story. The following list is the current set of connectors available in VisualAge for Java. As indicated earlier, you only need to know how to use the EAB tools in general in order to develop an application for any one of these connectors.

- **CICS ECI and CICS EPI Connectors**—Accesses CICS transactions.

- **Host-on-Demand (HOD) Connector**—Accesses 3270, 5250, CICS, and VT hosts.

- **IM™ TOC Connector**—Accesses IMS transactions.

- **J.D. Edwards® Connector**—Accesses Enterprise Resource Planning (ERP) data from the J.D. Edwards OneWorld® system.

- **MQSeries Connector**—Accesses MQSeries messaging software.

- **Oracle Applications Connector**—Accesses data from Oracle applications.

- **PeopleSoft Connector**—Accesses ERP data from PeopleSoft systems.

- **SAP® R/3 Connector**—Accesses the business object repository in SAP R/3.

17.4.2   References

- Green, John, Sandy Minocha, and Gary Bist. "Connectors in J2EE," *Web-Sphere Developer Domain Technical Journal,* May 2001. This article extends the subjects discussed here with material on managed and nonmanaged connections, connection pooling, performance recommendations, Quality of Service, JNDI, and other important areas linking connectors with J2EE. Available at `www.ibm.com/websphere/developer`.

- Monson-Haefel, Richard. *Enterprise JavaBeans*. O'Reilly, 1999. Though we have built a session bean with our EAB tool and avoided a discussion on enterprise beans themselves, many developers will want a better understanding of the enterprise bean architecture behind the tool. This book will help.

- Oya, Tsutomu, Bob Brown, Martin Smithson, and Tomohiro Taguchi. *CCF Connectors and Database Connection Using WebSphere Advanced Edition*. IBM Redbooks, 2000. This book looks at other connectors, particularly the IMS and MQSeries connectors. Though based on the previous architecture, Common Connector Framework (CCF), the material is still applicable. Remember that IBM provides migration tools to move CCF applications to J2EE. Available at `www.ibm.com/redbooks`.

- Picon, Joaquin, Regis Coqueret, Andreas Hutfless, Gopal Indurkhya, and Martin Weiss. *Design and Implement Servlets, JSPs, and EJBs for IBM Web-Sphere Application Server*. IBM Redbooks, 2000. This book looks at enterprise beans and their cousins, servlets and JSPs, from the application server perspective. It covers critical runtime areas such as scalability, caching, and performance trade-offs. Available at `www.ibm.com/redbooks`.

- Rowan, Ed. *Mastering Enterprise JavaBeans*. John Wiley & Sons, 1999. Another classic book on enterprise bean development with many examples. Look at the new sections on J2EE.

- Seelemann, Irene, Cyrus Soleimany, Richard Gregory, and Agnes Lisowska. "Working with the New ERP Connectors Available in VisualAge for Java," *VisualAge Developer Domain,* September 2001. This article looks at connectors in the Enterprise Resource Planning (ERP) arena. Tools, identical to the ones we have shown, are used to access data in J.D. Edwards, Oracle applications, and PeopleSoft ERP systems. Available at `www.ibm.com/vadd`.

- The product documentation for VisualAge for Java, Enterprise Edition, Version 4.0, product documentation contains many samples similar to the one shown here. In the online help, look in the Samples section under the Enterprise Access Builder. In the Concepts section, you will find topics about the JCA connector architecture, managed connections, connection pooling, JNDI, and comparisons of JCA with the older Common Connector Framework (CCF) architecture. The Tasks section has topics that show you how to migrate applications coded previously in CCF to JCA, and information on deployment. The online help topics are also available as a compilation in PDF format.

CHAPTER 18

Embracing the J2EE Connector Architecture: The BEA WebLogic Experience

Deb June and Mitch Upton[1]

BEA Systems Inc.'s commitment to the development of the J2EE platform runs deep, and this commitment is amply demonstrated by the ongoing evolution of its flagship WebLogic Server product, widely acknowledged to be the industry's top J2EE-compliant application server. WebLogic has maintained its reputation as the first application server on the market to offer robust implementations of new J2EE specifications by emphasizing aggressive development of important components like the J2EE Connector Architecture. WebLogic Server 6.1, released in the summer of 2001, supports the J2EE Connector Architecture Specification Version 1.0.

In addition to supporting the J2EE Connector Architecture 1.0 in WebLogic Server, BEA has been proactive in its support of Enterprise Application Integration technology through its WebLogic Integration product, which was also available in the summer of 2001. WebLogic Integration (WLI) 2.0 complements and extends the J2EE Connector Architecture by providing value-added features such as bi-directional and asynchronous communication with Enterprise Information Systems. WLI also provides facilities for allowing business analysts to define customized, business-focused interfaces to Enterprise Information Systems. These interfaces, called Application Views, allow a business analyst to use the capabilities of Enterprise Information Systems from within WLI's Business Process Management system. The combination of Business Process Management and Application Views allows business analysts to rapidly wire together enterprise class applications that are able to respond to ever-changing business needs. In addition to initiating interactions with an

---

1. Deb June is Connector Technical Lead, eCommerce Server Division, at BEA Systems.
  Mitch Upton is Application Integration Architect, eCommerce Integration Division, at BEA Systems.

Enterprise Information System, WebLogic/WLI-enabled applications can also respond to events that originate inside of an Enterprise Information System.

As part of BEA's ongoing commitment to J2EE standards, BEA is actively participating in the expert group (under the Java Community Process) for the J2EE Connector Architecture 2.0 specification. BEA will use the new concepts and technologies employed in the WebLogic Server 6.1 and WebLogic Integration 2.0 products as a guide in its interaction with the expert group for Connector Architecture 2.0.

This chapter discusses the WebLogic server-specific implementation of the J2EE Connector architecture.

18.1 WebLogic Server's Implementation of the J2EE Connector Architecture Specification

The release of WebLogic Server 6.1 provides support for the J2EE Connector Architecture Specification Version 1.0 by implementing the application server requirements for the Connection Management, Security Management, and Transaction Management contracts. As with other J2EE components such as EJBs and Web Applications, a resource adapter also uses WebLogic Server's deployment, configuration, monitoring and logging facilities. These facilities provide resource adapters and tools providers an environment for quickly and easily testing their implementations and a mature, full-featured runtime environment for integrating Enterprise Information Systems.

18.1.1 WebLogic Server Supplementary Deployment Descriptor

In addition to supporting the features of the standard resource adapter configuration file, `ra.xml`, WebLogic Server 6.1 defines an additional deployment descriptor file. This file, called `weblogic-ra.xml`, contains parameters specifically used for configuring and deploying a resource adapter within WebLogic Server. This deployment descriptor file contains elements for

- Defining the connection pool and logging parameters for the implementation of the Connection Management system contract

- Security Principal Mapping for the implementation of the Security Management system contract

- A Configuration Property Mapping to complement the *config-property* elements of the *ra.xml* deployment descriptor file

- Some additional elements for deploying a J2EE Connector Architecture-based resource adapter within the WebLogic Server environment

WebLogic Server requires a resource adapter archive (.RAR file) to include a `weblogic-ra.xml` deployment descriptor file in addition to the `ra.xml` deployment descriptor file specified in the J2EE Connector 1.0 specification. However, if a standard resource adapter acquired from a Resource Adapter Provider is deployed in WebLogic Server without a weblogic-ra.xml file, a template `weblogic-ra.xml` file populated with default element values will automatically be added to the resource adapter archive. This automatic resource file generation simplifies the process of establishing the parameters necessary to deploy the resource adapter in WebLogic Server and expedites the overall Enterprise Application Integration process.

18.1.1.1 Configuring Error Logging and Tracing Facilities for the Resource Adapter

The J2EE Connector Architecture specification describes how a resource adapter can produce tracing and logging messages by implementing the `ManagedConnectionFactory.set` and `getLogWriter` methods. The `weblogic-ra.xml` descriptor file supports two elements that allow administrators to configure logging and tracing for resource adapters deployed in WebLogic Server. The `logging-enabled` element can be used by a resource adapter deployer to enable or disable logging for a specific ManagedConnectionFactory at deployment time. The `log-filename` element is provided to specify the filename to write the logging information that the ManagedConnectionFactory produces.

These elements, in conjunction with the `ManagedConnectionFactory.set` and `getLogWriter` methods, enable the ManagedConnectionFactory to produce tracing and logging messages that can be used to diagnose and troubleshoot possible problems that occur with the resource adapter and its interactions with the WebLogic Server subsystems at both design time and runtime.

18.1.1.2 Configuring Resource Adapter Properties

The `ra.xml` deployment descriptor file supports a set of `config-property` elements used to specify the configuration settings for a ManagedConnectionFactory instance. The default values of these configuration properties are typically set by the resource adapter provider. However, if a configuration property is not set, it is the responsibility of the resource adapter deployer to provide a value for the property.

WebLogic Server provides the means to set configuration properties through the use of the `map-config-property` element in the `weblogic-ra.xml` deployment descriptor file. To configure a set of configuration properties for a resource adapter, the deployer specifies a `map-config-property-name` and `map-config-property-value` pair for each property.

The `map-config-property` element can also be used to override the values specified in the `ra.xml` deployment descriptor file. Upon WebLogic Server startup, the `map-config-property` values in the `weblogic-ra.xml` file will be compared against the `config-property` values in the `ra.xml` file and if the configuration property names match, WebLogic Server will use the `map-config-property-value` for the corresponding configuration property name.

18.1.1.3   Configuring Security Credentials

In BEA WebLogic Server 6.1, the Resource Principal on whose behalf the EIS-side sign-on is performed is implemented by means of a Security Principal Mapping mechanism. This mapping allows a resource principal to be determined from the identity of the initiating/caller principal for the application component requesting an EIS connection.

The Security Principal Map is specified in the `security-principal-map` element in the `weblogic-ra.xml` deployment descriptor file. Each resource principal known to WebLogic Server is mapped to a corresponding user name and password. The password is encrypted using an encryption tool that transforms a `weblogic-ra.xml` file containing clear text passwords into a new `weblogic-ra.xml` file containing encrypted passwords. Using the WebLogic Server Administration Console, the common tool for configuring J2EE components within WebLogic Server, the encryption tool is automatically invoked when new or modified mappings are committed.

A default resource principal can be defined for the Connection Factory in the `security-principal-map` element. This default resource principal is used whenever the current identity is *not* matched elsewhere in the security principal map. The default resource principal is an optional element, however. It must be specified in some form if container-managed sign-on is supported by the resource adapter and used by *any* client.

In addition, the deployment-time population of the Connection Pool with ManagedConnections is attempted using the defined "default" resource principal if one is specified.

18.1.1.4   Linking to a Resource Adapter Reference

As defined in the J2EE Connector specification, the Java classes needed to implement the resource adapter system contracts are specified in the `ra.xml` deployment descriptor file. On deployment of the resource adapter, these classes are loaded and the instantiated objects are configured using information from the `weblogic-ra.xml` deployment descriptor file.

WebLogic Server provides an optimization to the loading and configuration of resource adapter object instances. An element called `ra-link-ref` is supported in the `weblogic-ra.xml` deployment descriptor file. This element allows the specification of a link from one Resource Adapter to another resource adapter representing the same EIS but having a different configuration. The linked resource adapter can then simply instantiate any required Java objects using the referenced resource adapter and configure those objects as needed for the new Resource Adaptor instance. This performance optimization eliminates the need to load Java classes that have previously been loaded by the referenced resource adapter.

18.1.2   Extended Connection Pool Services

BEA WebLogic Server supports an advanced connection pooling facility by providing optional settings and services to configure and automatically maintain the size of the connection pool.

18.1.2.1   Decreasing Runtime Performance Cost for ManagedConnection Creation

Creation of ManagedConnections can be expensive. The actual cost of the creation process is dependent upon the complexity of the Enterprise Integration System that the ManagedConnection is representing. As a result, the resource adapter deployer may decide to prepopulate the connection pool with an initial number of ManagedConnections on startup of WebLogic Server and therefore avoid paying the performance price for creating these connections when they are later requested. This behavior can be configured with the `initial-capacity` element in the `weblogic-ra.xml` deployment descriptor file. Note, however, that it may not be possible to prepopulate ManagedConnections for certain resource adapters. For instance, this is true for resource adapters that must create ManagedConnections using runtime parameters that are only known at the time of a connection request.

As stated in the J2EE Connector specification, when a connection is requested the application server can first try to match the type of connection being requested with any existing and available ManagedConnection in the connection pool. However, if a match is not found, a new ManagedConnection may be created to satisfy the connection request. As mentioned above, the creation of a ManagedConnection can be an expensive runtime operation. WebLogic Server provides a setting that allows a number of additional ManagedConnections to be created and added to the pool whenever a match is not found. This feature allows the deployer greater control over when to incur the performance hit of connection pool growth. The behavior can be configured using the `capacity-increment` element in the `weblogic-ra.xml` descriptor file.

Because there is no initiating security principal or request context information available at WebLogic Server startup, the initial ManagedConnections are created with a default security context. The number of initial ManagedConnections that are created is controlled by the `initial-capacity` setting. When additional Managed-Connections are created (in batch sizes controlled by the `capacity-increment` element), the first ManagedConnection is created with the known initiating principal and client request information—the security context association—of the connection request. The remaining ManagedConnections, up to the `capacity-increment` limit, are created using the same default security context as used when creating the initial ManagedConnections.

18.1.2.2   Controlling Connection Pool Growth

As more ManagedConnections are created over time, the amount of system resources consumed by the connection pool increases. The amount of resources consumed as each new ManagedConnection is added is dependent on the Enterprise Integration System involved, but it is possible that the consumption of a large amount of system resources could affect the performance of the overall system.

To control the effect of connection pool growth on system resources, WebLogic Server provides the resource adapter deployer a means for specifying the maximum allowed number of allocated ManagedConnections. This value can be established using the `maximum-capacity` element in the `weblogic-ra.xml` descriptor file. If a new ManagedConnection (or more than one ManagedConnection in the case of `capacity-increment` being greater than one) needs to be created during a connection request, WebLogic Server will ensure that no more than the maximum number of allowed ManagedConnections are created.

If the maximum number has been reached, WebLogic Server will attempt to recycle a ManagedConnection from the pool. In the case of a recycling attempt, WebLogic Server looks in the free pool for the least commonly requested ManagedConnection. If there are no connections to recycle, a warning will be logged indicating that the attempt to recycle failed and that the connection request could not be granted.

18.1.2.3   Controlling Connection Pool Shrinkage

Although setting the maximum number of ManagedConnections prevents the server from being overloaded by more allocated ManagedConnections than it can handle, it does not efficiently manage the amount of system resources that is needed if the connection request level diminishes over time. WebLogic Server provides a service that monitors the activity of ManagedConnections in the connection pool when resource adapters are in use.

If connection pool usage decreases and remains at this diminished level for an extended period of time, the size of the connection pool will be reduced to the smallest amount necessary to adequately and efficiently service the current connection request level. This service is turned on by default. However, to turn off this service the resource adapter deployer can set the `shrinking-enabled` element in the `weblogic-ra.xml` descriptor file to false. The `shrink-period-minutes` element in the `weblogic-ra.xml` descriptor file is used to control how frequently WebLogic Server calculates the need for connection pool size reduction and selectively removes unused ManagedConnections from the pool if needed.

18.1.3   Example `weblogic-ra.xml` Deployment Descriptor

Code Example 18.1 shows a `weblogic-ra.xml` deployment descriptor file associated with the `blackbox-notx.rar` provided with the J2EE 1.3 package.

Code Example 18.1 Sample Deployment Descriptor

```xml
<?xml version="1.0" encoding="UTF-8"?>
<!DOCTYPE weblogic-connection-factory-dd PUBLIC '-//BEA Systems,
Inc.//DTD WebLogic 6.0.0 Connector//EN' 'http://www.bea.com/servers/
wls600/dtd/weblogic-ejb-jar.dtd'>
<weblogic-connection-factory-dd>
  <connection-factory-name>LogicalNameOfBlackBoxNoTx
    </connection-factory-name>
  <jndi-name>eis/BlackBoxNoTxConnectorJNDINAME</jndi-name>
  <pool-params>
    <initial-capacity>1</initial-capacity>
    <max-capacity>10</max-capacity>
    <capacity-increment>1</capacity-increment>
    <shrinking-enabled>false</shrinking-enabled>
    <shrink-period-minutes>15</shrink-period-minutes>
  </pool-params>
  <map-config-property>
    <map-config-property-name>ConnectionURL
    </map-config-property-name>
    <map-config-property-value>jdbc:cloudscape:demo;create=true
    </map-config property-value>
  </map-config-property>
  <security-principal-map>
    <map-entry>
      <initiating-principal>*</initiating-principal>
      <resource-principal>
        <resource-username>default</resource-username>
        <resource-password>{3DES}Gx3I+wWRT/IRhDqhSmgzVA==
        </resource-password>
      </resource-principal>
    </map-entry>
    <map-entry>
      <initiating-principal>foo</initiating-principal>
      <resource-principal>
        <resource-username>foo_user</resource-username>
        <resource-password>{3DES}Ow7TRhtU3ZU=</resource-password>
      </resource-principal>
    </map-entry>
  </security-principal-map>
</weblogic-connection-factory-dd>
```

18.1.4   Deployment Descriptor Editor

WebLogic Server 6.1 introduced a new feature to its graphical Administration Console called the Deployment Descriptor Editor (or DD Editor, for short). This tool enables the Administrator to view and configure deployment descriptor values for the J2EE components deployed within a WebLogic Server domain.

For a resource adapter, the elements of the `ra.xml` and `weblogic-ra.xml` deployment descriptor files can be viewed and their values modified. Once values have been modified, they can be validated against the DTD for the corresponding deployment descriptor file by the click of a single button in the interface. After the modified element values have been validated, the newly configured values can be written to a persistent resource adapter archive. If it is desirable to use these newly saved values in the current WebLogic Server runtime instance, the resource adapter is simply redeployed. The resource adapter can be redeployed from either the Administration Console or from the command line. Either method conveniently eliminates the need to manually extract the contents of the resource adapter archive and then edit the deployment descriptor files with an XML editor every time the resource adapter needs to be reconfigured.

18.1.5   Monitoring a Resource Adapter in the WebLogic Server Environment

Once a resource adapter is deployed and is actively being accessed, it is important for the administrator to monitor the activity of the connection pool so that bottlenecks or other performance inefficiencies can be quickly identified. If the administrator determines that a bottleneck or inefficiency exists, the DD Editor can then be used to tune the connection pool to correct the problem. The Administration Console provides a tool for monitoring the overall health of deployed J2EE components. For a resource adapter component, this tool allows the monitoring of several activity states applicable to ManagedConnections and their corresponding Connection handles. (See Figure 18.2.)

Figure 18.1 shows the ManagedConnection activity for a sample resource adapter since the time of its deployment in WebLogic Server. Based on the Connections Created Total Count, Free Connections High Count, and Connections Matched Total Count, we can conclude that only one ManagedConnection has been allocated and used to match 338 connection requests. If other connection requests had been received that did not match this ManagedConnection, we would expect to see a Connections Rejected Total Count greater than zero. If a new ManagedConnection needed to be created to satisfy a connection request but the maximum number of allocated ManagedConnections had been exceeded, the connection pool would need to destroy the least used ManagedConnection from the free pool and recycle the ManagedConnection connection pool slot for use by a new ManagedConnection that satisfied the connection request. In this scenario,

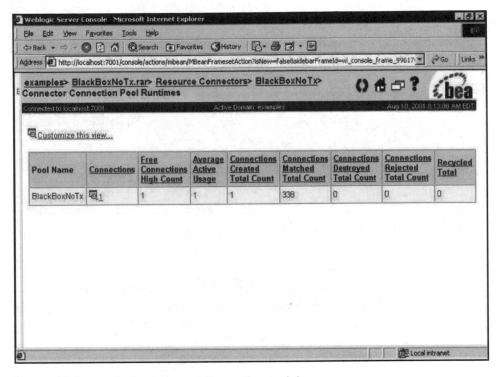

Figure 18.1 Monitoring ManagedConnection Activity

the Connections Destroyed Total Count and Recycled Total would have been greater than zero.

The Administration Console also provides information to monitor the Connection handle activity on the ManagedConnections, such as which Connection handles are currently active, which are involved in a transaction, and which are shared by more than one connection request.

18.2   WebLogic Integration 2.0

BEA WebLogic Integration (WLI) provides a WebLogic-based integration solution that supports open industry standards for connecting applications both within and between enterprises. It delivers application server, application integration, business process management, and Business-to-Business integration functionality that supports a *build to integrate* approach to enterprise application lifecycle management. The goal of WebLogic Integration is to speed development and deployment efforts, minimize the pain of integration, and lower the cost of ownership for IT investments.

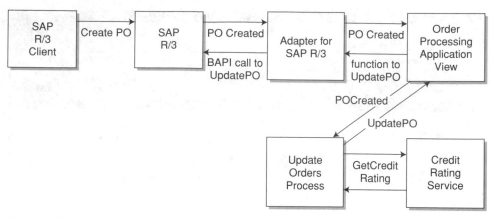

Figure 18.2 Business Process Management Component

The application integration component of WLI uses the J2EE Connector Architecture by building upon the Connector Architecture implementation in WebLogic Server 6.1 and adding the following value-added features:

- Bi-directional asynchronous communication with Enterprise Information Systems

- The definition of XML-based and business oriented interfaces to Enterprise Information Systems

- Rapid, simplified development and packaging of resource adapters

- Simplified communication model based on the concept of "services" to do work against an Enterprise Information System, and "events" to notify interested parties of work having been done against an Enterprise Information System. This communication model is embodied within an Application View.

WLI provides these additional features through the WLI Integration Framework and Adapter Development Kit (ADK). The Integration Framework is designed to host resource adapters that implement the value-added features defined by WLI. The Integration Framework provides services to these enhanced adapters and hosts Application Views that expose the adapter's capabilities as user-configured business-focused interfaces. The ADK provides base resource adapter implementations, and development frameworks that allow adapter developers to rapidly build resource adapters. Resource adapters built with the ADK are based on the J2EE Connector Architecture 1.0 specification, and can operate in any Connector Architecture 1.0 based application server. These same adapters can provide value-added features when running within the WLI Integration Framework and WebLogic Server.

18.2.1 Application Views

WLI defines all communication between Enterprise Information Systems and application components in terms of events and services. Events represent an occurrence of interest within an Enterprise Information System. An event is a Java object containing an XML document, making the data contained in the object available to any XML capable tool. The event contains XML data that describes the occurrence within the Enterprise Information System and the context in which it occurred. Services are business functions that can retrieve information from and cause changes within an Enterprise Information System. Services take request data in the form of an XML document, and return responses as an XML document. Because both the request and response are represented in XML, the data contained in them is available to any XML capable tool. Events and services are implemented using the capabilities of a WLI-compliant resource adapter. Thus, the combination of events, services, and a resource adapter bridges Enterprise Information System-specific data structures and capabilities into standard XML-based data structures and capabilities.

An Application View collects a set of events and services into an easy-to-use Enterprise Information System-neutral interface. Thus an Application View can be used to detect occurrences within, retrieve information from, and cause changes within an Enterprise Information System. Clients using an Application View can therefore make use of all the capabilities of an Enterprise Information System without knowing the communication and usage details of that system.

An Application View is used for a specific business purpose, and defines the events and services necessary to fulfill this business purpose. The Application View has a name and descriptive text that represents its business purpose.

Application Views are hosted within the WLI Integration Framework. The Integration Framework provides facilities for maintaining the metadata used to describe the Application View, and to deploy/undeploy the Application View within a running WebLogic Server instance. The Integration Framework also manages the relationship and communication between an Application View and its associated resource adapter.

For example, an Application View might be defined to handle the creation and maintenance of purchase orders within an SAP R/3 system. Such an Application View would use a resource adapter for the SAP R/3 system, and might be named "Order Processing". It might define events that indicate the creation of new purchase orders ("POCreated"), and the modification or deletion of existing purchase orders ("POUpdated" or "PODeleted"). It might also define services for creating new purchase orders ("CreatePO") and updating or deleting existing purchase orders ("UpdatePO" or "DeletePO"). This Application View thus provides an interface that allows the user to detect specific occurrences within SAP R/3 and to use a specific set of SAP R/3 functions. Because an Application View defines its events and services to use XML, the user can interact with SAP R/3 without having to use SAP R/3 data structures or communication methods.

An Enterprise Information System specialist defines an Application View at the request of a business analyst. This specialist applies knowledge of the Enterprise Information System to define events and services that meet the business needs described to him by the business analyst. Once the Application View is defined, the business analyst uses it within the Business Process Management component of WLI. Within the Business Process Management component, the business analyst uses business logic to wire together events and services from the Application View. In our example, the Business Analyst may define a business process called "Update Orders" that detects new purchase orders via a "POCreated" event, and updates them with information derived from other resources in the enterprise (for example, credit rating information), using the "UpdatePO" service. The Business Process Management component provides tools for extracting XML data from the incoming event, and composing the request XML document for the service.

18.2.2   Adapter Development Kit (ADK)

The J2EE Connector Architecture 1.0 specification defines a set of interfaces that must be implemented by a resource adapter that is based on the Connector architecture. The implementation of these interfaces can be development intensive. In addition, many adapter implementations contain a large set of common functionality. It would be wasteful for each adapter developer to independently implement this common functionality. The WLI Adapter Development Kit provides several application frameworks that embody common functionality required by adapters, allowing adapter developers to concentrate on adding value-added functionality specific to their Enterprise Information System.

The ADK can be used to rapidly build resource adapters that support the J2EE Connector Architecture. Resource adapters written using the ADK can be plugged into any J2EE compliant application server such as WebLogic Server 6.1. WLI defines adapters as having capabilities that are a superset of the capabilities defined by the Connector Architecture 1.0. WLI defines several components of an adapter to represent unique subsets of these capabilities. WLI defines adapters as being composed of three components:

- **Service Adapter**—Provides the ability to invoke functions within the Enterprise Information System and is used to implement Application View services

- **Event Adapter**—Provides the ability to detect occurrences within an Enterprise Information System and is used to implement Application View events

- **Design-time Component**—Provides the ability to browse metadata within an Enterprise Information System, and is used to define the events and services that make up an Application View

Adapters, as defined by the Connector Architecture 1.0 specification, fulfill the basic requirements of a WLI service adapter. Event adapters and design-time components of an adapter have no direct analog in the Connector Architecture 1.0 specification. The Connection Architecture 2.0 specification will address issues such as the implementation of additional WLI service adapter and event adapter features.

18.2.2.1 Service Adapters

A service adapter enables the execution of Application View services against an Enterprise Information System. The ADK provides an entire framework dedicated to the creation of service adapters. A service adapter written using the ADK fully supports Connector Architecture 1.0 based resource adapter. A service adapter is essentially a J2EE Connector Architecture based adapter that uses an enhanced form of Common Client Interface (CCI) to communicate with application components.

This enhanced CCI uses XML as the data structure for request and response data from an Enterprise Information System function and is named XML Common Client Interface (XCCI). The XCCI interface defines a custom CCI Record type that contains an XML document and is called a DocumentRecord. The DocumentRecord provides for the simple manipulation and extraction of XML data based on declarative hierarchical string expressions called XPaths. XPath is a standard XML data location facility specified by the W3C.

Any adapter that implements the XCCI interface can be used to implement services on an Application View hosted within the WLI Integration Framework. For example, an adapter that implements only the standard CCI interface needs to extend (to use the XCCI interface) before it can be used to implement services in WLI.

J2EE Connector Architecture-based adapters that do not implement the XCCI interface may be used as the starting point for implementing a WLI service adapter. Essentially, the adapter developer would build an XCCI interface that uses the underlying non-XCCI adapter. The ADK supports the development of such a hybrid adapter, and allows adapter developers to reuse existing adapters to reduce the effort and investment necessary to write a service adapter.

Service adapters are used by the WLI Integration Framework to implement services defined for an Application View. An Application View service corresponds directly to a function implemented by the service adapter. This function is accessed via the Interaction.execute method defined in CCI. The execute method takes a request Record, and a metadata object called an InteractionSpec. The InteractionSpec object contains the name of the function on the service adapter and, depending on the adapter implementation, any data needed by the function. An Application View service is always associated with an InteractionSpec object. At runtime, the Integration Framework handles mapping a service invocation on an Application View to the actual function on the service adapter by invoking Interaction.execute on the adapter.

The Integration Framework passes the request document provided by the user and the InteractionSpec object defined for the service to the Interaction.execute method. The execute method then invokes the named function on the service adapter passing data from the request document and InteractionSpec. The function on the service adapter thus has two "channels" of information to work with. The information in these two channels, taken together, must represent a set of information sufficient to perform the operation represented by the function on the service adapter. Placing more data in the InteractionSpec object allows the user to provide less data in the request document. This makes the function, and thus the service, easier to use. Thus, services can be used to hide complexity from the user (by placing more data into the InteractionSpec).

18.2.2.2   Event Adapters

An event adapter enables an application component to detect occurrences within an Enterprise Information System. The event adapter is used to implement events defined on Application Views representing business interfaces to that Enterprise Information System. Event adapters and the functions they perform are not defined by the Connector Architecture 1.0 specification. However, the capabilities of an event adapter are critical to achieving robust integration with an Enterprise Information System. Such capabilities will be addressed directly by the Connector Architecture 2.0 specification. BEA is committed to working with the Connector Architecture 2.0 expert group in defining these capabilities for the new specification.

An Event Adapter has the ability to listen and respond to events occurring within an EIS. The Event Adapter responds to events within an EIS by delivering an event object containing an XML payload into the WLI Integration Framework. The Integration Framework then notifies any application component interested in this type of event by delivering them a copy of the event object. This functionality provides bi-directional communication between the application component and the EIS. The WLI Integration Framework provides the infrastructure to host Event Adapters and to manage event subscriptions from application components.

An Event Adapter is composed of two main components; the event generator and the event router. The event generator is written by the adapter developer, and is specific to the Enterprise Information System. The event router is provided by the Integration Framework and is not specific to any Enterprise Information System. The event generator handles the detection of occurrences within the EIS and the creation of event objects that represent those occurrences. The event generator then hands the event objects over to the event router for delivery to application components. The event router maintains the subscription information from Application Clients that indicates each client's interest in certain types of events. The event router, upon receiving an event from the event generator, determines which application components are interested in the current type of event, and handles the delivery of the event into the Integration Framework.

The Event Adapter component of an adapter is logically separate from the service adapter component and is generally deployed separately. The service adapter is always deployed in the application server, and the event adapter is generally, though not always, deployed in a separate application server or servlet engine instance. The event router is logically associated with a single EIS instance, and not with the application server, and is thus deployed "closely" to the EIS. The term "close" in this case refers to the speed and reliability of the interprocess communication between the EIS and the event generator component of the event adapter. In most cases, the event adapter will actually run within an application server or servlet engine running on the same machine as the EIS. Figure 18.3 shows the relationship between the EIS, the event adapter, and subscribing application components.

From this diagram, we see that the event generator is completely isolated from the application components that will ultimately receive the events it creates. This allows the event generator to focus completely on the task of detecting EIS occurrences, and the events that represent them.

The ADK provides an entire framework for the creation of event generator components. This framework includes basic event generator implementations and utility classes for the creation of events.

18.2.2.3   Design-Time Components

The design-time component of an adapter is used to allow the user (business analyst or EIS specialist) to interactively define new Application Views using that

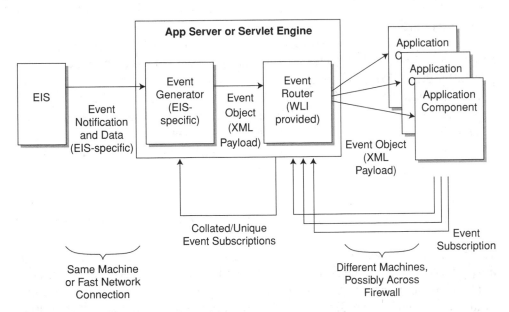

Figure 18.3 Component Relationships

adapter. The design-time component allows the user to "browse" metadata in the EIS and to interpret this metadata in terms of events and services. As the user browses the EIS, he or she defines events and services and collects them into an Application View.

How the user sees the metadata in the EIS, and what metadata corresponds to events and what metadata corresponds to services, is the choice of the adapter developer. The ADK includes a working sample database adapter (with source code), and a template adapter that serves as the starting point for new adapter development. The sample adapters each include a design-time component.

The database sample adapter defines events to represent inserts, deletes, or updates on rows in a database table. It defines services to represent the execution of SQL statements against the database. The database adapter allows the user to browse the tables defined in the database, and the columns defined for those tables. To create an event definition, the user selects a table, and indicates whether the event is to be fired for inserts, deletes, or updates on that table. To create a service, the user types in a SQL statement. The table browser can be used to assist the user in entering valid table and column names in that SQL statement. Other adapters will define events and services to represent different occurrences and functions, respectively, within the EIS.

The ADK provides base classes and Java Server Pages (JSP) templates for writing a JSP-based (Web-browser based) design-time interface. The design-time component, as supported by the ADK, is packaged as a J2EE Web application archive (WAR) file. Other client interface types (e.g., Swing GUI) are possible using the client application programming interface (API) for the WLI Integration Framework. However, the ADK only provides direct support for JSP-based design-time interfaces.

The design-time component can communicate with the EIS in any way the adapter developer wishes. However, the recommended approach, and the one employed by the design-time component of the database sample adapter, is to communicate with the EIS via the service adapter. This allows the design-time component to leverage the abilities already developed for the service adapter, and to guarantee similar results at both design-time and runtime. The service adapter for the DBMS sample adapter includes functions that help the design-time component retrieve and interpret the metadata for the database.

18.3   BEA Partners Adopting the J2EE Connector Architecture

The significant impact that the J2EE Connector Architecture is having on the industry has been clearly demonstrated in recent months by the high level of interest in the technology that has been shown by BEA's partners. By leveraging the capabilities of the WebLogic Server and WebLogic Integration products, system integrators and independent software vendors have already begun to build J2EE Connector Architecture-based resource adapters. These resource adapters will enable customers to leverage existing IT investments and build enterprise wide e-business solutions by integrating business-critical applications. Application integration tools built on top of the Connector Architecture will help to automate business processes both within the enterprise and over the public Internet for partners and customers alike.

The system integrators and independent software vendors that have shown interest in the Connector Architecture provide a wide array of software and services, including the production and integration of complex software systems like ERP, Supply Chain, Web to ERP, Web to mainframe, and Wireless Applications. These vendors cater to an extensive range of global markets such as finance, banking, health care, manufacturing, telecommunications, and government. The list of BEA partners that have already adopted the Connector Architecture and produced Resource Adapters includes such prominent companies as KPMG, Clarify (a Nortel Networks Company), Kana, Bull, Actional, Attunity, Stellcom, EzCommerce, Insevo (formerly B2B-ERP), Arsin Corporation, CSC, Infogain Corporation, and AMS. The resource adapters built by these companies support DBMS and ERP systems such as Oracle, CICS, DB2, VSAM, SAP, and even wireless messaging systems.

It is clear from this strong partner response that acceptance of the Connector Architecture is quickly growing not just among application server vendors but among ISVs and system integrators as well. In the long run, this strong adoption rate will mean nothing but good things for end users, who will be able to achieve a level of legacy application integration that was previously unobtainable.

18.3.1 Reference

Portions of this chapter are excerpted from the BEA WebLogic Server Programmer's Guide. Copyright BEA Systems, Inc. 2001. Reprinted with permission of BEA Systems. All rights reserved.

API Reference

THE J2EE Connector architecture defines a set of classes and methods for implementing both the application server side and resource adapter side of its system contracts. It also defines classes and interfaces for the CCI. This appendix provides a reference to these classes and methods, as defined by the Connector specification.

The Connector interfaces and classes are all found within the javax.resource package. The interfaces and classes are further organized into three packages beneath javax.resource:

- **javax.resource.cci**—Defines APIs for the Common Client Interface.

- **javax.resource.spi**—Defines APIs for system contracts.

- **javax.resource.spi.security**—Defines APIs for security contract.

A.1 javax.resource Package

The javax.resource package is the Connector architecture's top-level package. It includes one interface, Referenceable, and this interface extends the javax.naming.Referenceable interface.

This package also includes two exceptions: NotSupportedException and ResourceException. NotSupportedException is thrown to indicate that the caller, either a resource adapter or an application server for system contracts, cannot execute an operation because the operation is not supported. ResourceException is the root exception for the Connector architecture's exception hierarchy.

A.1.1 Referenceable Interface

The Referenceable interface extends the javax.naming.Referenceable interface. It provides support for the JNDI Reference mechanism, and this mechanism allows a connection factory to be registered in the JNDI namespace. Note that the implementation and structure of the Reference interface is specific to an application server.

An implementation class for a connection factory interface must implement both the java.io.Serializable and javax.resource.Referenceable interfaces to support JNDI registration.

This interface inherits the `getReference` method from the javax.naming.Reference interface.

setReference

```
public void setReference(javax.naming.Reference reference)
```

Sets the Reference instance. The deployment code calls this method to set the Reference that the `getReference` method can return later.

PARAMETERS:

`reference`   a Reference instance

A.2   javax.resource.cci Package

The javax.resource.cci package defines the Common Client Interface API.

A.2.1   Connection Interface

A Connection represents an application-level handle that uses a client to access the underlying physical connection. A ManagedConnection instance represents the actual physical connection associated with a Connection instance.

A client gets a Connection instance by using the `getConnection` method on a ConnectionFactory instance. A Connection instance can be associated with zero or more Interaction instances.

close

```
public void close() throws ResourceException;
```

Initiates close of the connection handle at the application level. Once a connection has been closed, a client should not use that closed connection to interact with an EIS.

EXCEPTIONS:

ResourceException   thrown when the close operation on a connection
                         handle fails

createInteraction

```
public Interaction createInteraction() throws ResourceException;
```

Creates an Interaction instance and associates it with this Connection instance. An Interaction enables an application to execute EIS functions.

RETURNS:
an Interaction instance for the Connection

EXCEPTIONS:
ResourceException   thrown when the method fails to create an Interaction

getLocalTransaction

```
public LocalTransaction getLocalTransaction() throws ResourceException;
```

Returns a LocalTransaction instance that enables a component to demarcate resource manager local transactions on the Connection. Some resource adapters may not allow a component to use the LocalTransaction interface to demarcate local transactions on a Connection. If so, the getLocalTransaction method should throw a NotSupportedException.

RETURNS:
a LocalTransaction instance

EXCEPTIONS:

ResourceException	thrown when the method fails to return a LocalTransaction instance because of a resource adapter error
NotSupportedException	thrown if this Connection does not support demarcation of resource manager local transactions

getMetaData

```
public ConnectionMetaData getMetaData() throws ResourceException;
```

Gets the information on the underlying EIS instance that is represented through an active connection.

RETURNS:
a ConnectionMetaData instance representing information about the EIS instance

EXCEPTIONS:

ResourceException   thrown when the method fails to get information about the connected EIS instance. The error may be internal to the resource adapter, specific to the EIS, or communication related.

getResultSetInfo

```
public ResultSetInfo getResultSetInfo() throws ResourceException;
```

Gets the information on the ResultSet functionality supported by a connected EIS instance.

RETURNS:

a ResultSetInfo instance representing ResultSet functionality supported by the EIS instance

EXCEPTIONS:

ResourceException   thrown when the method fails to get ResultSet-related information

NotSupportedException   thrown if ResultSet functionality is not supported

A.2.2   ConnectionFactory Interface

ConnectionFactory provides an interface that an application can use to get a connection to an EIS instance. A resource adapter is responsible for providing an implementation of the ConnectionFactory interface. The application code looks up a ConnectionFactory instance from the JNDI namespace, and then uses that instance to get an EIS connection.

The ConnectionFactory interface extends two interfaces: java.io.Serializable and javax.resource.Referenceable. An implementation class for ConnectionFactory is required to implement both these interfaces to support JNDI registration.

getConnection

```
public Connection getConnection() throws ResourceException;
public Connection getConnection(ConnectionSpec properties)
    throws ResourceException;
```

Gets a connection to an EIS instance. An application component should use the first variant of getConnection when the component wants the container to manage EIS sign-on. This is referred to as container-managed sign-on. When using this variant, the component does not pass any security information with the method.

A component should use the second `getConnection` variant, with the javax.resource.cci.ConnectionSpec parameter, if it needs to pass any resource adapter-specific security information and connection parameters. This variant of the method is often used in the component-managed sign-on case. An application component passes security information, such as user name and password, via the ConnectionSpec instance.

Note that the properties passed through the `getConnection` method should be specific to the client, such as user name, password, and language. These properties should not be related to the configuration of a target EIS instance, such as port number and server name.

The ManagedConnectionFactory instance is configured with a complete set of properties required for the creation of a connection to an EIS instance.

PARAMETERS:

`properties`   the Connection parameters and security information specified within a ConnectionSpec instance. (This parameter is used only in the second variant of the method.)

RETURNS:

a Connection instance

EXCEPTIONS:

ResourceException   thrown when the method fails to get a connection to the EIS instance. Examples of possible failures are:

- invalid specification of input parameters
- invalid configuration of a ManagedConnectionFactory instance. (For example, it may be configured with an invalid server name.)
- an error internal to the application server, such as an error related to connection pooling
- a communication error
- an error specific to the EIS, such as the EIS is not active
- an error internal to the resource adapter
- an error related to security, such as an invalid user
- a failure to allocate system resources

getMetaData

```
public ResourceAdapterMetaData getMetaData() throws ResourceException;
```

Gets metadata for the resource adapter. Note that the metadata information is about the resource adapter and not the EIS instance. You can invoke this method without first establishing an active connection to an EIS instance.

RETURNS:

a ResourceAdapterMetaData instance representing information about the resource adapter

EXCEPTIONS:

ResourceException   thrown when the method fails to get metadata information about the resource adapter

getRecordFactory

```
public RecordFactory getRecordFactory() throws ResourceException;
```

Gets a RecordFactory instance. The RecordFactory is used for the creation of generic Record instances.

RETURNS:

a RecordFactory instance

EXCEPTIONS:

ResourceException   thrown when the method fails to create a
                           RecordFactory
NotSupportedException   thrown when the operation is not supported

A.2.3   ConnectionMetaData Interface

The ConnectionMetaData interface provides information about an EIS instance connected through a Connection instance. A component calls the `Connection.get-MetaData` method to get a ConnectionMetaData instance.

getEISProductName

```
public java.lang.String getEISProductName() throws ResourceException;
```

Returns the product name of the underlying EIS instance connected through the Connection that produced this metadata.

RETURNS:

the product name of the EIS instance

EXCEPTIONS:

ResourceException   thrown when the method fails to get the information for
                       the EIS instance

getEISProductVersion

```
public java.lang.String getEISProductVersion() throws ResourceException;
```

Returns the product version of the underlying EIS instance connected through
the Connection that produced this metadata.

RETURNS:

the product version of the EIS instance

EXCEPTIONS:

ResourceException   thrown when the method fails to get the information for
                       the EIS instance

getUserName

```
public java.lang.String getUserName() throws ResourceException;
```

Returns the user name for an active connection as known to the underlying
EIS instance. The name corresponds to the resource principal under whose
security context a connection to the EIS instance has been established.

RETURNS:

a String representing the user name

EXCEPTIONS:

ResourceException   thrown when the method fails to get the information for
                       the EIS instance

A.2.4   ConnectionSpec Interface

An application component uses the ConnectionSpec interface to pass connection
request-specific properties to the `ConnectionFactory.getConnection` method.

It is recommended that you implement the ConnectionSpec interface as a Java-
Bean so that it supports tools. You must use the getter and setter methods pattern to
define the properties on the ConnectionSpec implementation class.

The CCI specification defines a set of standard properties for a Connection-Spec. The properties are defined either on a derived interface or an implementation class of an empty ConnectionSpec interface. In addition, a resource adapter may define additional properties specific to its underlying EIS.

A.2.5   IndexedRecord Interface

The IndexedRecord interface represents an ordered collection of record elements based on the java.util.List interface. This interface allows a client to access elements by their integer index (position in the list) and search for elements in the list.

IndexedRecord extends javax.resource.cci.Record, java.util.List, and java.io.Serializable. It inherits its methods from the Record and List interfaces.

A.2.6   Interaction Interface

The Interaction interface enables a component to execute EIS functions. An Interaction instance supports two execute methods that enable a component to interact with an EIS instance:

- One form of the execute method takes an input Record, an output Record, and an InteractionSpec. This method executes the EIS function represented by the InteractionSpec and updates the output Record.

- A second form of the method takes an input Record and an InteractionSpec. This method executes the EIS function represented by the InteractionSpec and produces the output Record as a return value.

An Interaction instance is created from a Connection and is required to maintain its association with the Connection instance. Execution of the close method releases all resources maintained by the resource adapter for the Interaction. However, the close of an Interaction instance should not close the associated Connection instance.

clearWarnings

```
public void clearWarnings() throws ResourceException;
```

Clears all the warnings reported by this Interaction instance. After a call to this method, the getWarnings method will return null until a new warning is reported for this Interaction.

EXCEPTIONS:

ResourceException   thrown when the method fails to clear the resource warnings associated with the Interaction

close

```
public void close() throws ResourceException;
```

Closes the current Interaction and releases all the resources held for this instance by the resource adapter. The close of an Interaction instance does not close the associated Connection instance. It is recommended that Interaction instances be closed explicitly to free any held resources.

EXCEPTIONS:

ResourceException   thrown when the method fails to close the Interaction instance. Invoking close on an already closed Interaction should also throw this exception.

execute

```
public boolean execute(InteractionSpec ispec, Record input,
    Record output) throws ResourceException;
```

```
public Record execute(InteractionSpec ispec, Record input)
    throws ResourceException;
```

Executes an interaction represented by the InteractionSpec. The first form of the method invocation takes an input Record and updates the output Record. The second form of the method takes an input Record and returns an output Record if the execution of the Interaction is successful.

PARAMETERS:

ispec   the InteractionSpec representing a target EIS data or function module
input   the Input Record
output   the Output Record

RETURNS:

The first form returns true if the execution of the EIS function is successful and the output Record has been updated; otherwise, it returns false. The second form returns the output Record if execution of the EIS function is successful; otherwise, it returns null.

EXCEPTIONS:

ResourceException   thrown when the method operation fails. Examples of possible errors are:

- invalid specification of an InteractionSpec, input, or output record structure
- errors in the use of input or output Record
- invalid connection associated with this Interaction
- a communication error
- an error specific to the EIS
- an error internal to the resource adapter

NotSupportedException   thrown when the operation is not supported

getConnection

```
public Connection getConnection();
```

Gets the Connection associated with the Interaction.

RETURNS:
the Connection instance associated with the Interaction

getWarnings

```
public ResourceWarning getWarnings() throws ResourceException;
```

Gets the first ResourceWarning from the chain of warnings associated with this Interaction instance.

RETURNS:
the ResourceWarning at the top of the warning chain

EXCEPTIONS:

ResourceException   thrown when the method fails to get the ResourceWarnings associated with the Interaction

A.2.7   InteractionSpec Interface

An InteractionSpec holds the properties that drive an Interaction with an EIS instance. An Interaction uses the InteractionSpec to execute the specified function on an underlying EIS.

The CCI specification defines a set of standard properties for an Interaction-Spec. An InteractionSpec implementation is not required to support a standard property if that property does not apply to its underlying EIS.

The InteractionSpec standard properties are:

- FunctionName—the name of an EIS function

- InteractionVerb—the mode of interaction with an EIS instance. The mode can be one of these values:

  - SYNC_SEND—This field indicates that the execution of an Interaction performs only a send to the target EIS instance. There is no synchronous response in terms of an output Record or ResultSet.

  - SYNC_SEND_RECEIVE—This field indicates that the execution of an Interaction sends a request to an EIS instance and synchronously receives a response.

  - SYNC_RECEIVE—This field indicates that the execution of an Interaction results in a synchronous receive of an output Record.

- ExecutionTimeout—the number of milliseconds an Interaction waits for an EIS to execute the specified function

The following standard properties can be used to give hints to an Interaction instance about ResultSet requirements:

- FetchSize

- FetchDirection

- MaxFieldSize

- ResultSetType

- ResultSetConcurrency

A CCI implementation can provide additional properties beyond that described in the InteractionSpec interface. Note that the format and type of the additional properties are specific to an EIS and are outside the scope of the CCI specification.

The InteractionSpec interface must be implemented as a JavaBean for toolability support. Thus the InteractionSpec implementation class must provide getter and setter methods for each of its supported properties, and properties can only be defined through these methods. The getter and setter methods convention should be based on the JavaBeans design pattern.

An implementation class for the InteractionSpec interface is required to implement the java.io.Serializable interface.

A.2.8   LocalTransaction Interface

A LocalTransaction defines a transaction demarcation interface for resource manager local transactions. Note that this interface is used for application-level local transaction demarcation. There is a comparable system contract-level LocalTransaction interface defined in the javax.resource.spi package that the container uses for local transaction management.

A local transaction is managed internal to a resource manager. No external transaction manager is involved in the coordination of such transactions.

A CCI implementation may implement the LocalTransaction interface, but this is not required. When a CCI implementation supports the LocalTransaction interface, the `Connection.getLocalTransaction` method should return a LocalTransaction instance. A component can then use the returned LocalTransaction to demarcate a resource manager local transaction (associated with the Connection instance) on the underlying EIS instance.

begin

```
public void begin() throws ResourceException;
```

Begins a local transaction on an EIS instance.

EXCEPTIONS:

ResourceException   thrown when the method fails to begin a local transaction. The method may fail because of a resource adapter internal error or an EIS-specific error, or because the Connection is already participating in a local or JTA transaction.

commit

```
public void commit() throws ResourceException;
```

Commits the current local transaction and releases all locks held by the underlying EIS instance.

EXCEPTIONS:

ResourceException   thrown when the method fails to commit a local transaction. Possible reasons for the method to fail are:

- a resource adapter internal error
- an EIS-specific error

- the Connection is already participating in an active JTA transaction
- there has been a violation of integrity constraints, deadlock detection, or a communication failure during transaction completion
- a retry requirement has occurred
- the transaction context is invalid. The `commit` operation was invoked without an active transaction context.

rollback

```
public void rollback() throws ResourceException;
```

Rolls back the current resource manager local transaction.

EXCEPTIONS:

ResourceException   thrown when the method fails to roll back a local transaction. The method may fail because of:

- a resource adapter internal error
- an EIS-specific error
- the Connection is already participating in an active JTA transaction
- the transaction context is invalid. The `rollback` operation was invoked without an active transaction context.

A.2.9   MappedRecord Interface

The MappedRecord interface is used for key-value map-based representations of record elements. The MappedRecord interface extends both the Record and java.util.Map interfaces.

A.2.10   Record Interface

The Record interface is the base interface for representing an input or output record to the `execute` methods defined on an Interaction.

It is possible to extend the Record interface to form one of the following representations:

- **MappedRecord**—A record represented by a key-value pair-based collection. This interface is based on the java.util.Map interface.

- **IndexedRecord**—A record represented by an ordered and indexed collection. This interface is based on the java.util.List interface.

- **JavaBean-based representation of an EIS abstraction**—For example, a custom record generated to represent a purchase order in an ERP system.

- **javax.resource.cci.ResultSet**—An interface that extends both java.sql.ResultSet and javax.resource.cci.Record. A ResultSet represents tabular data.

A MappedRecord or IndexedRecord can contain another Record. Thus you can use MappedRecord and IndexedRecord to create a hierarchical structure of any arbitrary depth. A basic Java type is used as the leaf element of a hierarchical structure represented by a MappedRecord or IndexedRecord.

clone

```
public java.lang.Object clone() throws
    java.lang.CloneNotSupportedException;
```

Creates and returns a copy of this object. The precise meaning of "copy" may depend on the class of the object. This method overrides the `java.lang.Object.clone` method.

EXCEPTIONS:

java.lang.CloneNotSupportedException   thrown when the object's class does not support the Cloneable interface. Subclasses that override the `clone` method can also throw this exception to indicate that an instance cannot be cloned.

equals

```
public boolean equals(java.lang.Object other);
```

Checks if this instance is equal to another Record.

PARAMETERS:

other   the other Record instance

RETURNS:
true, if the two instances are equal

getRecordName

```
public java.lang.String getRecordName();
```

Gets the name of the Record.

RETURNS:
a String representing the name of the Record

getRecordShortDescription

```
public java.lang.String getRecordShortDescription();
```

Gets a short description string for the Record. Application development tools primarily use this property.

RETURNS:
a String representing a short description of the Record

hashCode

```
public int hashCode();
```

Returns the hashCode for the Record instance.

RETURNS:
the hash code of this instance

setRecordName

```
public void setRecordName(java.lang.String name);
```

Sets the name of the Record.

PARAMETERS:
name   the name of the Record

setRecordShortDescription

```
public void setRecordShortDescription(java.lang.String description);
```

Sets a short description string for the Record. Application development tools primarily use this property.

PARAMETERS:

`description`   the description of the Record

A.2.11 RecordFactory Interface

The RecordFactory interface is used for creating MappedRecord and Indexed-Record instances. Note that the RecordFactory is only used for creation of generic record instances. A CCI implementation provides an implementation class for the RecordFactory interface.

createIndexedRecord

```
public IndexedRecord createIndexedRecord(java.lang.String recordName)
    throws ResourceException;
```

Creates an IndexedRecord. The method takes the name of the record that is to be created by the RecordFactory. The name of the record acts as a pointer to the meta information (stored in the metadata repository) for a specific record type.

PARAMETERS:

`recordName`   the name of the Record

RETURNS:

an IndexedRecord

EXCEPTIONS:

ResourceException   thrown when the method fails to create an
                         IndexedRecord. Examples of possible errors are:

- invalid specification of a record name
- an error internal to the resource adapter
- failure to access the metadata repository

NotSupportedException   thrown when the operation is not supported

createMappedRecord

```
public MappedRecord createMappedRecord(java.lang.String recordName)
    throws ResourceException;
```

> Creates a MappedRecord. The method takes the name of the record that is to be created by the RecordFactory. The name of the record acts as a pointer to the meta information (stored in the metadata repository) for a specific record type.

> **PARAMETERS:**
> recordName   the name of the Record

> **RETURNS:**
> a MappedRecord

> **EXCEPTIONS:**

ResourceException	thrown when the method fails to create a MappedRecord. Examples of possible errors are:
	• invalid specification of a record name
	• an error internal to the resource adapter
	• failure to access the metadata repository
NotSupportedException	thrown when the operation is not supported

A.2.12 ResourceAdapterMetaData Interface

The ResourceAdapterMetaData interface provides information about capabilities of a resource adapter implementation. Note that this interface does not provide information about an EIS instance that is connected through the resource adapter.

A CCI client uses a `ConnectionFactory.getMetaData` method to get metadata information about the resource adapter. The `getMetaData` method does not require an active connection to an EIS instance.

The ResourceAdapterMetaData can be extended to provide more information specific to a resource adapter implementation.

getAdapterName

```
public java.lang.String getAdapterName();
```

> Gets the name of the resource adapter in a form capable of being displayed by a tool.

RETURNS:

a String representing the name of the resource adapter

getAdapterShortDescription

```
public java.lang.String getAdapterShortDescription();
```

Gets a short description of the resource adapter in a form capable of being displayed by a tool.

RETURNS:

a String describing the resource adapter

getAdapterVendorName

```
public java.lang.String getAdapterVendorName();
```

Gets the name of the vendor that provided the resource adapter.

RETURNS:

a String representing the name of the resource adapter vendor

getAdapterVersion

```
public java.lang.String getAdapterVersion();
```

Gets the version of the resource adapter.

RETURNS:

a String representing the version of the resource adapter

getInteractionSpecsSupported

```
public java.lang.String[] getInteractionSpecsSupported();
```

Returns an array of fully qualified names of InteractionSpec types supported by the CCI implementation for this resource adapter. Note that the fully qualified class name is for the implementation class of an InteractionSpec. Tools vendors may use this method to find information on the supported InteractionSpec types. The method should return an array of length 0 if the CCI implementation does not define specific InteractionSpec types.

RETURNS:
an array of fully qualified class names of InteractionSpec classes supported by this resource adapter's CCI implementation

getSpecVersion

```
public java.lang.String getSpecVersion();
```

Returns a string representation of the version of the Connector architecture specification supported by the resource adapter.

RETURNS:
a String representing the supported version of the Connector architecture

supportsExecuteWithInputAndOutputRecord

```
public boolean supportsExecuteWithInputAndOutputRecord();
```

Returns true if the implementation class for the Interaction interface implements the `public boolean execute(InteractionSpec ispec, Record input, Record output)` method; otherwise, the method returns false.

RETURNS:
a boolean whose value depends on the method support

supportsExecuteWithInputRecordOnly

```
public boolean supportsExecuteWithInputRecordOnly();
```

Returns true if the implementation class for the Interaction interface implements the `public Record execute(InteractionSpec ispec, Record input)` method; otherwise, the method returns false.

RETURNS:
a boolean whose value depends on the method support

supportsLocalTransactionDemarcation

```
public boolean supportsLocalTransactionDemarcation();
```

Returns true if the resource adapter implements the LocalTransaction interface and supports local transaction demarcation on the underlying EIS instance through the LocalTransaction interface.

RETURNS:

true if the resource adapter supports resource manager local transaction demarcation through the LocalTransaction interface; otherwise, returns false

A.2.13 ResultSet Interface

A ResultSet interface represents tabular data that is retrieved from an EIS instance by the execution of an Interaction. The CCI ResultSet is based on the JDBC ResultSet. This interface extends the javax.resource.cci.Record and java.sql.ResultSet interfaces.

A.2.14 ResultSetInfo Interface

The ResultSetInfo interface provides information on the support provided for ResultSet by a connected EIS instance. A component calls the `Connection.getResultInfo` method to get the ResultSetInfo instance.

A CCI implementation is not required to support the ResultSetInfo interface. The implementation of this interface is provided only if the CCI supports the ResultSet facility.

deletesAreDetected

```
public boolean deletesAreDetected(int type) throws ResourceException;
```

Indicates whether a ResultSet has been deleted.

PARAMETERS:

type   the type of the ResultSet

RETURNS:

true if the ResultSet has been deleted; otherwise, returns false

EXCEPTIONS:

ResourceException   thrown when the method fails

insertsAreDetected

```
public boolean insertsAreDetected(int type) throws ResourceException;
```

Indicates whether a visible row insert can be detected by calling `Result-Set.rowInserted`.

PARAMETERS:
type   the type of the ResultSet

RETURNS:
true if result set type is changed; otherwise, returns false

EXCEPTIONS:
ResourceException   thrown when the method fails

othersDeletesAreVisible

```
public boolean othersDeletesAreVisible(int type) throws ResourceException;
```

Indicates whether deletes made by others are visible.

PARAMETERS:
type   the type of the ResultSet

RETURNS:
true if deletes by others are visible for the ResultSet type; otherwise, returns false

EXCEPTIONS:
ResourceException   thrown when the method fails

othersInsertsAreVisible

```
public boolean othersInsertsAreVisible(int type) throws ResourceException;
```

Indicates whether inserts made by others are visible.

PARAMETERS:
type   the type of the ResultSet

RETURNS:
true if inserts by others are visible for the ResultSet type; otherwise, returns false

EXCEPTIONS:
ResourceException   thrown when the method fails

othersUpdatesAreVisible

```
public boolean othersUpdatesAreVisible(int type) throws ResourceException;
```

Indicates whether updates made by others are visible.

PARAMETERS:
type   the type of the ResultSet

RETURNS:
true if updates by others are visible for the ResultSet type; otherwise, returns false

EXCEPTIONS:
ResourceException   thrown when the method fails

ownDeletesAreVisible

```
public boolean ownDeletesAreVisible(int type) throws ResourceException;
```

Indicates whether deletes are visible.

PARAMETERS:
type   the type of the ResultSet

RETURNS:
true if deletes are visible for the ResultSet type; otherwise, returns false

EXCEPTIONS:
ResourceException   thrown when the method fails

ownInsertsAreVisible

```
public boolean ownInsertsAreVisible(int type) throws ResourceException;
```

Indicates whether inserts are visible.

PARAMETERS:
type   the type of the ResultSet

RETURNS:
true if inserts are visible for the ResultSet type; otherwise, returns false

EXCEPTIONS:
ResourceException   thrown when the method fails

ownUpdatesAreVisible

```
public boolean ownUpdatesAreVisible(int type) throws ResourceException;
```

Indicates whether updates are visible.

PARAMETERS:
`type`   the type of the ResultSet

RETURNS:
true if updates are visible for the ResultSet type; otherwise, returns false

EXCEPTIONS:
ResourceException   thrown when the method fails

supportsResultSetType

```
public boolean supportsResultSetType(int type) throws ResourceException;
```

Indicates whether a resource adapter supports a specific ResultSet type.

PARAMETERS:
`type`   the type of the ResultSet

RETURNS:
true if the ResultSet type is supported; otherwise, returns false

EXCEPTIONS:
ResourceException   thrown when the method fails

supportsResultTypeConcurrency

```
public boolean supportsResultTypeConcurrency(int type, int concurrency)
    throws ResourceException;
```

Indicates whether a resource adapter supports the concurrency type in combination with the given ResultSet type.

PARAMETERS:
`type`   the type of the ResultSet
`concurrency`   ResultSet concurrency type defined in java.sql.ResultSet

RETURNS:
true if the specified combination is supported; otherwise, returns false

EXCEPTIONS:

ResourceException   thrown when the method fails

updatesAreDetected

```
public boolean updatesAreDetected(int type) throws ResourceException;
```

Indicates whether a visible row update can be detected by calling the `Result-Set.rowUpdated` method.

PARAMETERS:

`type`   the type of the ResultSet

RETURNS:

true if changes can be detected by the ResultSet type; otherwise, returns false

EXCEPTIONS:

ResourceException   thrown when the method fails

A.2.15 Streamable Interface

The Streamable interface enables a resource adapter to extract data from an input Record or to set data into an output Record as a stream of bytes.

The Streamable interface provides a resource adapter's view of the data that has been set in a Record instance by a component.

A component does not directly use the Streamable interface. A resource adapter implementation uses this interface. A component uses Record or one of its derived interfaces to manage records.

read

```
public void read(java.io.InputStream istream) throws java.io.IOException;
```

Reads data from an InputStream and initializes fields of a Streamable object.

PARAMETERS:

`istream`   InputStream that represents a resource adapter-specific internal representation of fields of a Streamable object

write

```
public void write(java.io.OutputStream ostream) throws
    java.io.IOException;
```

Writes fields of a Streamable object to an OutputStream.

PARAMETERS:

ostream   OutputStream that holds the value of a Streamable object

A.2.16 Exception ResourceWarning Class

ResourceWarning provides information on warnings related to the execution of an interaction with an EIS. Warnings are silently chained to the object whose method caused it to be reported. ResourceWarning extends ResourceException.

A.3   javax.resource.spi Package

The javax.resource.spi package defines a set of interfaces for the application server implementing the system contracts.

A.3.1   ConnectionEvent Class

The ConnectionEvent class provides information about the source of a connection-related event. The class implements the java.io.Serializable interface and extends java.util.EventObject.
A ConnectionEvent instance contains the following information:

- The type of the connection event

- The ManagedConnection instance that generated the connection event. The ConnectionEvent method getSource returns a ManagedConnection instance.

- The connection handle associated with the ManagedConnection instance. A connection handle is required for the CONNECTION_CLOSED event and is optional for other event types.

- Optionally, an exception indicating the connection-related error. Note that this exception is used for CONNECTION_ERROR_OCCURRED.

This class defines the following types of event notifications. Each event notification is defined as a `public static final int`.

- CONNECTION_CLOSED—Event notification that an application component has closed the connection

- LOCAL_TRANSACTION_STARTED—Event notification that a resource manager LocalTransaction was started on the connection

- LOCAL_TRANSACTION_COMMITTED—Event notification that a resource manager LocalTransaction was committed on the connection

- LOCAL_TRANSACTION_ROLLEDBACK—Event notification that a resource manager LocalTransaction was rolled back on the connection

- CONNECTION_ERROR_OCCURRED—Event notification that an error occurred on the connection. This event indicates that the ManagedConnection instance is now invalid and unusable.

A.3.2   ConnectionEventListener Interface

The ConnectionEventListener interface provides an event callback mechanism to enable an application server to receive notifications from a ManagedConnection instance. An application server uses these event notifications to manage its connection pool, clean up any invalid or terminated connections, and manage local transactions.

An application server implements the ConnectionEventListener interface. It registers a connection listener with a ManagedConnection instance by using the `ManagedConnection.addConnectionEventListener` method.

This interface extends the java.util.EventListener interface.

connectionClosed

```
public void connectionClosed(ConnectionEvent event);
```

Notifies that an application component has closed the connection.

A ManagedConnection instance notifies its registered set of listeners by calling the `ConnectionEventListener.connectionClosed` method when an application component closes a connection handle. The application server uses this connection close event to put the ManagedConnection instance back into the connection pool.

PARAMETERS:

event   event object describing the source of the event

connectionErrorOccurred

```
public void connectionErrorOccurred(ConnectionEvent event);
```

Notifies of a connection-related error. The ManagedConnection instance calls the `ConnectionEventListener.connectionErrorOccurred` method to notify its registered listeners of the occurrence of a physical connection-related error. The event notification happens just before a resource adapter throws an exception to the application component using the connection handle. The `connectionErrorOccurred` method indicates that the associated ManagedConnection instance is now invalid and unusable. The application server handles the connection error event notification by initiating its application server-specific cleanup—such as removing the ManagedConnection instance from the connection pool—and then calling the `ManagedConnection.destroy` method to destroy the physical connection.

PARAMETERS:
event   event object describing the source of the event

localTransactionCommitted

```
public void localTransactionCommitted(ConnectionEvent event);
```

Notifies that a resource manager local transaction was committed on the ManagedConnection instance.

PARAMETERS:
event   event object describing the source of the event

localTransactionRolledback

```
public void localTransactionRolledback(ConnectionEvent event);
```

Notifies that a resource manager local transaction was rolled back on the ManagedConnection instance.

PARAMETERS:
event   event object describing the source of the event

localTransactionStarted

```
public void localTransactionStarted(ConnectionEvent event);
```

Notifies that a resource manager local transaction was started on the ManagedConnection instance.

PARAMETERS:

event   event object describing the source of the event

A.3.3   ConnectionManager Interface

The ConnectionManager interface provides a hook for the resource adapter to pass a connection request to the application server.

An application server provides the implementation of the ConnectionManager interface. This implementation is not specific to any particular type of resource adapter or connection factory interface.

The ConnectionManager implementation delegates the quality of services (QoS) role to the application server. The application server provides these services, which consist of security, connection pool management, transaction management, and error logging/tracing. An application server implements these services in a generic manner, independent of any resource adapter and EIS-specific mechanisms. The Connector architecture does not specify how an application server implements these services, and each implementation is specific to an application server.

After a connection request has been initiated and an application server has hooked in its services with the resource adapter, the connection request is delegated to a ManagedConnectionFactory instance. The ManagedConnectionFactory determines whether to create a new physical connection or to match the request to an already existing physical connection.

A class that implements the ConnectionManager interface is also required to implement the java.io.Serializable interface.

In a nonmanaged application scenario, either an application developer provides the ConnectionManager implementation class or a resource adapter provides a default ConnectionManager implementation. In both cases, third-party vendors can provide quality of services as separate components.

allocateConnection

```
public java.lang.Object allocateConnection
    (ManagedConnectionFactory mcf, ConnectionRequestInfo cxRequestInfo)
    throws ResourceException;
```

A connection factory instance for a resource adapter calls the `allocateConnection` method to pass a connection request to the ConnectionManager instance.

The `ConnectionRequestInfo` parameter represents information specific to the resource adapter for handling the connection request.

PARAMETERS:

`mcf`	used by the application server to delegate a request for connection matching or creation
`cxRequestinfo`	connection request information

RETURNS:

a connection handle with an EIS-specific connection interface

EXCEPTIONS:

ResourceException	thrown when the method fails
ApplicationServerInternalException	indicates an application server-specific exception
SecurityException	thrown when a security-related error occurs
ResourceAllocationException	thrown when the method fails to allocate system resources for the connection request
ResourceAdapterInternalException	thrown when a resource adapter-related error condition occurs

A.3.4   ConnectionRequestInfo Interface

The ConnectionRequestInfo interface enables a resource adapter to pass its own request-specific data structure across a connection request flow. A resource adapter extends this empty interface to support its own data structures for a connection request.

Typically a resource adapter uses this interface to handle application component-specified per-connection request properties, such as client ID and language. The application server passes these properties to the resource adapter with `matchManagedConnection` and `createManagedConnection` calls. These properties remain opaque to the application server during the connection request flow.

A resource adapter can use this additional per-request information from the `matchManagedConnection` and `createManagedConnection` calls to do connection creation and matching.

equals

```
public boolean equals(java.lang.Object other);
```

Checks whether this ConnectionRequestInfo instance is equal to another instance of ConnectionRequestInfo. Because ConnectionRequestInfo is defined specific to a resource adapter, the resource adapter is required to implement this method. The conditions for equality are specific to the resource adapter.

PARAMETERS:
other   the other ConnectionRequestInfo instance

RETURNS:
true if the two instances are equal

hashCode

```
public int hashCode();
```

Returns the `hashCode` of the ConnectionRequestInfo.

RETURNS:
the hash code of this instance

A.3.5   LocalTransaction Interface

The LocalTransaction interface provides support for transactions that are managed internal to an EIS resource manager. Such transactions do not require an external transaction manager.

A resource adapter implements the javax.resource.spi.LocalTransaction interface to provide support for local transactions that are performed on the underlying resource manager. If a resource adapter supports the LocalTransaction interface, then the application server can choose to perform local transaction optimization. Local transaction optimization is when the application server uses a local transaction instead of a JTA transaction for a single resource manager case.

Refer also to the next section, "ManagedConnection Interface."

begin

```
public void begin() throws ResourceException;
```

Begins a local transaction.

EXCEPTIONS:

ResourceException	thrown when the method fails
LocalTransactionException	indicates an error condition related to the local transaction management
ResourceAdapterInternalException	thrown when a resource adapter-related error condition occurs
EISSystemException	thrown when an EIS instance-specific error condition occurs

commit

```
public void commit() throws ResourceException;
```

Commits a local transaction.

EXCEPTIONS:

ResourceException	thrown when the method fails
LocalTransactionException	indicates an error condition related to the local transaction management
ResourceAdapterInternalException	thrown when a resource adapter-related error condition occurs
EISSystemException	thrown when an EIS instance-specific error condition occurs

rollback

```
public void rollback() throws ResourceException;
```

Performs a rollback of a local transaction.

EXCEPTIONS:

ResourceException	thrown when the method fails
LocalTransactionException	indicates an error condition related to the local transaction management
ResourceAdapterInternalException	thrown when a resource adapter-related error condition occurs
EISSystemException	thrown when an EIS instance-specific error condition occurs

A.3.6   ManagedConnection Interface

A ManagedConnection instance represents a physical connection to the underlying EIS. A ManagedConnection instance provides access to two interfaces:

- javax.transaction.xa.XAResource
- javax.resource.spi.LocalTransaction

A transaction manager uses the XAResource interface to both associate and dissociate a transaction with the underlying EIS resource manager instance. It also uses this interface to perform a two-phase commit protocol. Note that the transaction manager does not directly use the ManagedConnection interface.

The application server uses the LocalTransaction interface to manage local transactions.

addConnectionEventListener

```
public void addConnectionEventListener
    (ConnectionEventListener listener);
```

Adds a connection event listener to the ManagedConnection instance. A registered ConnectionEventListener instance is notified of connection events, including connection close and error events and events on the ManagedConnection instance related to local transactions.

PARAMETERS:
listener   a new ConnectionEventListener to be registered

associateConnection

```
public void associateConnection(java.lang.Object connection)
    throws ResourceException;
```

Changes the association of an application-level connection handle with a ManagedConnection instance. This method is used by the container. The container is responsible for locating the correct ManagedConnection instance. Once it has located the correct instance, the container calls the associateConnection method.

The resource adapter is required to implement the associateConnection method. The method implementation should dissociate the connection handle, which is passed to the method as a parameter, from its currently associated

ManagedConnection instance and then associate the new connection handle with itself.

PARAMETERS:

connection   an application-level connection handle

EXCEPTIONS:

ResourceException	thrown when the method fails to associate the connection handle with this ManagedConnection instance
IllegalStateException	thrown when this method is invoked from an illegal state
ResourceAdapterInternalException	thrown when a resource adapter-related error condition occurs

cleanup

```
public void cleanup() throws ResourceException;
```

Performs a connection cleanup on the ManagedConnection instance. An application server calls this method to force such cleanup on the Managed-Connection instance.

The cleanup method initiates a cleanup of the client-specific state maintained by a ManagedConnection instance. Successful cleanup should invalidate all connection handles that were created using this ManagedConnection instance. Any attempt by an application component to use the connection handle after a cleanup of the underlying ManagedConnection instance should result in an exception.

Cleaning up a ManagedConnection instance is always driven by an application server. An application server should not invoke the cleanup method while an incomplete transaction associated with the ManagedConnection instance is in progress.

Invoking the cleanup method on an already cleaned-up connection should not throw an exception.

Cleaning up a ManagedConnection instance resets its client-specific state and prepares the connection to be put back into a connection pool. The cleanup method, however, should not cause a resource adapter to close the physical pipe and to reclaim system resources associated with the physical connection.

EXCEPTIONS:

ResourceException   thrown when the method fails

| IllegalStateException | thrown when this method is invoked from an illegal state. This error might occur if a current in-process local transaction does not allow connection cleanup. |
| ResourceAdapterInternalException | thrown when a resource adapter-related error condition occurs |

destroy

```
public void destroy() throws ResourceException;
```

Destroys the physical connection to the underlying resource manager. To manage the size of the connection pool, an application server can explicitly call the destroy method to destroy a physical connection. A resource adapter should destroy all allocated system resources for this ManagedConnection instance when this method is called.

EXCEPTIONS:

| ResourceException | thrown when the method fails |
| IllegalStateException | thrown when this method is invoked from an illegal state |

getConnection

```
public java.lang.Object getConnection
    (javax.security.auth.Subject subject,
    ConnectionRequestInfo cxRequestInfo) throws ResourceException;
```

Creates a new connection handle for the underlying physical connection represented by the ManagedConnection instance. The application code uses this connection handle to refer to the underlying physical connection. A connection handle is tied to its ManagedConnection instance in a resource adapter implementation-specific way.

The ManagedConnection instance uses the Subject and additional ConnectionRequestInfo data to set the state of the physical connection. Note that the ConnectionRequestInfo data is specific to a resource adapter and opaque to an application server.

PARAMETERS:

| Subject | JAAS (Java Authentication and Authorization Service) subject representing the security context |
| cxRequestInfo | ConnectionRequestInfo instance |

RETURNS:

a generic Object instance representing the connection handle. For the CCI, the connection handle created by a ManagedConnection instance is of the type javax.resource.cci.Connection.

EXCEPTIONS:

ResourceException	thrown when the method fails
SecurityException	thrown when a security-related error occurs
CommException	thrown when the method fails to communicate with the EIS instance
EISSystemException	thrown to indicate an internal error condition in the EIS instance. This exception occurs if the EIS instance is involved in setting the state of the ManagedConnection.
ResourceAdapterInternalException	thrown when a resource adapter-related error condition occurs

getLocalTransaction

```
public LocalTransaction getLocalTransaction() throws ResourceException;
```

Returns a javax.resource.spi.LocalTransaction instance. The container uses the LocalTransaction interface to manage local transactions for an RM (resource manager) instance.

RETURNS:

a LocalTransaction instance

EXCEPTIONS:

ResourceException	thrown when the method fails
ResourceAdapterInternalException	thrown when a resource adapter-related error condition occurs

getLogWriter

```
public java.io.PrintWriter getLogWriter() throws ResourceException;
```

Gets the log writer for this ManagedConnection instance. The log writer is a character output stream to which all logging and tracing messages for this ManagedConnection instance are printed. The ConnectionManager manages the association of the output stream with the ManagedConnection instance, based on connection pooling requirements.

The log writer associated with a ManagedConnection instance can be set specifically for the instance by the application server. Or, the log writer for the ManagedConnection instance can be the default log writer set from the ManagedConnectionFactory instance that created this connection.

RETURNS:

a character output stream associated with this ManagedConnection instance

EXCEPTIONS:

ResourceException   thrown when the method fails

getMetaData

```
public ManagedConnectionMetaData getMetaData() throws ResourceException;
```

Gets the metadata information for this connection's underlying EIS resource manager instance. The ManagedConnectionMetaData interface provides information about the underlying EIS instance associated with the Managed-Connection instance.

RETURNS:

a ManagedConnectionMetaData instance

EXCEPTIONS:

ResourceException   thrown when the method fails
NotSupportedException   thrown if the operation is not supported

getXAResource

```
public javax.transaction.xa.XAResource getXAResource()
    throws ResourceException;
```

Returns a javax.transaction.xa.XAResource instance. An application server enlists this XAResource instance with the transaction manager if the ManagedConnection instance is used in a JTA transaction coordinated by the transaction manager.

RETURNS:

an XAResource instance

EXCEPTIONS:

ResourceException	thrown when the method fails
NotSupportedException	thrown if the operation is not supported
ResourceAdapterInternalException	thrown when a resource adapter-related error condition occurs

removeConnectionEventListener

```
public void removeConnectionEventListener
    (ConnectionEventListener listener);
```

Removes an already registered connection event listener from the Managed-Connection instance.

PARAMETERS:

listener   a registered ConnectionEventListener to be removed

setLogWriter

```
public void setLogWriter(java.io.PrintWriter out)
    throws ResourceException;
```

Sets the log writer for this ManagedConnection instance. The log writer is a character output stream to which all logging and tracing messages for this ManagedConnection instance are printed. An application server manages the association of an output stream with the ManagedConnection instance based on the connection pooling requirements.

When a ManagedConnection object is initially created, the default log writer associated with the object is obtained from the ManagedConnection-Factory. An application server uses the setLogWriter method to set a log writer specific to this ManagedConnection for logging or tracing errors.

PARAMETERS:

out   a character output stream to be associated with the log writer

EXCEPTIONS:

ResourceException	thrown when the method fails
ResourceAdapterInternalException	thrown when a resource adapter-related error condition occurs

A.3.7   ManagedConnectionFactory Interface

A ManagedConnectionFactory interface is a factory of both ManagedConnection and EIS-specific connection factory instances. The ManagedConnectionFactory interface supports connection pooling by providing methods for matching and creating ManagedConnection instances.

The ManagedConnectionFactory interface extends the java.io.Serializable interface.

createConnectionFactory

```
public java.lang.Object createConnectionFactory()
    throws ResourceException;
```

```
public java.lang.Object createConnectionFactory
    (ConnectionManager cxManager) throws ResourceException;
```

Creates a connection factory instance. The first form of the method initializes the connection factory instance with a default ConnectionManager that is provided by the resource adapter.

The second form of the method initializes the connection factory instance with the passed ConnectionManager parameter. In a managed scenario, the application server provides the ConnectionManager.

PARAMETERS:

cxManager   a ConnectionManager to be associated with the created EIS connection factory instance

RETURNS:

an EIS-specific connection factory instance or a javax.resource.cci.ConnectionFactory instance

EXCEPTIONS:

ResourceException	thrown when the method fails
ResourceAdapterInternalException	thrown when a resource adapter-related error condition occurs

createManagedConnection

```
public ManagedConnection createManagedConnection
    (javax.security.auth.Subject subject,
    ConnectionRequestInfo cxRequestInfo) throws ResourceException;
```

Creates a new physical connection to the underlying EIS resource manager. A ManagedConnectionFactory instance uses the security information and additional ConnectionRequestInfo to create this new connection. The security information is passed as the `subject` parameter. The ConnectionRequestInfo is specific to the resource adapter and is opaque to the application server.

PARAMETERS:

`subject`	security information for the caller
`cxRequestInfo`	additional resource adapter-specific connection request information

RETURNS:

a ManagedConnection instance

EXCEPTIONS:

ResourceException	thrown when the method fails
SecurityException	thrown when a security-related error occurs
EISSystemException	thrown when an internal error condition occurs in the EIS instance
ResourceAllocationException	thrown when the method fails to allocate system resources for the connection request
ResourceAdapterInternalException	thrown when a resource adapter-related error condition occurs

equals

```
public boolean equals(java.lang.Object other);
```

Checks if this ManagedConnectionFactory is equal to another ManagedConnectionFactory. This method overrides the `equals` method in the java.lang.Object class.

RETURNS:

true if the two instances are equal; otherwise, returns false

PARAMETERS:

`other`   another ManagedConnectionFactory instance

getLogWriter

```
public java.io.PrintWriter getLogWriter() throws ResourceException;
```

Gets the log writer for this ManagedConnectionFactory instance. The log writer is a character output stream to which all logging and tracing messages for this ManagedConnectionFactory instance are printed.

An application server manages the association of an output stream with the ManagedConnectionFactory instance. When a ManagedConnectionFactory object is created, the log writer is initially null. That is, logging is initially disabled.

RETURNS:
a PrintWriter

EXCEPTIONS:
ResourceException   thrown when the method fails

hashCode

```
public int hashCode();
```

Returns the hash code for the ManagedConnectionFactory instance. This method overrides the `hashCode` method in the java.lang.Object class.

RETURNS:
the hash code for the ManagedConnectionFactory instance

matchManagedConnections

```
public ManagedConnection matchManagedConnections
    (java.util.Set connectionSet, javax.security.auth.Subject subject,
    ConnectionRequestInfo cxRequestInfo) throws ResourceException;
```

Returns a matched connection from the candidate set of connections. A ManagedConnectionFactory instance finds a matching connection using the security information passed to it through the subject parameter, plus the information provided through the ConnectionRequestInfo parameter and additional resource adapter-specific criteria. Note that the criteria used for matching are specific to a resource adapter and are not prescribed by the Connector specification.

This method returns a ManagedConnection instance that is the best match for handling the connection allocation request.

PARAMETERS:

connectionSet	a candidate connection set
subject	security information pertinent to the caller
cxRequestInfo	additional resource adapter-specific connection request information

RETURNS:

a ManagedConnection if the resource adapter finds an acceptable match in the candidate connection set; otherwise, returns null

EXCEPTIONS:

ResourceException	thrown when the method fails
SecurityException	thrown when a security-related error occurs
NotSupportedException	thrown if the operation is not supported
ResourceAdapterInternalException	thrown when a resource adapter-related error condition occurs

setLogWriter

```
public void setLogWriter(java.io.PrintWriter out)
    throws ResourceException;
```

Sets the log writer for this ManagedConnectionFactory instance. The log writer is a character output stream to which all logging and tracing messages for this ManagedConnectionFactory instance are printed.

An application server manages the association of an output stream with the ManagedConnectionFactory instance. When a ManagedConnectionFactory object is created, the log writer is initially null; that is, logging is disabled. Associating a log writer with a ManagedConnectionFactory instance enables logging and tracing for that ManagedConnectionFactory instance.

The ManagedConnection instances created by a ManagedConnectionFactory "inherit" the ManagedConnectionFactory log writer. An application server can override this inherited log writer using the ManagedConnection method setLogWriter to set specific logging and tracing for the ManagedConnection instance.

PARAMETERS:

out   a PrintWriter representing an output stream for error logging and tracing

EXCEPTIONS:

ResourceException	thrown when the method fails
ResourceAdapterInternalException	thrown when a resource adapter-related error condition occurs

A.3.8   ManagedConnectionMetaData Interface

The ManagedConnectionMetaData interface provides information about the underlying EIS instance associated with a ManagedConnection instance. An application server uses this information to get runtime information about a connected EIS instance.

The ManagedConnection.getMetaData method returns a ManagedConnection-MetaData instance.

getEISProductName

```
public java.lang.String getEISProductName() throws ResourceException;
```

Returns the product name of the underlying EIS instance connected through the ManagedConnection instance.

RETURNS:
the product name of the EIS instance

EXCEPTIONS:
ResourceException   thrown when the method fails

getEISProductVersion

```
public java.lang.String getEISProductVersion()
    throws ResourceException;
```

Returns the product version of the underlying EIS instance connected through the ManagedConnection instance.

RETURNS:
the product version of the EIS instance

EXCEPTIONS:
ResourceException   thrown when the method fails

getMaxConnections

```
public int getMaxConnections() throws ResourceException;
```

Returns the maximum limit for the number of active concurrent connections that an EIS instance can support across client processes. The method returns zero (0) if an EIS instance either does not know or does not have a maximum limit.

RETURNS:

the maximum number of active concurrent connections supported by an EIS instance

EXCEPTIONS:

ResourceException   thrown when the method fails

getUserName

```
public java.lang.String getUserName() throws ResourceException;
```

Returns the name of the user associated with the ManagedConnection instance. The name corresponds to the resource principal under whose security context a connection to the EIS instance has been established.

RETURNS:

the name of the user

EXCEPTIONS:

ResourceException   thrown when the method fails

A.3.9   ApplicationServerInternalException Class

An ApplicationServerInternalException indicates that an internal error to the application server has occurred.

A.3.10   CommException Class

A CommException indicates errors related to failed or interrupted communication with an EIS instance. Common error conditions represented by this exception type are communication protocol errors and invalidated connection errors due to a server failure. This class extends ResourceException.

A.3.11 EISSystemException Class

An EISSystemException indicates EIS-specific system-level error conditions. Error conditions that cause this exception to be thrown include:

- Failure or inactivity of an EIS instance

- Communication failure

- An EIS-specific error in the creation of a new physical connection

  This class extends ResourceException.

A.3.12 IllegalStateException Class

An IllegalStateException is thrown from a method if the caller—either a resource adapter or an application server for system contracts—is in an illegal or inappropriate state for the method invocation. This class extends ResourceException.

A.3.13 LocalTransactionException Class

A LocalTransactionException represents error conditions related to the local transaction management contract. This class extends ResourceException. Note that the JTA specification specifies the javax.transaction.xa.XAException class for exceptions related to XAResource-based transaction management contracts.

The LocalTransactionException is used for the local transaction management contract to indicate the following error conditions:

- Invalid transaction context when a transaction operation is executed. For example, it is an error to call a LocalTransaction `commit` method without an active local transaction.

- Attempting to roll back a transaction in the LocalTransaction `commit` method.

- Attempting to start a local transaction from the same thread on a ManagedConnection that is already associated with an active local transaction.

- Any resource adapter or resource manager-specific error condition related to local transaction management. Examples of such error conditions are violation of the integrity of resources, deadlock detection, communication failure during transaction completion, retry required error, or any internal error in a resource manager.

A.3.14 ResourceAdapterInternalException Class

A ResourceAdapterInternalException indicates the occurrence of an error internal to the resource adapter.

A.3.15 ResourceAllocationException Class

A ResourceAllocationException indicates an error resulting from the insufficient allocation of resources.

A.3.16 SecurityException Class

A SecurityException indicates an error condition related to the security contract between an application server and a resource adapter. This class extends ResourceException. A SecurityException represents such error conditions as:

- Invalid security information (represented as a Subject instance) passed across the security contract. Invalid security information might be credentials that have expired or that have an invalid format.

- Lack of support for a specific security mechanism in an EIS or resource adapter.

- Failure to create a connection to an EIS because of failed authentication or authorization.

- Failure to authenticate a resource principal to an EIS instance.

- Failure to establish a secure association with an underlying EIS instance.

- An access control exception to indicate the denial of a requested access to an EIS resource or a request to create a new connection.

A.4   javax.resource.spi.security Package

The javax.resource.spi.security package defines security-related interfaces.

A.4.1   GenericCredential Interface

The GenericCredential interface defines a security mechanism-independent interface for accessing the security credential of a resource principal. The GenericCredential interface provides a Java wrapper over an underlying representation of a security credential. For example, the GenericCredential interface can be used to wrap Kerberos credentials.

The Connector architecture does not define standard formats or requirements for security mechanism-specific credentials. For example, a security credential wrapped by a GenericCredential interface can have a native representation that is specific to an operating system.

The GenericCredential interface enables a resource adapter to extract information about a security credential. The resource adapter can then manage EIS sign-on for a resource principal by either:

- Using the credentials in an EIS-specific manner if the underlying EIS supports the security mechanism type represented by the GenericCredential instance.

- Using the GSS-API (Generic Security Service-API) if the resource adapter and underlying EIS instance support GSS-API.

equals

```
public boolean equals(java.lang.Object another);
```

Tests if this GenericCredential instance refers to the same entity as the supplied object. The two credentials must be acquired over the same mechanism and must refer to the same principal.

PARAMETERS:
another   the Object to which GenericCredential is to be compared

RETURNS:
true if the two GenericCredentials refer to the same entity; otherwise, returns false

getCredentialData

```
public byte[] getCredentialData() throws SecurityException;
```

Gets security data for a specific security mechanism represented by the GenericCredential. For example, this method gets authentication data required for establishing a secure association with an EIS instance on behalf of the associated resource principal.

The `getCredentialData` method returns the credential representation as an array of bytes. Note that the Connector architecture does not define a standard format for the returned credential data.

RETURNS:
a connection handle with an EIS-specific connection interface

EXCEPTIONS:
SecurityException   thrown when a security-related error occurs

getMechType

```
public java.lang.String getMechType();
```

Returns the mechanism type for the GenericCredential instance. The mechanism type definition for GenericCredential should be consistent with the Object Identifier (OID) representation specified in the GSS specification. In the GenericCredential interface, the mechanism type is returned as a stringified representation of the OID specification.

RETURNS:
mechanism type

getName

```
public java.lang.String getName();
```

Returns the name of the resource principal associated with a GenericCredential instance.

RETURNS:
name of the principal

hashCode

```
public int hashCode();
```

Returns the hash code for this GenericCredential instance. This method overrides the `hashCode` method in java.lang.Object.

RETURNS:
hash code for this GenericCredential

A.4.2   PasswordCredential Class

The PasswordCredential class acts as a holder for user name and password. This class extends java.lang.Object and implements java.io.Serializable.

equals

```
public boolean equals(java.lang.Object another);
```

Compares this PasswordCredential instance with the specified object for equality. The two instances are the same if they are equal in user name and password. This method overrides the `equals` method in the java.lang.Object class.

PARAMETERS:

another   the Object to which PasswordCredential is to be compared

RETURNS:

true if the specified object is a PasswordCredential whose user name and password are equal to this instance; otherwise, returns false

getManagedConnectionFactory

```
public ManagedConnectionFactory getManagedConnectionFactory();
```

Gets the target ManagedConnectionFactory for which the application server has set the user name and password. A ManagedConnectionFactory uses this field to determine if it should use this PasswordCredential instance for sign-on to the target EIS instance.

RETURNS:

a ManagedConnectionFactory instance for which the user name and password have been specified

getPassword

```
public char[] getPassword();
```

Returns the user password. Note that this method returns a reference to the password. It is the caller's responsibility to zero out the password information after it is no longer needed.

RETURNS:

the password

getUserName

```
public java.lang.String getUserName();
```

Returns the name of the user associated with a PasswordCredential instance.

RETURNS:
name of the user

hashCode

```
public int hashCode();
```

Returns the hash code for this PasswordCredential instance. This method overrides the hashCode method in java.lang.Object.

RETURNS:
hash code for this PasswordCredential

setManagedConnectionFactory

```
public void setManagedConnectionFactory(ManagedConnectionFactory mcf);
```

Sets the target ManagedConnectionFactory instance for which the user name and password have been set by the application server.

PARAMETERS:
mcf   a ManagedConnectionFactory instance for which the user name and password have been specified

Glossary

Access objects—High-level objects that abstract the complexity and low-level details of an EIS access API. Access objects may be command beans, data access objects, and custom records.

ACID—The acronym for the four properties guaranteed by transactions: atomicity, consistency, isolation, and durability.

Application assembler—An individual who combines enterprise beans, and possible other application components, into larger, deployable application units.

Application client—A first-tier client component that executes in its own Java virtual machine. Application clients have access to some J2EE platform APIs (JNDI, JDBC, RMI-IIOP, JMS).

Application server—A generic term for a middle-tier component server that is compatible with the J2EE platform.

Authentication—A step that occurs as part of the security process, during which a user proves his or her identity to the enterprise network security manager.

Authorization—A step that occurs as part of the security process, during which the target application or database server verifies whether or not that user has the authority to access the requested application or data.

Bean developer—The programmer who writes the enterprise bean code implementing the business logic and produces enterprise beans.

Bean-managed persistence—An approach to managing entity object state persistence where the entity bean itself manages the access to the underlying state in a resource manager.

Bean-managed transaction demarcation—An approach to managing transactions where the bean developer manages transaction boundaries programmatically from within the application code.

Business entity—A business object representing some information maintained by an enterprise.

Business process—A business object that encapsulates an interaction of a user with business entities.

Caller principal—A principal associated with an application component instance during a method invocation.

Command bean—A JavaBean used by an application to encapsulate a call to another application or a database call. Enterprise applications frequently use this design pattern.

Commit—The point in a transaction when all updates to any resources involved in the transaction are made permanent.

Common Gateway Interface (CGI)—One of the interfaces for developing dynamic HTML pages and Web applications.

Common Object Request Broker Architecture (CORBA)—A language-independent, distributed object model specified by the Object Management Group (OMG).

Compensating transaction—A transaction or operation that undoes the work of a previously committed transaction.

Component—An application-level software unit supported by a container. The J2EE environment defines four types of components: enterprise beans, Web components, applets, and application clients.

Connection factory—An object that produces connections.

Connector—A standard extension mechanism for containers to provide connectivity to enterprise information systems. A connector is specific to an enterprise information system and consists of a resource adapter and application development tools for enterprise information systems.

Connector architecture—An architecture for the integration of J2EE applications with enterprise information systems. There are two parts to this architecture: a resource adapter provided by an enterprise information system vendor and the J2EE server that allows this resource adapter to plug in. This architecture defines a set of contracts that a resource adapter has to support to plug in to a J2EE product, for example, transactions, security, and connection management.

Container—A standardized runtime environment that provides services to components. Services include life cycle management, security, deployment, and runtime services.

Container-managed persistence—An approach to managing entity object state persistence where the container manages the transfer of data between the entity bean instance variables and the underlying resource manager.

Container-managed transaction demarcation—An approach to managing transactions where the EJB container defines the transaction boundaries by using the transaction attributes provided in the deployment descriptor.

Conversational business process—A business process with a single actor. A conversational business process means that a single actor engages in a conversation with the application. An example of a conversational business process is an application that displays a sequence of forms to the user and validates the data input by the user.

Credential—A credential contains or references security information that can authenticate a principal to additional services.

Declarative transaction demarcation—Container-managed transaction demarcation. Also referred to as declarative transactions.

Deployer—The deployer is an expert in the target operational environment who installs J2EE software modules into the operational environment, usually a container. The deployer may also customize the software modules for the target operational environment.

Deployment descriptor—An XML document that contains the declarative information about the enterprise bean. The deployment descriptor directs a deployment tool to deploy enterprise beans with specific container options and describes configuration requirements that the deployer must resolve.

Document Object Model (DOM)—An interface that provides a set of objects to represent XML documents, allowing applications to dynamically access and update the content, structure, and style of XML documents.

Document Type Definition (DTD)—DTDs define the elements, attributes, and rules for the XML tags used by a particular document or set of documents.

ear file—An enterprise application archive file that contains a J2EE application.

EJB container—A programming environment for the development, deployment, and runtime management of enterprise beans.

ejb-jar file—A Java ARchive (JAR) file that contains one or more enterprise beans with their deployment descriptor.

EJB server—Software that provides services to an EJB container. For example, an EJB Container relies on a transaction manager that is part of the EJB server to perform the two-phase commit across all participating resource managers. The J2EE architecture assumes that an EJB container is hosted by an EJB server from the same vendor, so it does not specify the contract between these two entities. An EJB server may host one or more EJB containers.

EJB server provider—A vendor that supplies an EJB server.

End user—In security terms, an end user is an entity that acts as a source of a request.

Enterprise Application Integration (EAI)—The process by which an enterprise integrates its existing applications and systems and adds new technologies and applications.

Enterprise bean—A component that is part of a distributed enterprise application and that implements a business process or business entity. There are two types of enterprise beans: session beans and entity beans.

Enterprise bean class—A Java class that implements the business methods and the enterprise bean object life cycle methods.

Enterprise bean deployment—The process of installing an enterprise bean in an EJB container.

Enterprise bean objects—Distributed objects that implement the enterprise bean's remote interface. The EJB container implements these objects.

Enterprise Information System (EIS)—The services that support the enterprise information systems that manage and store enterprise-critical data and functions.

Enterprise Resource Planning (ERP)—Applications that cover the complete range of enterprise business functions, including inventory management, production control, human resources, financials, and logistics.

Entity bean—A type of enterprise bean that can be shared by multiple clients and the state of which is maintained in a resource manager. An entity bean can implement a business entity or a business process.

Entity object—Distributed objects that implement an entity bean's remote interface. These objects are object-oriented representations of real-life business entities and business processes.

Home interface—One of two interfaces for an enterprise bean. The home interface defines zero or more methods for creating and removing an enterprise bean. For session beans, the home interface defines create and remove methods, whereas for entity beans, the home interface defines create, finder, and remove methods.

HTTP—Hypertext Transfer Protocol. The Internet protocol used to fetch hypertext objects from remote hosts. HTTP messages consist of requests from client to server and responses from server to client.

HTTPS—HTTP layered over the SSL protocol.

Hypertext Markup Language (HTML)—A markup language for hypertext documents on the Internet. HTML enables the embedding of images, sounds, video streams, form fields, references to other objects with URLS, and basic text formatting.

Initiating principal—The security principal representing the end-user that interacts directly with the application.

ISV—Independent software vendor.

Java API for XML Messaging (JAXM)—A Java standard, based on SOAP technology, for sending XML messages over the Internet.

Java API for XML Processing (JAXP)—Java APIs for parsing and manipulating XML documents.

Java API for XML Registries (JAXR)—Java APIs that provide a standard way to access XML-based business registries over the Internet.

Java API for XML-based RPC (JAX-RPC)—Java APIs that make it possible to access Web services using remote procedure calls.

Java Architecture for XML Binding (JAXB)—A Java architecture that enables applications to manipulate XML documents in the same way they manipulate Java objects.

Java™ 2 Platform, Enterprise Edition (J2EE)—An environment for developing and deploying enterprise applications. The J2EE platform consists of a set of services, application programming interfaces (APIs), and protocols that provide functionality for developing multi-tiered, Web-based applications.

Java™ 2 Platform, Standard Edition (J2SE)—The core Java technology platform.

JavaServer Pages™ (JSP)—An extensible Web technology that uses template data, custom elements, scripting languages, and server-side Java objects to return dynamic content to a client. Typically, the template data is HTML or XML elements, and in many cases the client is a Web browser.

Markup—A set of tags and other code used to describe the content of text.

Persistence—The protocol for making an object's state durable.

Primary key—An object that uniquely identifies an entity bean within a home.

Principal—An entity that can be authenticated by an authentication mechanism. It is identified using a principal name and authenticated using authentication data.

Protection domain—See *security domain*.

Remote interface—One of two interfaces for an enterprise bean. The enterprise bean remote interface defines the business methods callable by a client.

Remote Method Invocation (RMI)—A technology that allows an object running in one Java virtual machine to invoke methods on an object running in a different Java virtual machine.

Resource adapter—A system level software library used by an application server or a client to connect to a resource manager. A resource adapter may provide additional services beyond the connection API.

Resource manager—A resource manager provides access to a set of shared resources. A resource manager participates in a transaction. An example of a resource manager is a relational database management system (RDBMS).

Resource manager connection—An object that represents a session with a resource manager.

Resource manager connection factory—An object used for creating a resource manager connection.

Resource principal—A security principal under whose security context a connection to an EIS instance is established.

RMI-IIOP—A version of RMI implemented to use the CORBA IIOP protocol. RMI-IIOP provides interoperability with CORBA objects implemented in any language if all the remote interfaces are originally defined as RMI interfaces.

Rollback—The point in a transaction when all updates to any resources involved in the transaction are reversed.

Secure Socket Layer (SSL)—A security protocol that provides privacy over the Internet. The protocol allows client-server applications to communicate in a tamper-free way that cannot be eavesdropped. Servers are always authenticated, and clients are optionally authenticated.

Security attributes—A caller's identity attributes and shared authorization attributes contained in the caller's credential.

Security context—An object that encapsulates the shared state information regarding security between two entities.

Security domain—A scope within which certain common security mechanisms and policies are established. An enterprise can contain more than one security domain. Thus an application server and an EIS can be in the same security domain or they can be in different security domains.

Session bean—A type of enterprise bean that implements a conversational business process. The state of a session bean is maintained by the container and is not externalized to a resource manager.

Session bean objects—Distributed objects that implement a session bean's remote interface.

Simple API for XML (SAX)—A standard interface for event-based XML parsing.

Simple Object Access Protocol (SOAP)—An XML-based protocol for accessing objects.

Stateful session bean—A type of a session bean class that retains state on behalf of its client across multiple method invocations by the client.

Stateless session bean—A type of a session bean class that does not retain any client-specific state between client-invoked methods. All instances of a stateless session bean are identical.

System Administrator—The system administrator configures and administers the enterprise computing and networking infrastructure, which includes the EJB server and container. The system administrator is also responsible for most security-related administration responsibilities.

Transaction—An atomic unit of work that modifies data. A transaction encloses one or more program statements, all of which either complete or roll back. Transactions enable multiple users to access the same data concurrently.

Transaction attribute—A value specified in an enterprise bean's deployment descriptor that is used by the EJB container to control the transaction scope when the enterprise bean's methods are invoked. A transaction attribute can have the following values: `Required`, `RequiresNew`, `Supports`, `NotSupported`, `Mandatory`, `Never`.

Transaction manager—Provides the services and management functions required to support transaction demarcation, transactional resource management, synchronization, and transaction context propagation. A transactional manager coordinates transactions across multiple resource managers.

Transaction service—A transaction service is the same as a transaction manager.

War file—A Web archive file containing the class files for servlets and JSPs.

Web application—An application built for the Internet with Java technologies, such as JavaServer Pages and servlets, as well as with non-Java technologies, such as CGI and Perl.

Web component—A component, such as a servlet or JSP page, that provides services in response to HTTP requests.

Web container—A programming environment for the development, deployment, and runtime management of servlets and JavaServer Pages.

XA transaction—A transaction that is controlled and coordinated by a transaction manager external to the resource manager.

XML—eXtensible Markup Language. A markup language that allows you to define the tags, or markup, needed to identify data and text in XML documents. The deployment descriptors are expressed in XML.

XML Schema—A standard that supports the expression of DTD rules for XML documents.

XML tag—A label applied to a piece of data that indicates the meaning of the data.

XSL—eXtensible Style Language. A language for defining style sheets for XML content.

XSL Transformation (XSLT)—A standard associated with XSL that defines the mechanism to transform an XML document into a specific format.

Index

Compensating transactions, 62–63
Component-managed sign-on, 73,
    74–75
Component-managed transaction
    demarcation, 226
Components, defined, 27
Configured identity approach, 75
Connection, security of, 77
Connection factory
    in application development,
        286–288
    creation of, 196, 200
    described, 175–176
    function of, 173, 204
    managed, 176–177
    view of, 200
Connection handle, 179
Connection interface, 112, 118,
    120–121, 218
    in JMS, 97
    methods in, 316–318
    types of, 118–122
Connection management architecture,
    47
    aspects of, 48–50
    classes and interfaces in,
        217–223
    schematic of, 48
Connection management contract, 33,
    47
    error handling in, 223
    features of, 204
    function of, 203–204
    implementation of, 172–175
    in nonmanaged environment,
        214–217
    object diagram for, 207
    overview of, 204–205
    uses of, 205–217
Connection pool(ing), 203
    controlling growth of, 302
    controlling shrinkage of, 302

importance of, 45
J2EE Connector architecture and,
    46–47
WebLogic Server support of,
    301–303
Connection timeout, 288
    connectionClosed method, 214,
        340
    connectionErrorOccurred method,
        341
ConnectionEvent class, 222,
    339–340
ConnectionEventListener interface,
    205, 230
    methods in, 340–342
ConnectionFactory interface,
    118–119, 217–218
    in JMS, 97
    methods in, 318–320
ConnectionManager interface, 173,
    177, 204, 219, 220, 250
    methods in, 342–343
ConnectionMetaData interface, 127,
    128
    methods in, 320–321
ConnectionRequestInfo interface, 173,
    180
    methods in, 343–344
    using, 181–182
Connections
    establishment of, 50–52, 115,
        129–130, 206–210
    handling, 182–183, 212–214
    importance of, 45
    matching of, 210–212
    minimum and maximum, 288
    pooling of, 45–47
    requesting, 174
    sharing of, 237–239
ConnectionSpec interface, 118,
    119–120, 267
    methods in, 321–322

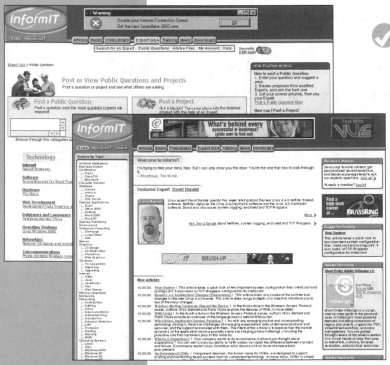